Greenwich Council
Library & Information Service

IN HOUSE
QUALITY
SYSTEMS

COUSINS DIVIDED

George V and Nicholas II

For G. W. K.

COUSINS DIVIDED

George V and Nicholas II

A N N M O R R O W

SUTTON PUBLISHING

First published in the United Kingdom in 2006 by
Sutton Publishing Limited · Phoenix Mill
Thrupp · Stroud · Gloucestershire · GL5 2BU

British Library Cataloguing in Publication Data
A catalogue record for this book is available from the British Library.

ISBN 0-7509-3372-0

Typeset in 11/13.5pt Sabon.
Typesetting and origination by
Sutton Publishing Limited.
Printed and bound in England by
J.H. Haynes & Co. Ltd, Sparkford.

Contents

Illustrations

A young Nicholas Romanov, 1871 *(Getty Images)*
His cousin George, later king and emperor, 1868 *(Getty Images)*
Members of the British and Russian royal families at Cowes, Isle of
    Wight, 1909 *(Getty Images)*
Prince John *(Ian Shapiro, Argyll Etkin Archives)*
Queen Alexandra and her sister Dowager Marie Feodorovna of
    Russia, 1911 *(The Royal Archives © HM Queen Elizabeth II)*
The Russian imperial family, 1914 *(Private Collection)*
Tsar Nicholas II's coronation procession *(Getty Images)*
King George V's coronation *(Getty Images)*
Nicholas II and Prince George with their sons at Cowes, 1909
    (Roger Short)
Nicholas with the Duke of Connaught at Balmoral *(Ian Shapiro,*
    Argyll Etkin Archives)
The British royal family, 1905 *(Getty Images)*
The Tsar inspecting Russian troops at Peterhof, 1910 *(Getty Images)*
George V on the Western Front *(The Royal Archives © HM Queen*
    Elizabeth II)
Nicholas and George, 1913 *(Getty Images)*
Kaiser Wilhelm II with the Tsar, 1913 *(Roger Short)*
Sir George Buchanan, British Ambassador to St Petersburg
    (Getty Images)
The British royal family at the wedding of the then Duke of York to
    Lady Elizabeth Bowes-Lyon, 1923 *(The Royal Archives*
    © HM Queen Elizabeth II)
Nicholas and three of his daughters while in the hands of the
    revolutionaries *(Getty Images)*
Nicholas alone as a prisoner *(Roger Short)*
The Times' report of the death of the Tsar, July 1918 *(News*
    International/Times Syndication)
Prince Michael of Kent at the reburial service of the Romanovs,
    July 1998 *(EPA Agency)*
Nicholas II's tomb in St Petersburg *(G.W.K. Fenn-Smith)*

Acknowledgements

First may I acknowledge the gracious permission of Her Majesty the Queen for allowing access to her grandfather King George V's diaries and letters to Nicholas II, held in the Royal Archives at Windsor Castle, for which she owns the copyright. It was a privilege to sit in the Round Tower at Windsor Castle and read these guileless, sometimes moving, documents.

To Pamela Clark, the Registrar at the Royal Archives, my thanks for her guidance; and to Frances Dimond, curator of the Royal Photographic Collection, for her discerning help in choosing from the incomparable range of photographs in the Royal Family collection.

My thanks go also to the following:

In Russia, to Professor Zoia Belyakova, a guiding light in St Petersburg who opened rare doors, sharing her intimate knowledge of the Romanovs; also to Ivan and Vassily, her grandsons; Dr Ushakov of the Russian State Archives Federation (GARF); to Vera Rachevsky, curator of the Galitzine Library in St Petersburg; to Valentine Vailevna at the Alexander Palace at Tsarskoe Selo; and the custodians of the Crow's Nest, Livadia, the imperial summer palace in the Crimea.

In Switzerland, to Prince Nicholas Romanov, ambassador for the imperial family, for his elegant overall view and memorable pasta.

In France, to Angela Cotterell, the spirit of Paris, who tracked down the Tsar's favourite Russian tea and who is treasured by Russian exiles, among others; to Tamara Rybakova at the Maison Russe and its special residents for their charming but inevitably sad memories; and to Lena Petrossian for sharing her knowledge of the delights of imperial caviar.

In the United States, to Philippa Bowers in Virginia; in Washington, to Joan Whittington for research at the Library of Congress; also to Dr Dick Whittington; to Henry B. Thomas and Lynn Wardle for invaluable sleuthing; in New York, to Jerry Minkow and Jeannie Sakol, who always encouraged.

In Finland, to Ossi Laurila for his expert advice, and his wife Mary Anne Evans; to Petri Tuomi-Nikula, Press Counsellor at the Embassy of Finland, London; in Helsinki, to his brother Jorma Tuomi-Nikula, author of *Emperors' Summer Holidays in Finland*.

In London, a huge debt of gratitude goes to Kenneth Rose, for the clarity and distinction of his advice and generous access to precious private papers; and to Countess Mountbatten of Burma, the Tsarina's great-niece, for sharing sensitive, humorous memories; to Dominic Lieven, for a stimulating insight into Russia's history; to William Clarke, an enlightened mentor on the lost fortune of the last Tsar; to Count Nicolai Tolstoy, for his incisive historian's perspective; to Tania Tolstoy, an ambassador for Russia, for sensitive guidance and generous introductions; to Kyril Zinoviev, who epitomises the best of an *ancien regime*; and to Katya Galitzine, who loves her two countries and flits between St Petersburg and Cirencester.

My thanks go also to the following people for their help; John Barnes, for his introduction to Sophie Joan Mead-King, née Bolitski, the mother of his late wife, Anthea; to Edomé Broughton-Adderley, for a private view of her own cup of sorrows; to Marion Mitten and Trevor Turner, for opening a door to Fabergé; to Jim Coyle and his team at British Library Newspapers; and to Charlie and Blue Hodgson.

In Scotland, to Helen Murray Threipland, née Molchanoff, actor Richard Marner and Pauline, his widow; to Elena and Tom Snow, and their son Alexander, for his evocative film *St Petersburg Symphony*; to Karen McAulay, Music & Academic Sciences Librarian, Royal Scottish Academy of Music & Drama, Edinburgh.

Exceptional thanks go also to Sonia and Philip Goodman, who shared captivating and perceptive memories of the Tsar's sisters in exile; to Michael Allen, who is the son of the Tsarina's Yorkshire godchild; to Randle Meinertzhagen, for access to his father's extraordinary life; to Mary Lovell, who trustingly lent invaluable documents; to Malcolm Bury, for sharing his grandfather's engaging description of meeting the Tsar; to Coryne Hall, for her entertaining anecdote about the Queen Mother and others; to Donald and Susan Crawford for hospitality and encouragement; to Elliot Philipp, for medical advice, and to Graham Thompson of the Haematology

Department at the Chelsea and Westminster Hospital; to Lieutenant-Colonel Roger Binks, The Royal Scots Dragoon Guards Depot, Edinburgh, for valued guidance about their Colonel-in-Chief, and to Major Mark Ravnkilde and Major James Scott; and to Colonel Charles Webb, Militaria consultant at Spink of London.

To Jeremy Barnett and Marina Bowater, for private recollections of life at Tsarskoe Selo; to brothers the Reverend Eric Flood and the Reverend Gerald Flood and Kirsten Gill, for advice on Denmark and Hvidøre; to Nicolas Guedroitz, Madame Olga Kulikova, John van der Kiste and Shay McNeal; to Stephen Poliakoff for his sensitive guidance on the lost prince; and to Peter Day.

To Russian expert Richard Davies, Archivist, Russian Archives, Brotherton Library at the University of Leeds; to Lucy McCann, deputy librarian, the Bodleian Rhodes House; to Edda Tasiemka and her treasure-trove newspaper archive; to Ros Watson and Barbara Blakeson, Royal Pump Room Museum, Harrogate; and to Zena Dickinson, Secretary to the Wernher Collection, Luton Hoo.

To the London Library, my appreciation for the unfailing and exceptional help given by Jean Strathdee-Cook, Bridie Mcmahon, Colin Stevenson, Head of Loans for over forty-six years, and the rest of the team.

To David Gillings at Westland Helicopters, and to Clive Richards, Air Historical Branch, Bentley Priory, for expert detail on aircraft used for the 'rescue attempts' from Ekaterinburg.

I am also indebted to Roger Short for unfailing kindness and advice, for sharing expert knowledge and allowing access to his jewel of a collection of imperial photographs and rare documents; to Ian Shapiro and Jim Hanson of Argyll Etkin Limited, London, for inspiring and generous help.

To Raja Halder for his help and his beautiful music; and to Dominic Baker, a technical wizard who can calm computers.

To Catherine Theakstone, for unflappable research at Hulton Getty; to Helen Bowen, for her patience; to Neil Hudd, N.I. Times Syndication; to Steve Dennish and his obliging team at Swift Print, Silver Street, Cirencester; to Kate O'Meara at Hodder & Stoughton for securing copyright permissions; and to Dominic Garwood for his assistance.

Thanks as always go to Angie Montfort-Bebb at Universal Aunts Ltd, for her introduction to the multi-talented Caroline Wolff, to whom my thanks also go for all her graceful help and good humour.

To my agent Jonny Pegg at Curtis Brown, for strong support; to Jaqueline Mitchell at Sutton Publishing, who masterminded the idea, for her clever guidance; to Anne Bennett, Julian Beecroft and Hazel Cotton for their editorial support, and to Chris Jones, special thanks.

Finally, to favourite cousins everywhere. But above all to my husband, for his immeasurable contribution, *spasiba* – this book is for him.

Author's Note

Researching *Cousins Divided*, works of reference, memoirs, printed letters, diaries, archive sources, unpublished works, periodicals and past and contemporary newspapers have been consulted, and material has also been drawn from radio and television, from documentaries and film. A number are mentioned in the text and source notes, but it would be impossible to credit all of them, though every effort has been made to trace copyright holders.

Russia adhered to the old-style Julian calendar until 1 February 1918. This was twelve days behind the more commonly used Gregorian calendar in the west; but in the nineteenth century, to confuse things, the Russians decided to alter this to thirteen days behind in the twentieth century. Some of the dates mentioned may have escaped conversion in the text. Nicholas II abdicated on 2 March 1917 according to the Russian calendar but on 15 March 1917 following the Western calendar.

There were three Russian Revolutions. The first was a small but meaningful event in 1905. The second Russian Revolution in February 1917, which resulted in the mutiny of 160,000 garrison peasant conscripts in Petrograd, toppled the Tsar.

The third Revolution began when warning shots were fired at the Winter Palace from the cruiser *Aurora* on 25 October (7 November) 1917. Lenin, heading the Bolsheviks in February (actually 3 March) 1918, gave away a third of Russia's western territories when he signed the Brest-Litovsk treaty with Germany and Austria.

Generally, St Petersburg will be the name given to that city thoughout the text, as it was only briefly known as Petrograd; with Soviet influence it became Leningrad before reverting once again to its old tsarist name St Petersburg.

References are made throughout the text to the Emperor and Empress; Tsar and Tsarina. Nicholas and Alexandra are sometimes abbreviated to Nicky and Alix (Princess Alix of Hesse). Their daughters were grand duchesses. The Dowager Empress Marie

Feodorovna was known as Dagmar by her Danish relatives and as 'Aunt Minnie' by King George V. Nicholas II's third daughter was christened Maria but usually known by family and friends as Marie; this was partly due to the influence of the French at the imperial court.

Introduction

The Tsar was God. Each morning, schoolchildren recited prayers reverently facing Nicholas II's portrait, those infinitely tragic eyes looking down on his young subjects. He was their 'Little Father, Lord and Judge'.

The word 'Tsar' meant Caesar. He rode a white horse like a hero in a Pushkin fairy tale, with an escort of *Chevalier Gardes* in silver and gold uniforms. His kingdom stretched from 'Arctic ice-fields to the Aral Sea, from Warsaw to the walls of Tartary'.[1] He was indestructible.

From the gilded windows of the Winter Palace, Nicholas II looked out with satisfaction at his 300-year-old imperial city, tantalising in the opaqueness of May mornings, with teasing glimmers of cupolas and slender gold spires as the angels on St Isaac's above the cathedral's great Vitali bronze and oak doors emerged still swathed in pearly clouds. In the Palace Square, children chased each other, sometimes stopping to look up at the Alexander Column, the highest in the world, with its messenger carrying a cross of peace. Théophile Gautier's lyrical view on his first visit to St Petersburg in 1858 was: 'Nothing is more beautiful than this city of gold, on a horizon of silver, where the sky retains the paleness of dawn.'

The Russian Empire was so vast that, when the sun rose on one side, it was already setting on the other. The Romanovs owned 326 palaces and relied on 15,000 servants, all capable of spectacular subservience, bowing low before their Emperor in a reception hall of gold mirrors lit by 696 candles.

Nicholas II was one of the richest men in the world, but his reign heralded the swansong of a dazzling *ancien régime*. 'The most magnificent in Europe' was Prince Christopher of Greece's description of the Russian court, yet he felt there was 'something barbaric' about 'its splendour'. The lifestyle of the imperial elite was indulgent, improvident, reckless and cultivated.

Few of the privileged Russian aristocracy were philanthropic or driven by any Puritan ethic. The Stroganovs, who were partial to stew with sour cream, lived in a baroque green and white Rastrelli palace filled with Greek sculpture, and had an orchestra of 600 serfs, who moved about silently in felt-wrapped shoes. A Yussopov, unable to think of a birthday present for his wife, gave her a mountain in the Crimea.* They had impossibly grand titles and were joyously part of the Silver Age of Russia.

Discerning, travelled, privileged and literary, attracted by Empire French-style classicism, they knew excellence and demanded it from round the world for their palaces and sumptuous tall houses on the English Embankment, overlooking the River Neva.

Sophisticated, liberal, connoisseurs of the arts, they led lives of strenuous leisure. Their imperial baroque palaces, shimmering with gold leaf, were aesthetic examples of the best by Russian and European craftsmen. They ordered agate cabinets, and Karelian birchwood floors with Pompeian motifs, and their colonnaded porticoes were decorated with sculpted marble chariots drawn by deer, swans, horses and peacocks.

Walls hung with paintings by Fragonard and Watteau were lined with silk; ceilings were in Arabic geometric design or porcelain *trompe l'œil*; coats of arms showed Roman legion eagles; sculpted cherubs clung with crossed podgy legs to floor-length Versailles mirrors.

French was the language of the imperial court. Francomania was chic. Gone was any conflict between being European and Asian. Smart Russians thought of themselves as European, yet it was the eastern blood that inspired the exotic.

While England had Elgar and Holst, in Russia in the years before the First World War, Rachmaninov, who finished his admired Second Symphony in 1906, Stravinsky, with his *Firebird*, Glazunov and Rimsky-Korsakov, with his *Scheherazade*, all blossomed under the patronage of a Tsar who loved music and ballet. Nicholas personally liked to organise the artistic entertainment. Often the cream of St Petersburg was given a private view of ballets; *Swan Lake* was put on by impresario Sergei Diaghilev with costumes by Bakst, and danced by Pavlova or Karsavina. Chagall and Kandinsky were producing exciting avant-garde art, and portrait painters Repen and Serov were capturing flattering images of their Tsar. The Futurists, recognised by their 'gilded noses and dyed faces', wore

* The mountain of I-Petri on the south coast of the Crimea.

radishes in their buttonholes.[2] In this receptive climate for the arts, where more literature and art was being created than anywhere else in Europe, audiences in the Mariinskiy Theatre with its bas-reliefs, cornices from Homer's *Iliad*, thought they had touched paradise.

In winter, the young went ice skating or slid down *katki* (ice hills) and then jumped into brightly painted troikas, 'jingling, whistling and whooping away', to race across the blue-tinged ice into a pink sunset. At dusk, as candles and braziers were lit, girls stood before long mirrors in pearl-encrusted evening dresses and put on furs and diamonds before joining their escorts, resplendent in the ornate uniform of the Emperor's Guards, which made even the weediest look impressive.

On these translucent 'White Nights' during the height of the season,* with only two hours of darkness, brightly painted sleighs drawn by prancing horses equipped with special spiked winter shoes, spurred on by coachmen in purple-blue tailored coats, they went speeding along Nevsky Prospekt, an elegant wide leafy copy of the Champs-Elysées in Paris, to one of the Tsar's banquets for three thousand[3] at the Winter Palace.

When they arrived, uniformed trumpeters played as flutes of vintage champagne were offered before *zakhouska*, a delectable choice of hors d'oeuvres laid out on long tables with white cloths; three different kinds of caviar, lemon vodka, tiny salted cucumbers, smoked salmon, fish from the Volga, and little mushrooms 'boiling in a rich cream sauce' – all presented just to whet the appetite.

Then it was time to sit down to an imperial banquet in Nicholas Hall in St Petersburg under the crystal-roped Murano chandeliers, where a scarlet-uniformed Cossack stood to attention behind each guest's chair. Often the Tsar's preference was for Russian Church music, and he liked his guests to hear this haunting *a capella* singing while they dined. There were never fewer than thirty-five courses, which might include watermelon in a silver container with crushed ice, bowls of steaming borscht with blobs of sour cream and pastry, followed by a little sturgeon, roast venison or a small tree partridge, until finally the rum baba,† a large cake covered with rum-flavoured icing. Nicholas usually chose an 1880 sweet wine called Seventh

---

* The height of the season from late May to early June, when the sun hardly sets and there is barely more than two hours' change of light.

† *baba* meaning 'peasant woman'.

Heaven, from the Crimean Royal Vineyards, which his guests
enjoyed in a rarefied atmosphere smelling of *chypre* and chocolate,[4]
before retiring to smoke small, yellow cigarettes and join the
dancing. In the palace ballroom, the green of the palm trees from the
Crimea, contrasted with the gold-embroidered crimson livery of
black footmen offering liqueurs to men with scented beards.

The winter season ritually began with a 'grand costume ball' in
the Assembly Hall of the Nobles.[5] The Tsar would select a girl and
then call for a glass of water, which he held high as he waltzed with
his starry-eyed partner – it being a matter of pride never to spill a
single drop.[6] Orchestras, seated in alcoves garlanded with blowsy
pink roses and jonquils all brought from the French Riviera, played
schottishes, oriental quadrilles and polonaises until four in the
morning, when the imperial guests flew off in their sleighs to Strelna
and other fashionable nightclubs. It was an era of gypsy choirs,
duels at daybreak, of guardsmen with magnificent plumes galloping
with abandon through a tsarist fairyland.

The *Folle Journée* was the last great revel before Lent, which
began officially as the clock struck twelve on the Sunday night
before Ash Wednesday, when the music stopped dramatically and a
penitent supper of cabbage and mushrooms was served. Pink-faced
old *babushkas* spent Ash Wednesday in the kitchens making thin
blinis from buckwheat, served with caviar, or home-made berry jam,
to soften the beginning of this important religious season, with its
emphasis on fasting. During the Lenten months of deprivation, the
more imaginative ate a mush of gherkins, caviar, horseradish, oil
and potato. Sprays of 'silvery catkins tied with ribbons'[7] in the
absence of palm were carried in church processions, especially in
Archangel, where Palm Sunday was known as the Sunday of the
Pussy Willows.

When ice floes covered the Neva like a protective white sheet,
St Petersburg and Moscow held no charms for the Tsar's coterie. In
the country, the winter came early, candles and *lampadi* (lamps)
were lit at lunchtime, washerwomen broke through the ice with bare
hands to rinse the laundry, and servants put cotton wool between
the double window frames, adding a sprinkling of borax to make it
glint in an increasingly elusive sun, all a signal for the privileged
owners to escape. They left behind the worst of the Russian winter
when *muzhiks* (Russian peasants) in white aprons and brown fur
hats shovelled snow from the streets into the River Neva, and

boarded '*le train des grands ducs*' to Europe: to Biarritz, Baden-Baden, Nice, Cannes and Monte Carlo. They enjoyed wintry sunshine abroad and the comforting smell of olive-wood fires.

As soon as the orange blossom appeared they went back to Russia, when fur-lined sleighs were being replaced by horses and carriages. At Easter, the palace kitchens smelt once more of baking, of raisins, almonds, vanilla and cardamom for the kulich cake, decorated with the words 'Christ is risen' on the icing.

In the spring of 1917, refreshed, they returned to St Petersburg, expecting to enjoy, as usual, the starry delights of their own 'Venice of the North', the soirées at the Winter Palace reeking of incense as cavalry officers with diamond-studded double-eagle epaulettes clicked their heels and swore fidelity to their Tsar.

In an atmosphere of elegant inertia, the first intimation of the Revolution in Russia was a household being reduced to one pastry chef and unable to find another because the servants had joined a leftist uprising. Basic foodstuffs – eggs, butter, bread – were now beyond the reach of the average man or woman, who watched their children become wan and close to death from starvation. Strikes, fuelled by resentment, sparked the 1917 October Revolution.

Still Nicholas II remained detached, even when the cobblestones outside the Winter Palace were spattered red with revolution. As if coping with a minor diary change he noted, 'I shall take up dominoes again in my spare time.' Dogged by an inability to confront these problems, he became a tragic figure. Forced to abdicate in March 1917, he brought down with him the Romanov dynasty which had dominated *rossiiskaia imperia*[8] for three centuries. Now the aristocracy who had enjoyed the lavishness of the imperial court fled to safe havens in Western Europe: one dressed in rags ended up selling the insides of cigarette butts in Paris; another, rabbit skins in Normandy.

It had been assumed that Nicholas might be given a home in England with King George V. The two men were first cousins and held dear their close friendship. They looked alike, fair-haired and with slightly protruding big blue eyes, and were about the same height, 5ft 7in; both men also wore a nautical-style beard. They much enjoyed being mistaken for one another. George was affectionately known by the Romanovs as the Tsar's 'twin brother'. Their bearded profiles on gold roubles and sovereigns were indistinguishable.[9] A touching photograph of them with arms linked at Cowes is haunting in its trust, and the steady, unruffled gaze of these almost identical cousins.

Their mothers were sisters, daughters of the Danish King Christian IX, the Sea King, highly eligible princesses in the European marriage market. Alexandra had married the Prince of Wales, while her sister Dagmar became the wife of Tsar Alexander III of Russia. When Alexandra's husband, King Edward VII, came to the throne he was known affectionately in both families as 'Uncle Wales'. The family bonds were all the closer because his niece, Princess Alix of Hesse, who was the daughter of Princess Alice, his favourite sister, had married Nicholas II, Tsar of All the Russias.

They were one big happy family ruling three empires. There was the King and his two cousins, the Tsar and the Kaiser. They all knew each other simply as 'Nicky', 'Georgie' and 'Willy'. The German Emperor Wilhelm II was never a favourite at Windsor, but Nicholas II was loved like a true brother.

Born in 1865, George V was three years older than the Tsar. One became a midshipman at the age of twelve and wanted nothing more than a career in the navy; the other was happiest being a soldier. They wrote to each other as 'My dearest Nicky' and 'My dearest Georgie'. Each deeply conservative, they were single-minded in their devotion to their wives and families. They shared the same respect for their destiny but lacked their fathers' flamboyance. George V never wanted to be king and succeeded only on the death of his older brother Eddy Duke of Clarence.* Nicholas was born to be Tsar but was quite unprepared.

In the intermingling of the two families, one was noticeably exotic, the other steadily unostentatious. There was a theatrical edge to Russian ceremonial occasions; for instance, the annual blessing of the Neva before the river's iridescent summer journey through lagoons and under curving bridges to the Gulf of Finland. Wherever the Tsar travelled, he was escorted by the 'Konvoy', a quartet of black-cloaked Cossacks of the Imperial Bodyguard, with long blue cloaks lined with scarlet, and silver cartridge cases strapped across their chests.

The decorous English court on the other hand had a propriety inspired by King George and Queen Mary. This came as something of a shock to those who had enjoyed Edward VII's exuberantly

* Prince Albert, Duke of Clarence, b. 1864, d. 1892.

hedonistic reign. Shaking off the stern Lutheran pall imposed by his father Prince Albert and carried on by Queen Victoria, when Edward succeeded in 1901, new millionaires met old aristocrats round the King's dining table; an eclectic mix of *nouveaux riches* and old aristocracy enjoying an indulgently Edwardian decade. But when George V came to the throne, he imposed a new sedateness and sobriety. Informal meals never lasted longer than twenty-five minutes. But on ceremonial occasions there was still the unrivalled pageantry of the English court, so admired around the world.

While Nicholas himself may not have enjoyed the opulence of the court in St Petersburg, its continuing existence tarnished his image. Unlike his English cousin he was not blessed with much instinct for self-preservation and was unable to give any outward impression of thrift or restraint. The deliberately orchestrated, quiet frugality seen at Windsor and Buckingham Palace, in such contrast to the Russian court, would be the salvation of the British royal family. They ate cold rice pudding, wore tweeds, drank tea, exercised their dogs and played charades; it was all comfortingly routine, but that same dullness would save the British monarchy. There were no banquets given by the British royal family to rival those of St Petersburg, where guests enjoyed larks' tongues and nightingales' livers and gargantuan Escoffier creations, with only a sprinkling of social conscience.

George V had none of his cousin's grand-sounding titles: Nicholas was known as Tsar of All the Russias, Emperor and Autocrat, Supreme Commander, God of All the Russias, Lord and Judge, and Little Father. But the King earned respect given voluntarily, not engendered by slavish adulation. He acted as a constitutional monarch, even if this meant suppressing an emotional attachment and ignoring family ties.*

By the beginning of the twentieth century, the cousins appeared invincible, ruling over flourishing empires. One had supremacy over

---

* *King George V*, by Harold Nicolson, page 178. He had tried to help the Portuguese royal family when revolutionaries overthrew King Manuel in 1911. His impulsive reaction was to respond to a request to send a British warship to rescue them. But his Foreign Secretary, Sir Edward Grey, was against this, mindful of the importance of recognising the new republic in Portugal. Fond as he was of King Manuel, the King had to rein in feelings of support but insisted on sending the royal yacht *Victoria and Albert* to bring the dethroned King and his mother Queen Amélir to England.

the sea, the other over land. But then in 1917 the Revolution crept up like a pack of starving wolves, and, finding a plump and unwary victim, they pounced. Nicholas II was the prey, the obvious scapegoat, as he well knew long before seven assassins arrived at the cellar in Siberia on 18 July 1918. His only son and heir was haemophiliac, a strain inherited from his great-grandmother Queen Victoria, the boy's short life expectancy adding to his father's agony. Today there is a plaque on a dark-red-stoned ruin at the Lower Dacha at Peterhof: 'On this spot the heir to the throne, Tsarevich Alexander, was born'; instead of flowers, there is only litter, sweet papers blowing squalidly around an empty wine bottle.

During his 25-year reign, George V saw emperors overthrown, killed, despised, left penniless and homeless. When Nicholas II's life was in danger during the Bolshevik uprising in 1917, he did not hesitate to extend a warm invitation to him to come to England and be safe. But then, in one of the more painful episodes in British royal history, George quickly changed his mind. This is the prerogative of kings.

The thought of the spread of Bolshevism to England unnerved him; all too easily George could imagine being taken away unceremoniously with Queen Mary in a cart covered with pig straw, to be executed like Marie Antoinette and Louis XVI. He had no appetite for further involvement in the plight of his troubled Russian cousin.

The relationship between the two cousins is as dramatic and poignant as a Shakespeare tragedy. It is a tale of family affection, of privilege, hesitancy, self-preservation and public duty. Like a beautiful glass sculpture which has splintered, some of the pieces are still jagged, memories are sharp, while others are rounded by time. These two Emperors were kinsmen. One survived and one died. This is their story.

ONE

Grandmother of Europe

Queen Victoria presided imperturbably, if not always contentedly, over an empire which covered a quarter of the earth's surface. Respectfully known as 'Grandmother of Europe', ruling England for sixty-four years, her dream was to consolidate the dynasty even further through marriage. Already in the courts of Europe her children and grandchildren held sway.

It helped that most of the crowned heads of Europe were inter-related, so these various rulers all knew each other only too well. Kaiser Wilhelm II of Germany was George V's first cousin, and both were grandsons of Queen Victoria. Tsar Nicholas II of Russia's wife, Princess Alix of Hesse, was also one of the Queen's grandchildren.

Eight of Victoria's grandchildren wore crowns either as reigning monarchs or royal consorts. Her scheme to dominate Europe heading one big royal family had some success for a time, with goodwill visits and exchanges of pleasantries, usually in English, their common language.

Her eldest son, the future King Edward VII, considered the best-dressed man in Europe, was a popular figure, especially with the Danish royal house. The Danish King Christian IX's daughter Alexandra had been an entrancing eighteen-year-old, with pale skin, clear blue eyes and a cloud of brown hair, when she arrived from Copenhagen on 7 March 1863 at the Bricklayers' Arms railway station in the London borough of Southwark. She would marry the Prince of Wales three days later.

A warm and generous personality, Alexandra's beauty endured, but it was not enough for her wandering-eyed husband. His attachment to Mrs Keppel, once described as 'the most perfect mistress in the history of royal infidelity', proved to be the most emotionally destructive. Known as 'La Favorita', she was the great-grandmother of the former Mrs Camilla Parker Bowles, now HRH Duchess of Cornwall and Prince Charles's second wife. Mrs Keppel's daughter, Sonia, cherished memories of visits by her mother's portly admirer, known to her as 'Kingy', who smelt of cigars, gave her Fabergé eggs at Easter and tolerantly allowed the children to roll slices of bread and butter in a race down the seams of his trousers.[1]

Yet the Prince and Princess loved each other and their six children, who were born in fairly quick succession.* The heir to the throne Prince Eddy, Duke of Clarence, was born in 1864, and a second son followed eighteen months later. Not expecting this second baby for another month, the highly social Princess of Wales, who was not quite twenty-one, had been out at a concert, and only reluctantly opted out of a dinner party when she went into labour. Prince George was born at 1.30 a.m. on 3 June 1865 at Marlborough House in London. His name was chosen for its Englishness. An uncomplicated child, he appealed to Queen Victoria because, unlike his siblings, whom she dismissed as being 'puny', he was 'always merry and rosy'.[2]

Not burdened with the prospect of ever being King, George enjoyed an exceptionally loving and carefree start in life. Alexandra was a tactile mother who liked nothing more than the chance to run up to the nursery, put on a flannel apron, wash the children herself 'and see them asleep in their little beds'.[3]

But with the birth of her third child, Princess Louise, in 1867, her stamina declined after a bout of rheumatic fever. In addition, Alexandra's deafness now became more pronounced; she had inherited the disability from her mother Princess Christian, who suffered from otosclerosis.[4] This deafness prevented her joining in general conversation and became a psychological barrier; but it helped her close her ears to whispers about her husband's losses at the gaming tables and the expensive jewels being lavished on his mistresses. The cruel thing was that this deafness could give the misleading impression that Alexandra was featherbrained. It is true she was not always steeped in the works of Kierkegaard, the Danish philosopher, preferring the fairy tales of Hans Christian Andersen, but she had a quick mind and expressed strong political views, hating the Germans when the Duchy of Holstein broke away from

---

*   Prince Albert, Eddy, Duke of Clarence, 1864; Prince George, later King George V, 1865; Princess Louise, 1867, married the Duke of Fife; Princess Victoria, 1868, unmarried; Princess Maud, 1869, married Haakon VII of Norway; Prince Alexander, born 6 April, died 7 April 1871.

Denmark. Royal adviser Lord Esher thought Alexandra often had more original things to say 'than any other member of the family' and believed 'her cleverness has always been under-rated because of her deafness'.[5] Her sister Dagmar was always considered the clever child in the Danish royal family.

A sybarite who smoked 'one small cigar and two cigarettes before breakfast and twelve huge cigars and twenty cigarettes during the day',[6] the Prince of Wales was a kindly father but hardly an example of moral frugality to his growing sons. When he became King, he stripped away the stultifying formality of Queen Victoria's reign, his court now became opulent and hedonistic, and some thought it positively vulgar.

His second son George, in spite of a shy solemnity as he stared out above a large Eton collar, was a high-spirited child. Nursery staff thought him a bit of a 'pickle', especially when they caught him pulling the pigtails of Chinese mandarins at a banquet.[7]

George should have been a confident, uncomplicated child. He rarely experienced his father's wrath. The Prince of Wales believed restraint was needed only for the reins of an excitable racehorse. George himself would be a strict, almost tyrannical father, although 'this attitude . . . of querulous disapproval melted away . . . as his children married', and he was a solicitous father-in-law, charming his sons' wives.

Much of George's childhood was spent away from the panoply of monarchy, and he was thankful he would never be King. For him, life at Sandringham with cricket, tennis and outdoor pursuits was idyllic. This boy, with his true love of nature, absorbed the names of flowers and shrubs on the Norfolk marshes and learned to shoot well under those great, liberating skies of East Anglia. He took a keen interest in farming and knew 'every dog in the kennels and every horse in the royal stables'.[8] These players in rural life remained close to the heart of this country-squire King.

Growing up speaking English and German, attention was paid to young George's English, carefully eradicating any hint of a guttural German accent. His father was always sensitive about received pronunciation and worried that at times he did not sound quite British enough. He was also anxious that his sons should have the sort of well-rounded education he had been denied. Literature had never been an integral part of his education, prompting Lady Frederick Cavendish to say of the Prince of Wales and his wife that

'The melancholy thing [is] that neither he nor the darling Princess ever care to open a book'.[9]

He appointed an austere 32-year-old, the Revd John Dalton, who had first-class honours in theology, as tutor to Eddy and George, his two eldest sons. The clergyman was a martinet, who disapproved of the future King's lifestyle, but he steered the Princes over fourteen years with strait-laced devotion. Dalton set the boundaries for George V's love of order and distaste for louche living. He instilled in him a balanced approach between right- and left-wing political theory.[10] He was less successful with Prince Eddy.

From the age of six, George and his brother had lessons with Dalton. Their day began at seven in the morning with geography and English before breakfast. The clergyman's insistence on timekeeping, sartorial correctness and dedication to duty had less influence on the heir to the throne than on his younger brother. They were fond of Dalton, although he was rigorous and stern. But he did teach them how them to shoot with a bow and arrow, and proved an unexpectedly game target for the Princes.

Years later, George would affectionately point to a favourite spot at Sandringham and recall, 'Down there he ran', referring to the dutiful Dalton, who 'allowed us to shoot at him as the running deer'. But this did not impress Queen Mary, who declared that it was disgraceful that Dalton had never educated the Princes properly.[11]

For George and his siblings social life revolved around the other important royal families of Europe. Holidays were spent with cousins destined to be kings of Denmark, Germany and Russia.

Confident about their immutable destinies, these princely children never felt the need to be overtly competitive, though in every family there is a vexatious relative: everyone found Wilhelm, the future German Kaiser, impossible. He was jealous of the bond between the British and Russian royal families. 'Uncle Bertie' was brother-in-law to Tsar Alexander III, and their formidable empires covered almost a quarter of the world's surface; this he found deeply irritating.

The Queen often complained to his mother, Princess Victoria,* about his bombastic behaviour. But the Kaiser had a withered arm,

---

* Princess Victoria married Frederick III, Emperor of Germany and King of Prussia.

so allowances were made for this disability when he over-compensated for this weakness with aggression. The Queen came to dread the Kaiser's visits, because he could be rude and disruptive. 'It seems,' she grumbled once, 'as if someone is constantly stirring him up against his relations.'[12] His biggest sin was being unforgivably late for dinner, engrossed in the latest P.G. Wodehouse, his favourite reading. To Queen Victoria, death was the only acceptable excuse for not appearing punctually at dinner. Princess Alexandra, who could not stand the Kaiser, dismissed him as a 'mad and a conceited ass'. Her sister Dagmar, Empress Maria Feodorovna of Russia, shared this view and never forgave Wilhelm for playing Cupid in what she believed was her son Nicholas's disastrous marriage.*

Nicholas on the other hand was a charming and cultivated cousin of whom George was particularly fond. Although he was heir to a mighty empire, Nicholas found Queen Victoria formidable. The Romanovs always felt that she was contemptuous of them. Grand Duchess Olga, the Tsar's sister, once said, 'I may be wrong, but [Queen Victoria] wasn't really fond of anyone except her German relations. She certainly did not like us . . . she said that we possessed a "bourgeoisie".'[13] Ironic, since Russian society was made up mainly of aristocracy and serfs.

The Queen's feelings of unease about the Russian royal family had been exacerbated by the marriage in 1874 of her second son, Prince Alfred of Edinburgh, to Grand Duchess Maria, who was Tsar Alexander II's only surviving daughter. He brought his bride to England, installed her in Clarence House and even created a Russian Orthodox chapel for her on the first floor. But Maria, spoilt by an adoring father, found life at the English court tedious and made no secret of her boredom. Her whims were tolerated – all her shoes were specially made so that they were interchangeable, with no left and right – but not her haughty view that as the Russian Emperor's daughter she was infinitely superior to the English royals and their German forebears.†

None of this helped relations with Russia. Alexander III had dismissed Queen Victoria as 'pampered, sentimental . . . selfish', and

---

* See Chapter 7.

† The marriage was far from happy; Alfred went back to Germany to continue his career as a naval officer and in 1893 succeeded as Duke of Saxe-Coburg-Gotha.

thought her 'a self-indulgent old babushka'.[14] The Queen spoke disparagingly of him as 'the fat Tsar' and blamed Dagmar, his altogether too vivacious wife, for this antipathy.

The Sea King's two daughters, Alexandra and Dagmar, were confident enough in their own impeccable royal lineage as children of King Christian IX not to be easily intimidated by their foreign royal in-laws. They took every opportunity to be together in England, Denmark or Russia at family festivities. Edward VII once described these get-togethers as the 'trade union of the continent's crowns'.[15]

All seemed set fair for these two powerful royal families. The two cousins, Nicholas and George, would play a crucial role in world affairs and would be a force in some of the more cataclysmic events of the twentieth century.

TWO

Motherless Alicky

Queen Victoria treated her family like pieces on a chessboard, to be positioned in alliances which would enhance the dynasty. This frequently involved marriage between cousins who may not have been attracted to each other. Nobody ever seemed to worry about the genetic wisdom of these alliances. Most of the pawns were biddable, but some resisted. One of these was Princess Alix of Hesse, motherless from the age of six and brought up at the British court.

A dedicated meddler, the Queen had her eye on Alix as wife for Prince Eddy, Duke of Clarence, the future King. Love did not enter into the equation. They were first cousins: her mother, Princess Alice, and his father, the Prince of Wales, were brother and sister.

Princess Alice, who was Queen Victoria's second daughter, was nineteen when she married Prince Louis, Grand Duke of Hesse. In 1862, Alice gave up a comfortable royal lifestyle in England to become the chatelaine of a far from Ruritanian castle in the small, impoverished Hesse-Darmstadt principality in Germany.

But the Hesses, with their distinctive red and white flag, were one of the oldest royal houses in Europe and would produce the last Tsarina of Russia. Once a cultural oasis, Darmstadt had attracted Schiller and Goethe and other writers who felt inspired by the friendly atmosphere of the palace and were seduced by the charm of the old town, with its cobbled streets and literary history.

The cultivated Princess Alice, who appreciated books and music, tried to continue this tradition, and house guests sometimes included John Ruskin and Alfred, Lord Tennyson. But when Hesse lost its independence and became part of the German Empire, it ceded its artistic elan to Weimar.

The wedding of 'English Alice' had been a dismal event following the death of her father Prince Albert on 14 December 1861. The Queen, who could be mournful at the drop of a lace handkerchief, in low voice never missed an opportunity to remind the family how regrettable it was that he never saw his 'poor dear Alice' becoming Grand Duchess of Hesse and by Rhine.

The Prince Consort, who always involved himself in family matters, was so relieved that this daughter, never a great beauty, had found a husband, he personally ordered her wedding dress. But he never saw her marry, and, six months after his death, on 1 July 1862 the unfortunate bride had to choose a black trousseau. Her wedding was positively funereal. Inconsolable, Queen Victoria insisted that the ceremony to the good-looking Leopold, Duke of Hesse should be in the dining room at Osborne, rather than in the formal grandeur of St James's Palace. The toll of arranging her father's funeral and supporting the Queen in her elaborate grieving ritual sparked off the start of Alice's nervous headaches, a frailty inherited by her daughter Alix.

Settling into her German home by the banks of the Rhine, Alice nostalgically filled the white New Palace with English wallpaper and furniture from Maples, with sentimental paintings of stags at bay, silver-framed photographs of shooting and skating parties, and watercolours of Balmoral and Sandringham.

When Alice became pregnant, her mother felt excessively for her. 'Oh, if it could be I who was to wear the shift,'[1] the Queen wailed with that little bit of self-absorption which was never a million miles away, adding, 'that it could be I who was to undergo the trial, that I could be giving another child to Albert'. Aged forty-four, Victoria was reduced to hugging her dead husband's red dressing gown. Her protestation that she longed to wear a maternity smock again was questionable as she had given birth to nine children and found babies positively 'repulsive', often describing them as 'frightful . . . nasty objects'.[2]

Alice gave birth to seven children in fairly quick succession. Her first, Victoria, born in 1863, married thirty-year-old Prince Louis of Battenburg,* then serving in the British Navy and described by the Kaiser as the 'most handsome man in Europe'.

---

*   Later given the more English-sounding title of Milford Haven. Their children included Earl Mountbatten of Burma and Princess Alice of Greece, who was Prince Philip's mother. But the marriage in 1884 very nearly did not take place, because the night before the wedding the 21-year-old Princess had eaten shellfish. An hour and a half before the wedding, which was due to start at 4.30 p.m., the execrable lobster had its revenge and she became violently ill. As if that were not enough, the unfortunate bride had to hobble up the aisle because she had hurt her ankle falling over a coal scuttle.

Alice's second child, Elizabeth, 'Ella', described by Queen Victoria as 'a wonderfully pretty girl', was born in 1864.* The eldest son and heir, Ernst, was born in 1868; a younger boy, Frederick, known in the family as 'Frittie', died dramatically when he was three years old.

Absorbed playing Chopin's *Funeral March* on the piano,[3] Alice was unaware that her small son had opened one of the bow windows, climbed out and crashed to the ground, where servants found his body on the stone terrace. He died of a brain haemorrhage. Although haunted by grief and guilt, Alice knew that, because he was haemophiliac, his life would have been short and troubled. Queen Victoria was the carrier but always protested, 'This disease has nothing to do with our family.' But there was incontrovertible evidence: in 1876 her youngest son Leopold, Duke of Albany, died of the blood disorder.

Princess Alix of Hesse, the second youngest daughter, was born in 1872. This future Empress of Russia inherited the haemophilia strain from Queen Victoria, this dynastic curse which would have a profound effect on Russian history. Described by her mother as a 'sweet . . . little person, always laughing', Alix's godparents included two Emperors, Edward VII and Alexander III, an auspicious start for this delicate child with a dimple.

It was a loving childhood with an English influence: *Alice in Wonderland* was favourite nursery reading. The Hesse children were brought up to make their own beds, to dust their rooms and look after their pets, which included a fox and a wild boar. But from an early age, Alix began to complain of pains in her legs, later diagnosed as sciatica but stemming from a childhood accident when, chasing her brother and sisters, she had fallen through a glass cloche in the garden, ripping her leg open.

Some of the blame for Alix's bossy inflexibility, so misunderstood and damaging to her later, can be attributed to her English governess, 'Orchie', Mary Anne Orchard, who instructed Alix on the importance of the Bible and rectitude.

When the Hesse family was struck by diphtheria, a scourge heralded by a sore throat, Alice devotedly nursed her family, but in

---

*   Princess Irène, born in 1866, married the Kaiser's younger brother, Prince
    Henry of Prussia, in 1888. Ernst, heir to the title Grand Duke of Hesse, was
    born in 1868.

1878 lost her youngest child, four-year-old May, to what Queen Victoria described as 'that horrid disease'.[4] Alice herself, aged thirty-five, died of diphtheria on 14 December that same year during a blizzard, when gales like harbingers of death rattled the window frames of the sickroom at the New Palace.

This reprise of the Queen's grief seventeen years to the day after Albert's death was a coincidence which she thought 'almost incredible and most mysterious', and was certainly a heaven-sent reason for another protracted spell of mourning. Revisiting Darmstadt in 1880, Victoria approved when she saw that her daughter's bedroom was still draped in black, exactly as it had been the day she died.

'It is the good who are always taken,' the Prince of Wales cried in an outburst of sentimentality when he heard about the death of his sister. Taking the news equally badly, his wife Alexandra sobbed, 'I wish I had died instead of her.'[5]

The Prince of Wales had been close to this delicate sister and liked visiting Darmstadt in springtime when the woods were sprinkled with lily of the valley as they picnicked in pine forests near sandy inlets by the Rhine. They were so devoted that, when he was ill with typhoid in 1871, Alice, although three months pregnant, rushed home to be at his bedside at Sandringham and did not return to Darmstadt until she was sure he was out of danger. Every year after her death he always made a point of visiting her grave in the family mausoleum.

The trauma of losing her mother when she was six altered Alix's personality. This engaging child now became remote and withdrawn. A cold carapace hid the vulnerability of a highly strung child missing the sheltering love of an exceptionally close family.

The Queen now seized the moment to become a second mother to her Hesse grandchildren. In a distraught letter from Windsor Castle to Alice's 'poor dear children' in Darmstadt, she told them, 'You have had the most terrible blow which can befall children,' and promised that, as their 'poor old Grandmama' she would try to be a mother to them, signing it, 'Your devoted and most unhappy Grandmama, VRI'.*

Barely a month after his wife's death, Grand Duke Louis responded gratefully to Queen Victoria's sympathetic letter and

---

* Victoria Regina Imperatrix.

asked if he could bring his motherless children to England. He had tried hard to compensate but they pined for their mother, their old toys had been burnt and the nursery smelt of disinfectant.

Sympathetic as she was to her widower son-in-law, Prince Louis of Hesse, the Queen's moist-eyed compassion ran dry when he had the temerity to marry again. The Prince's second wife, Alexandrine von Kolemine, was soon being described as a 'depraved' and 'scheming' woman, and soon eased out, dispatched with a large compensatory sum of money. Only with the abrupt end to this second marriage was the Grand Duke forgiven.

'Uncle Bertie', the future Edward VII, met the sad little party from Darmstadt at Flushing in Holland in January 1879. He welcomed them on board the royal yacht as they set sail for Cowes and the enveloping warmth of Osborne. They were taken then to Windsor Castle, where Queen Victoria thought six-year-old Alix, with her long fair hair and wistful smile, a child to be spoilt and moulded.

Acting *in loco parentis*, the Queen was delighted to sweep up the Hesse children into court life. The motherless 'darling . . . gentle, little, simple Alicky', versed in the art of pleasing, called the Queen 'Gangan', and revelled in being the clear favourite among twenty-seven grandchildren. Alix was soon at home in the British court, which still retained comforting familiar German touches created by the Prince Consort. Used to the heel-clicking formality in Germany, Alix was not surprised on visits to England when servants bowed low to the Queen or removed their shoes to walk on tabletops arranging the epergnes and candelabra.

The Hesse children all spoke English, lapsing into German only occasionally in the excitement of hide-and-seek in the turrets of Windsor Castle or as they bowled their hoops down the Long Corridor.[6] Soon Alix thought of herself as an English princess enjoying a closeness to her kingly cousins 'George' and 'Eddy'; their lives would be inextricably linked. Absorbed in his life in the Royal Navy, George never thought of Alix, this appealing if sometimes prim German cousin, as anything other than a little sister. One day he would have her life in his hands.

The Hesse children were less in awe of the Queen than their English cousins. George V's future wife, Princess May, had as a child burst into tears when she first saw Queen Victoria. The Duke of Windsor remembered his great-grandmother as a daunting figure, with such an aura of majesty that 'she was almost regarded as a divinity'. Alix recalled her own terror once when, on a guttural order from the Queen, she was asked to play the piano to amuse the royal guests, and how, with 'clammy hands . . . literally glued to the keys', she obeyed.[7] Years later she would happily play Grieg, the Queen's favourite composer.

But most memories for Alix and her siblings were of the fun they had as children at Windsor Castle, recalling how their 'wild romps were often interrupted by one of the pages bringing a message from the Queen that she would not have so much noise'.

Knowing she was favoured, Alix felt comfortable walking alongside the Queen, a four-foot eleven-inches tall, thirteen-stone, black-bombazined figure gliding authoritatively in ribboned satin sandals to intimidate generals and gillies. Smelling of orange-water cologne, a tulle cap with streamers covering her bun, Victoria ruled over colonies and country, unsmiling in public but warmly receptive to this granddaughter, this 'dear little thing'.

Both were happiest at Osborne and Windsor, disliking the formality of Buckingham Palace, where Alix, grey eyes wide, listened as courtiers, advisers and politicians competed for the attention of the Empress of India. When she found this sombre atmosphere too boring, she skipped off to the nursery, where she got such pleasure from cranking up the tail of a toy lion which, when it opened its mouth, swallowed a Russian soldier.[8]

Alix also learned practical things at the British court. Years later in captivity, helping an attendant struggling with blankets and sheets, she told her, 'When I was a girl my grandmother, Queen Victoria, showed me how to make a bed. I'll teach you *à la mode de Windsor*.'[9]

Growing into a slender young girl with sensitive features, Alix became increasingly prone to melancholy. Her childhood pet name 'Sunny' was unfortunate. In common with women called 'Kitten' or 'Baby', they often have reason to regret these childhood soubriquets later as they put on weight or become prematurely wrinkled or, in Alix's case, increasingly sour.

As she grew older, Alix, though beautiful and with a tiny waist, often had a disagreeable, unsmiling, pinched look. A German cousin, Marie Louise of Schleswig-Holstein, once said, 'Alix, you always play at being sorrowful,' adding prophetically, 'One day the Almighty will send some real crashing sorrows and then what are you going to do?'

Her brooding nature and irritability would later be seen as an expression of disapproval at the Russian court. They mocked their English Tsarina's nervous tendency to flush scarlet. Queen Victoria and certain cynics might mourn the absence of the blush, but this nervous trait was cruelly scrutinised by the imperial courtiers, who were quick to notice Alix's telltale blood-red flush, which no Romanov jewelled necklace could ever disguise.

Yet two future emperors, one Russian, one British, had sought her hand in marriage.

THREE

'We Bathe Every Day'

Osborne House, that happiest and most informal of the royal homes, was loved by generations as a snug royal haven on the Isle of Wight. It was a favourite place for holidays, especially for royal women. The weather was gentle enough for tea on the velvety lawns and a little croquet, unlike Balmoral, where they had to accompany the guns, turning blue with cold in the Highlands.

An Italianate villa, Osborne had been transformed by Albert the Prince Consort, with the initials 'V' and 'A' entwined on the ceilings, and antler-horn furniture he brought from Hamburg. It was heavy with Teutonic sentiment. After Albert's death, the children knew they must tiptoe past his bedroom, where everything was kept as if he were alive: his clothes laid out, his watch fully wound, his handkerchief on the sofa and always fresh flowers in the room.

They stood silently before the Landseer picture, commissioned by the Queen in 1841, of Eos, the favourite greyhound bitch that Prince Albert had brought over from Germany. This portrait of the speedy animal sniffing her husband's hat and gloves on a doeskin stool could reduce Victoria to tears.

The children had the Prince Consort to thank for the Swiss Cottage which he created in the grounds, where they played games and had nursery tea. Years later, Alix like to reminisce about the pretty thatched cottages on the Isle of Wight, 'I always loved the little houses . . . dear little houses set in their pretty gardens'. Already she knew all about Osborne. It was the place where her mother had been married and was as integral a part of her English upbringing as Windsor.

Osborne, for her, was associated with dreamy holidays, sailing, building sandcastles on the beach, merry picnics and playing with toys used by generations of royal children. It was here Alix really got to know 'Uncle Bertie's' children, her English cousins, who were in Queen Victoria's opinion a handful and 'wild as hawks'. They knew each other already because, after her mother's death, the

Prince of Wales brought his children to Germany, hoping to comfort his late sister's broken family, and they all stayed in a pretty hunting lodge above a forest at Wolfsgarten, not far from Frankfurt.

The royal children had been spoilt by their parents and were full of self-confidence, but they never forgot their privileged place in the royal pecking order. Although Alix and George shared formative years together, these two cousins had little in common except a shared love of Osborne. In an enthusiastic letter written to his tutor, Dalton, dated 20 August 1876,[1] George told him in a neat, firm hand how 'we catch crabs nearly every day . . . we bathe every day'.

Taken under her grandmother's black-silk wing, Alix now enjoyed the most carefree times she had ever known, shrimping, playing tennis, racing round the oak and chestnut trees, drinking lemonade and competing with her cousins for favourite 'curly biscuits' and chocolate cake at tea. The German children tried to behave well during ten-course lunches and not put sticky fingers on the original gold hand-blocked wallpaper at Osborne, and they marvelled at the exotic livery of Grandmama's two Indian servants.

Osborne was the Queen's idea of a simple family holiday. The royal party was accompanied by over a hundred servants, who moved like silent, swift-footed gazelles and were rarely seen or heard. On late summer days, with huge house parties and surrounded by generations of royal children, Alix felt the reassuring glow of continuity.

The Queen liked to play at being 'ordinary', using her bathing machine on the 'charming beach'. How wonderful it was having it 'quite to ourselves', she liked to say, unaware of the phalanx of sturdy royal retainers waving away any bathers straying too close. There were fishing trips *en famille*; on one occasion, nineteen whiting were caught and taken proudly by the royal children to the chefs in the kitchens.

In Queen Victoria's eyes, Alix was 'a most lovely child'.[2] She was to be indulged, and so was allowed to join her grandmother for breakfast on the jasmine-scented terrace. The Queen fussed over Alix, who picked at her food while enjoying her own boiled egg served in a solid-gold egg cup shaped like a chicken. Victoria preferred the seaside souvenir egg cup bought for her by John Brown, her beloved factotum.[3]

Curry, created by the exotic-looking Indian servant known as the munshi, Hefiz Abdul Karim, who wore a scarlet uniform and turban, was not a favourite. This *Spitzbube* – scamp – of a granddaughter was not too enthusiastic about toad-in-the-hole either. Food at Hesse had never been light, but English puddings defeated Alix's sister, Princess Victoria, who could never stand the 'awful bread and butter puddings . . . without a raisin' or 'stodgy tapioca . . . full of lumps'. On crisp evenings the children were often summoned to the crimson drawing room, where they sat by the beechwood fire. Coal was not allowed.

Years later, Alix would return to the Isle of Wight as Tsarina. The Kaiser came to Cowes Regatta every summer, bringing with him a large suite, his great white yacht dominating the Solent. The Prince of Wales sometimes dreaded 'Willy's' disruptive presence, but the Tsar on the other hand was warmly welcomed. He arrived with Alix and his children just before the Regatta Week in 1909 on board the graceful 4,500-ton *Standart*, with its black and gold stripe and gold imperial double eagle at the stern. Built in Denmark, with polished teak decks, chintzy sitting rooms and a balalaika orchestra, it was, unlike his cousin George's yacht, designed for pleasure rather than competitive racing. The Tsar's children, who had hardly ever been abroad, scampered about 'the Island' enjoying a rare freedom. For some reason, the Prince of Wales had been unable to accommodate Nicholas and his family at the big house, and instead installed them in the much smaller Barton Lodge.

Prince John thought his Russian cousins, especially the tsarinas in their white lace dresses and becoming hats, were like exotic birds. While the Tsar admired Britain's battleships from the deck of the *Victoria and Albert*, John was capturing him in a series of irreverent, comical drawings.[4] His older brother, David, the future Duke of Windsor, given the task of showing Nicholas II round Isle of Wight, did not find the Russian Emperor a man 'of marked personality'.[5] But he had captured Alix's heart.

As the Hesse girls grew up, Victoria saw them as a potential harvest of suitable wives and was increasingly determined to marry 'Alicky' off to her eldest grandson, Prince Eddy, Duke of Clarence and heir to the throne; so much more convenient than having to cope with some unmalleable foreign princess. A tall, slight figure with a waxed moustache and a hearing problem, Prince Eddy, according to his tutor Dalton, was always slipping away into low dives in seaports and keeping questionable company. His younger brother George, on the other hand, an exemplary royal son, industrious, with a keenly developed sense of duty, was not in need of the steadying influence of a Hesse princess. The Queen began taking Alix on public engagements, giving her a taste of the public life she would lead as a future consort.

Alix had always loved Balmoral, cantering over the hills on her mountain pony, visiting the keeper's cottage in the woods and stopping by the small shops selling tam-o'-shanter caps, sweets and fishing tackle.[6] The Queen now arranged a meeting for her seventeen-year-old granddaughter with Prince Eddy, hoping the charm of her tartan home, walks through the heather, a little stalking and the wail of the bagpipes would encourage romance.

But Alix was no longer appreciating the hearty outdoor pursuits enjoyed by her English royal cousins and was mentally sophisticated, already reading books on philosophy, mathematics and astronomy. Her English cousin George, on the other hand, preferred newspapers to books, vaudeville to opera, and was happiest when outdoors sailing, playing polo, riding or shooting. For indoor pursuits, he might pick up a billiard cue or a magnifying glass to examine his stamp collection rather than play the piano or go to the royal library.

Any antipathy George later felt for Alix may have begun with what he saw as her intellectual superiority, not to mention the way she took for granted her privileged place at the British court, never a suitably grateful poor relation. There were those at court who thought the young German Princess far too pleased with herself.

An opinionated and independent young woman, she would not be bullied into a marriage by a grandmother constantly extolling Prince Eddy's virtues, who was not to know that Alix had been in love with the future Tsar of Russia since the age of twelve.

FOUR

Their Mothers' Darling Boys

The cousins Nicholas and George had boisterous, chivalrous fathers. But it was their mothers who had intensely emotional ties with their sons. There was a slim age difference between Nicholas and George; they shared a restrained humour, a love of uniforms and a devotion to their mothers, who continued to indulge them long after they became emperors.

This was quite unlike the relationship the Prince of Wales had with his mother, Queen Victoria, which was so unrelentingly stern and repressive that, when she died, the life of a playboy became irresistible. A bon viveur who loved cigars, racing, gambling and pretty women, King Edward VII was smarter than his hedonistic image allowed. Astute politically, and experienced, having waited so long to succeed, he was quick to assimilate the public mood and he understood foreign diplomacy. He was also an indulgent father.

Alexander III, on the other hand, was uncomplicated, less diplomatic, commanding respect if only for his girth. Fond of drink and horseplay, he was a loving parent. 'I do not need porcelain, I want normal, healthy Russian children,' he told the children's tutors. Wearing peasant clothes, he worked at his huge desk with his dogs at his feet, scribbling away and often shouting, 'Fools! Idiots!' when he came across an unsatisfactory document.

He became Russian Emperor as a result of two tragedies: one was the death in 1865 of his elder brother, Grand Duke Nicholas 'Nixa' Alexandrovich, Crown Prince of Russia; and the second was the murder in March 1881 of his father Alexander II. The only positive outcome for him was his marriage to Dagmar, Queen Alexandra's sister, who had been engaged to his older brother. This proved a love match. She was adored by her brown-bearded husband, who indulged her love of clothes and jewellery. A sparkling presence at the Russian court, she was not liked by other women.

Queen Victoria, however, did approve of Dagmar, thinking her a 'very nice girl', cleverer than her daughter-in-law Princess Alexandra, but not as ravishing. Dagmar did not, she thought, have 'the distinguished face and appearance of dear Alix'.

Dagmar and Alexander had five children, three sons and two daughters.* Dagmar never found pregnancy easy, or her sister's advice to eat raw ham when feeling nauseous. 'Did you suffer much? My poor little Minny – or did you have a little chloroform this time?'[1] her sister Alexandra anxiously enquired after a difficult labour. All her children were christened in the Winter Palace church wearing special detachable bibs, embroidered with the gold Romanov double-headed eagle and imperial crown.

Nicholas II was born at 12.30 a.m. on 6 May 1868, the saint's day of the Old Testament figure Job the Long-suffering, and this always made him feel that he was ill-starred. Nothing he touched, he once said, ever really worked, and he blamed this on the luckless Job. When the French Ambassador, Maurice Paléologue, congratulated the Tsar on his association with the saint's day of Job, celebrated in the Orthodox Church, Nicholas replied mournfully that he thought he was doomed. 'I am unlucky,' he said simply. Had his uncle survived, he would have been merely the nephew of the Tsar, and could have been an enlightened patron of the arts he so enjoyed, appearing at Mariinskiy† first nights and ceremonial occasions in Moscow and St Petersburg.

When his father had his first sight of Nicholas as a tiny baby, the doctor told him, 'Your son's no use, you must have him shot.' Instead the doctor was shot and the baby flourished, cherished by his mother, who never forgot his early frailty. The guns boomed out from the Peter and Paul Fortress, in salute to this tiny bundle, the last of the Romanov family to wear the imperial crown.

At the time of his birth, 'among his contemporaries in the 1870s only two men faced an inheritance as awesome as his own'.[2] One was the young Emperor of China,‡ and the other was the Habsburg Crown Prince Rudolph, who committed suicide with his mistress§ at Mayerling in 1889.

---

* Nicholas, 1868, George, 1871 and Michael, 1878; also two daughters, Xenia, 1875 and Olga, 1882. Another son, Alexander, was born on 26 May 1869 and died of meningitis a year later.

† Theatre and now home of the Bolshoi Ballet in St Petersburg.

‡ Guangxu of the Qing Dynasty.

§ Baroness Maria Vetsera.

The Empress, like her sister Alexandra, was such a loving mother, it was to the detriment of Nicholas, who as a result was distinctly immature, even after he became Emperor in 1894. 'The great trouble with your Russian Grand Dukes is that while they are brought up quite simply, they are never allowed to think themselves as simple mortals,' Emperor Frederick of Germany told Princess Catherine Radziwill.[3] Nicholas was cocooned in the inalienable belief that as Tsar he was untouchable.

The maternal bond between Nicholas and Dagmar had been strengthened when Alexander III went off to command an army corps in the Russo-Turkish War. Nicholas, aged nine, grieved not so much for his burly father but for his mother, and desperately tried to comfort her. He had never seen her cry before and, putting his arms around her neck, he kissed her as she lovingly encircled him in her arms.[4]

Alexandra was an equally clingy mother. She found it difficult ever to think of George as anything but as her own 'Darling Little Georgie'. He reciprocated. Once, homesick on board HMS *Dreadnought* in Corfu in 1886 and pining for Sandringham, he wrote to his mother, telling her he longed to be with her so much, 'it almost makes me cry when I think of it. I wonder who will have that sweet little room of mine, you must go and see it sometimes and imagine that your little Georgie dear is living in it.' He was, at the time, a 21-year-old naval officer. Even as the bearded commander of a warship, she sent him solicitous letters warning him not to get his feet wet.

The two men grew to be tautly correct, but their mothers' exuberance never failed to work its magic, especially when they went to Denmark for uninhibited Danish royal family reunions with lots of practical jokes and horseplay. This usually involved the simple fun of spraying each other with soda siphons.

George gradually developed a less oedipal attitude towards his mother. Devoted though he was to 'Darling Motherdear', he could be impervious to her influence, which was never more in evidence than in 1917 when he made the decision to refuse her nephew, the Tsar, safe haven. He was equally adamant in refusing to help when his cousin, King Constantine I of Greece, had fallen from favour. George pointed out to his distraught mother that he was powerless to help 'Tino', her favourite brother William's son. She always had a soft spot for this boy.[5]

Brother 'Willi', born in 1845, had been an eighteen-year-old naval cadet when he was asked one evening at Marlborough House by Lord Palmerston if he might like to become King of Greece. Not hugely academic, the boy accepted with alacrity, and became George I of Greece, confirming once more that the map of Europe was a royal chessboard.[6] In spite of his mother's wheedling, George remained firm: 'I am not prepared now on account of the strong feeling which certainly exists in this country against him, to do anything.'[7]

Despite Dagmar's emotional indulgence at Gatchina, an 'English style' natural-stone palace with a moat, Nicholas and his siblings slept on camp beds, had cold baths and ate black bread for breakfast. Once he was so famished that he ate the beeswax from around a gold crucifix. An English nanny, Miss Elizabeth Franklin, occasionally prepared porridge for breakfast.

It was a warm, relaxed upbringing; the Russian imperial family was never afraid to be tactile. Xenia and Olga were closer to their father, who 'was built like a butcher, powerful and extremely muscular. In his youth, he could straighten horseshoes with his bare hands and smash in doors with his bare shoulders.' Alexander could sometimes make Nicholas, a sensitive child, nervous, saying things like 'You are a little girlie',[8] not the kind of remark calculated to inspire early confidence. Yet, if he had been particularly rough or outspoken, Alexander would later go up secretly to Nicholas's bedroom to reassure the boy and next day take him off to shoot bear. In this loving environment the children listened to legends passed down the centuries and were brought up on Pushkin's stories, illustrated by frescoes in the 'Fairy Tale Room'.

For Nicholas, summers were long and carefree, spent on the Baltic coast building sandcastles or riding his bicycle in the grounds of his grandparents' (King Christian IX and Queen Louise) castle in Denmark.

When he was five, he made his first visit to England on board the imperial yacht, sailing into Woolwich with his parents. His mother and his aunt Alexandra created a stir by dressing identically in frothy long white dresses and picture hats brimming with cherries.

Early on, Nicholas and George had surprisingly clear ideas about their lives. One wanted to be a sailor, the other a soldier. They were both educated at home. One of Nicholas's tutors, Charles Heath, was responsible for his perfect English; he also spoke and read

French and German. It was a well-rounded education with emphasis on music, calligraphy, chemistry and biology. He was also taught fencing, and enjoyed riding, shooting and the open-air life.

George was still a child when he told his parents that he wanted nothing more than a life at sea. Although Alexandra fretted, there was no real reason why George should not follow his dream and join the Royal Navy. For his father, it was a relief that his second son had such definite ambition. But, as he was too young to go away by himself, it was decided that Prince Eddy should accompany him. The hope was that a rigorous life at sea might instil in the heir to the throne 'those habits of promptitude and method, of manliness and self-reliance' in which he was, according to Dalton, 'somewhat deficient'.[9]

Eddy was not capable of taking much responsibility and was inclined toward lethargy. He was a frail child.* The Princes' father insisted that Dalton should accompany them. George was just twelve and was one of the youngest cadets ever, apart from Nelson, when in September 1877 they joined 'the old wooden training ship Britannia . . . at the mouth of the river Dart'.[10]

A tough initiation, during which he 'reefed the sail and swabbed the deck' and learned what it was to have 'blistered hands and tired feet',[11] shaped George into a straightforward, no-nonsense future king.

He found being royal was a positive disadvantage; naturally diffident, he confessed, 'It never did me any good to be a Prince . . . and many was the time I wished I hadn't been. Nicknamed 'Sprat', he was on his own admission 'awfully small', a ripe target for bullying: 'I'd get a hiding time and again.'[12] Highly strung, George had a tendency to lie awake worrying, and the salty, abrasive manner which he cultivated later disguised this vulnerability.

Neither was he spared fagging, that old public-school ritual. But he was also a scapegoat and was often caught when sent off to the tuck shop ashore to bring back food forbidden on the ship. Apart from having the sweets confiscated, and being reprimanded, he complained, 'The worst of it was it was always *my* money; they never paid me back.'

When he was fourteen, George joined HMS *Bacchante*,[13] a 4,000 ton fully rigged cruise corvette with auxiliary engines. He stayed for

---

*   He was two months premature, and weighed 3lb 4oz.

three years, went round the world, acquired a vocabulary of swear words, and got used to being covered in grime in the stokehold. He learned to get on with the other midshipmen, not really making friends, but learning how to handle people. He showed an aptitude for mathematics and found learning the geography of his father's empire at first hand much more compelling than struggling with constitutional history and languages, closeted with the patient Dalton, resident tutor on board.

George began to keep a diary in May 1880 using a lined copybook in which he wrote in a firm schoolboy hand, recording the weather but rarely what was in his heart. He found spelling a challenge; later in a letter he referred to a telephone call in which he had been 'wrung up'.[14]

Nicholas had also been fairly protected, but, early on, he became familiar with the great armies he would be expected to command and the principles of 'high service' of the Tsar to his people. It was this military section of his education with Danielovich, Director of the Second St Petersburg Military School, that he loved, and aged sixteen he joined the celebrated Preobrazhensky Regiment.

Two eminent professors painstakingly tried to instil the rudiments of economics into this amiable young man, but his diary for the time reveals how trying he found this instruction, complaining that 'one of the professors . . . bored me to the point that I nearly fell asleep'. Nicholas showed little interest in state council meetings, and once his father, exasperated, threw nuggets of bread at him, which did not help financiers trying to concentrate on the funding needed for the launch of the Trans-Siberian Railway.

The importance of his spiritual role was impressed upon him by his political tutor, Konstantin Pobedonostsev, Chief Procurator of the Most Holy Synod, but even he could not help noticing how often his important pupil became apathetic, yawning and languid as soon as any mention of the business of government arose. Pobedonostsev instilled in Nicholas the belief that the Tsar had an inviolable place in the hearts of the Russian people: after all, Tsar meant Caesar; it was an almost mystical bond, which meant that any move towards democracy in Russia would inevitably prove fatal for the Romanovs.[15]

An early warning of the vulnerability of any Emperor of Russia was stamped on Nicholas's young mind when, in 1881, assassins successfully murdered his grandfather Alexander II at the second attempt. A bomb had been thrown at the Emperor's armoured carriage as it passed along the Catherine Embankment. Fatally, the Tsar got out of the carriage, wanting to help the wounded. Someone in the crowd asked, 'Are you hurt, sir?' 'No, thank God,' the Emperor replied. Then another voice shouted, 'It is too early to thank God', and a second grenade was thrown, blowing his legs away. He asked to be taken home to die in the Winter Palace, where he bled to death within an hour.

Nicholas never forgot the traumatic sight of his grandfather, the man he called 'Anpapa', being carried on to a sofa, his legs shockingly mangled. Doctors were unable to save the Tsar or ease his pain. Nicholas remembered, 'My father took me up to the bed and said to Alexander II, "Papa, your ray of sunshine is here".' At this the dying man smiled and there was a tremble in his eyelashes. Then the Tsar Liberator was dead.

The Prince of Wales came to Russia for the funeral and now invested the new Tsar, Alexander III, with the Order of the Garter. But the moment when the Prince strode into the throne room at the Anichov Palace accompanied by courtiers, one carefully carrying the insignia on blue velvet cushions, was virtually ruined. The new Empress, Dagmar, dissolved into helpless laughter and irreverently nudged her sister the Princess of Wales, whispering, 'Oh! My dear! Do look at them. They look exactly like a row of wet-nurses carrying babies!' The Tsar himself admitted afterwards that he had the greatest difficulty smothering his laughter as 'Uncle Bertie' placed the Garter round his neck.[16]

The new Tsar inherited £9 million and had a personal account at the Bank of England. Like all rich people, he was parsimonious, watching housekeeping bills; soap and candles were to be used down to the last scrap, there was no need to change the table linen every day, and a hundred eggs need no longer be used for an omelette for twenty people.

Alexander II had been an enlightened Tsar, and on the verge of signing a manifesto granting the people a constitutional government, but his successor, 'Sasha', while privately a loving husband and father, became a furious and implacable emperor, launching repressive measures and setting back any hope of reform.

'Orthodoxy, autocracy and patriotism' was now the imperial maxim. The serfs, who had barely had time to enjoy their new-found emancipation, were once again being controlled by bullying landlords, and living in perpetual fear. But an industrialised working class was beginning to emerge in the cities of Kiev, Moscow and St Petersburg, and Marxist ideas were beginning to take hold, offering hope for the struggling, downtrodden masses.

In 1887, there was yet another assassination attempt, this time on Alexander III; it was foiled, and the unsuccessful band of revolutionaries, including Lenin's brother, was executed. Lenin himself, then a radical young lawyer, was determined to avenge his brother's death and set out to destroy the imperial family.

When Alexander died in 1894, of kidney disease at Livadia, there had been some economic progress during his reign, but also a continuing backdrop of repression and hardship. Ordinary people were as poor as ever after thirty years of industrialisation. As Tsar, Alexander had the distinction of having kept the peace throughout his entire reign, and also his huge personal fortune, which so emphasised the continuing contrast between the poverty of his subjects and the wealth of the imperial family.

Nicholas II did not inherit his father's financial acumen or natural authority. When he succeeded he was one of the richest men in the world, but he was an ill-equipped successor, and eventually lost both his vast wealth and his glorious Byzantine heritage.

Alexander III once said of his heir that he was 'just a boy with childish instincts'. Tolstoy described Nicholas as a kind man with a goodwill, but predicted he would be ruined by sycophants and his domineering uncles.

The English monarchy was vulnerable too. Prince Eddy was leading a dissipated life and attracting scandalous rumours. He was certainly not facing up to his responsibilities as heir apparent. He did seem to realise his own inadequacy, and once said of his younger brother, Prince George, 'It is he who ought to be the King and not I!'[18]

FIVE

'Little Darling'

As young men, Nicholas and George enjoyed a little essential philandering. Of the two, Nicholas was the more immature. As a young cavalry officer charmed by the romance of military life, which endured until his death, he loved military parades and dining in the mess.

Carrying out an inspection on horseback, seeing 'A white sea of soldiers in a pretty country on a warm summer day', Nicholas said was one of the most impressive sights he could imagine. There could be nothing finer for him he said, except perhaps seeing 'a squadron of large ships'.[1] His memories were not solely of manoeuvres, but also of drinking bouts with fellow officers, as he recorded in his diary. 'Got stewed, we wallowed in the grass and drank . . . tasted six sorts of port and got soused, felt owlish,' was one entry.

A *Chevalier Gardes* dinner at the barracks might begin formally enough. After an orgy of drinking, their idea of fun was to dash outside, take off all their clothes and sit on the ground, howling like wolves at the night sky.[2] Then the Tsarevich and his cavalry officer companions would jump into sledges and speed off to carouse among the ice hills, often ending up in a gypsy settlement listening to the wild emotive tzigane gypsy music until dawn. On cue, liveried servants brought out huge bowls of champagne, then, biting and kicking each other, the officers rushed on all fours, jockeying for position to lap at the deep-rimmed jorum.

Tsar Alexander III was aware of his son's bacchanalian 'potato* parties', which included casual sex with *poules de luxe*, who were high-class prostitutes, all a far cry from Nicholas's first crush on 'Toria', George's sister, his sedate cousin, a princess. They first met when they were both fifteen, but it was nothing more than an adolescent flirtation. The Tsar decided the time had come to find

* The slang expression for girlfriends and mistresses in use at that time.

Nicholas a suitable mistress, ideally from the *demi-monde*, socially and physically accomplished.

For George, known sometimes as 'Royal George', there was no such helpful introduction from his father, Edward VII, who was too busy with his own libidinous activities. George also was lacking in confidence, but had enjoyed a two-year formative experience at Southsea, where there was an accommodating girl. Solace was also provided by a woman he shared with Prince Eddy in north London, who in his opinion was a 'ripper'.[3] Apart from these trysts in St John's Wood, romantic liaisons with girls in his own circle were few. He was seriously attracted by Julie Stonor, the daughter of one of the Princess of Wales's ladies-in-waiting, and a granddaughter of Sir Robert Peel. Her mother died when she was young, and the Prince and Princess of Wales had cared for her almost like one of their own children. There had been memorable Christmases at Sandringham – in 1885 especially, when George and Julie played the piano together, sang songs, and enjoyed card games and bowls.

But George had to return to naval duties, and was soon posted to Malta. He may have cherished romantic notions, but any future together was out of the question because Julie Stonor was a Roman Catholic. When he returned, this comely girl who, according to the acerbic Lady Geraldine Somerset, a royal lady-in-waiting, had considerable appeal also to George's father, had married the Marquis d'Hautpoul. But they stayed in touch and, long after he was married and as King, he always enjoyed visiting the d'Hautpouls at their home at Turville Heath in Surrey, where it was noted 'his cares and anxieties fell away and he renewed his youth and high spirits as he talked of old times with one of his first and closest women friends'.[4] His devoted mother, who always thought of him as her 'Georgie boy', was quick to sympathise over his broken romance with Julie Stonor. 'Alas, rather a sad case I think for you both,' Alexandra said, 'my two poor children,' though she was not altogether *desolée* at the prospect of her stalwart favourite son staying single a little longer. She enjoyed late breakfast with him around eleven in the morning, when George read Thackeray to her while she was having her hair done.[5]

In Malta, where his uncle Alfred, Duke of Edinburgh, was Commander-in-Chief of the Mediterranean Fleet, there was no shortage of well-connected girls ready to dance with and amuse 'P.G.', as George was known by friends.

Fairly inexperienced and rather susceptible, he was charmed by his uncle's wife, Grand Duchess Marie, the daughter of Alexander II of Russia, who had been scathing about what she saw as the lacklustre British court.

He then became seriously attracted to their daughter, his cousin 'Missy', Marie of Edinburgh. Queen Victoria approved but his mother did not. He kissed Missy once and thought this was the only preliminary needed before marriage. But Marie's ambitious parents quickly propelled her towards the Crown Prince of Romania, which was taken as a slight by the Prince and Princess of Wales. Later, Marie of Romania was a charming if provocative guest at Buckingham Palace.

As his Commander-in-Chief, Alfred was only too glad to arrange parties and receptions for George in Malta, which were just what the Prince of Wales dreaded, knowing only too well the social temptations of this seductive climate. Messages were being sent with advice that 'The dear boy ought to put the muzzle on in hot climates or else he will be seedy.'[6] Instead of a muzzle, George grew a beard.

The Prince of Wales kept up a barrage of instructions: his son was to be kept busy, he should be sent away on exercises at sea so he would not be 'kicking his heels'. Emphasising his concern to Captain Henry Stephenson, who was in charge of Prince George's naval training, he stressed, 'I am most anxious that my son should not be for long at Malta, as I am sure in every respect it is undesirable.' In another urgent, private and confidential note to Stephenson dated 27 July 1887 the Prince of Wales took things further, saying that Malta was a complete 'waste of time', a place where 'there was nothing but tittle-tattle . . . and . . . coffee-housing!'

Even his mother joined the chorus of protective anxiety, urging Captain Stephenson to get her darling second son away from the iniquities of Malta and 'its dissipations'. It might have been some comfort to his parents to know that George's fleshpot excesses were limited to being luridly tattooed when his ship had put in at Tokyo in 1882, a fashionable trend among the aristocracy, often later regretted. Only his mother and his personal valet ever saw the bright yellow-and-red fiery dragons created by a Japanese tattooist called Hori Chyo on his arms and shoulders. 'These will not be seen again,' he told his manservant after his coronation in 1911.

George would have reason to echo his father's aversion to Malta later, calling this pleasant Mediterranean port 'a bloody place'. On the eve of his engagement to Princess May, he was embarrassed by a rumour that he had been secretly married in Malta already and had three children. An English newspaper called the *Star* had picked up the titillating allegation from the *Liberator*, a magazine published in Paris. This scandal would haunt him later when he became King. Under the provocative headline 'Sanctified Bigamy', it was claimed that, as a naval officer stationed in Malta, George had morganatically married Laura, the younger daughter of a British Admiral, Sir Michael Culme-Seymour.

While his father believed the worst, imagining his son in the unsavoury dives of Sliema, the port, in reality George was more preoccupied with sailing, cricket, billiards and seaside picnics. He did find time for dancing and reading undemanding romantic novels, enjoying particularly *Wrong on Both Sides*. 'Such a lovely book,' he said. 'I always cry over it.'[7] George's affections were more for his polo pony, who was called Real Jam, than for any admiral's daughter.

While the Prince of Wales fretted about his son being attracted to the wrong sort of woman in Malta, Alexander III had taken positive steps to direct his heir's emotional development. He orchestrated a romantic encounter with a sociable leading dancer, Mathilde Kschessinska, who had trained from the age of nine at the Imperial Ballet School. He took his diffident heir to a graduation performance at the yellow and white Empire-style Imperial Theatre School, where the children were astonished to see Alexander III, his wife and the Tsarevich backstage afterwards.

'Where is Kschessinska?' cried the Tsar. Then, spotting seventeen-year-old Mathilde, he boomed, 'Sit next to me,' elbowing aside a star pupil who had been selected for the honour. He ordered Nicholas to sit on Mathilde's other side and, with heavy humour and a broad grin, warned, 'Careful now! Not too much flirting!'

Mathilde, born on 19 August 1872, was the youngest of thirteen children. Four feet eleven inches tall, she would become one of Russia's most celebrated ballerinas, and would be crowned with wreaths and palms in silver and gold. Her Polish father, Adam Felix Kschessinska, had brought his native dances, including the mazurka, to St Petersburg. Mathilde enjoyed a happy childhood with traditional Polish Easters celebrated with special creamy fish soups and baked *koulitchs*, these being twelve loaves, one for each apostle, and always cooked by Mathilde's father.

It was not long before the Tsarevich was saying openly, 'I've fallen madly in love with Little K.' Alexander III's strategy had taken off dangerously well. He now feared his inexperienced son might even want to marry the dancer, so Nicholas was sent off on a world tour, often the royal recipe for princely personal development.

Nicholas left on 23 October 1890, and enjoyed Egypt, where he played chess, rode a donkey, learned to eat the Arab way with his fingers while looking at dancing girls, got drunk and did a little sightseeing round the famous temple at Luxor. But he formed a jaundiced opinion of Japan, where a crazed policeman in Otsu leapt out at him, cutting his forehead to the bone and giving him headaches for the rest of his life. His cousin, Prince George of Greece, gamely fought off the assailant with a walking stick. It was popularly rumoured that his attacker had not been a policemen but an enraged husband who thought Nicholas was paying too much attention to his lotus-blossom wife. Nicholas never got over his antipathy to the Japanese. Once when an envoy of the Mikado was coming to see him he declared, 'An insufferable morning. I received the Swedish Minister and the Japanese monkey.' For such a gentle man, he could be intolerant; he was anti-Semitic but fond of his Muslim subjects.

On his return after nine months, Nicholas was desperate to see Kschessinska and was soon assiduously attending ballet rehearsals. The Emperor's choice had been clever, because she was worldly and sophisticated and would give Nicholas self-confidence. Not conventionally beautiful, she had exceptional energy and developed a style of dancing which some thought wanton. Her way of twirling her leg over four chairs placed in a square became the talk of St Petersburg, and balletomanes marvelled at the way she could execute thirty-two fouettés, occasionally insouciantly followed by another thirty-two. News of her legendary legs and very short tutus prompted crowned heads including the Shah of Persia to show an intense interest in Russian ballet. All the men in the imperial family genuinely enjoyed classical dance, so it was never a surprise to see a great strapping grand duke sitting in the stalls riveted by the jetés of a Sugar Plum Fairy.

The romance between Nicholas and Mathilde began like a children's story, when a young guards officer called one evening at Kschessinska's parents' house. Giving his name as Eugene Volkoff, he was shown into the sitting room, where the mystery visitor was then revealed as the Tsarevich, who bowed low and said softly, 'Since our meeting I have been in the clouds!' This not very large house is now a sweet factory in a dilapidated part of St Petersburg.

This was the start of the Tsarevich's intense love affair with a worldly, sophisticated opportunist. They began to be seen publicly, enjoying tête-à-têtes over the samovar in the imperial box, where Nicholas was attentive, calling her his 'canary', instructing his servants in their gold-eagle-embossed red jackets to present his mistress with a porcelain cup of delicate tea and almond-scented milk. He took her to supper at Restaurant Cuba, one of the most glamorous restaurants in St Petersburg, where once in a fracas he had hurled a crystal bowl of caviar in a city prefect's face during a police raid.

Socially assured, 'Little K', although tiny, liked making an entrance, appearing on one occasion at a ball in a 'black domino with a lace mask', saying later that she had 'only showed my teeth and . . . my smile'.

As the affair gained momentum, gifts from 'Niki' followed: gold bracelets studded with diamonds, necklaces, and a house in a more prestigious part of St Petersburg. As a house-warming present he gave her a vodka service with eight gold glasses studded with precious stones, and a photograph inscribed 'To my dear Panni'.*

Kschessinska's house, with elaborate candelabras studded with gold-swan ballet symbols and her Louis XVI drawing room with Russian Empire-style furniture, was created solely for the Tsarevich's pleasure; here he was entertained with champagne and coquetry. They enjoyed sublime food, served on Limoges porcelain with Catherine the Great gold cutlery. At Christmas, tiny diamonds glittered on the branches of small fir trees.

In the rose garden dotted with sensual marble nymphs, Kschessinska served tea in a little temple. Her swimming pool, a fashionable asset though hardly used in this cold city in the far north of Europe, was decorated with flowers and leaves to give a *trompe l'oeil* effect of a set from the ballet *Swan Lake*. Her pet goat, which appeared with her in the ballet *Esmeralda*, had its own special servant.

As a hostess in one of her sculptured, long satin dresses with a low-cut silk bodice and bird-of-paradise feathered headdress,

* A Polish endearment.

Mathilde entertained not only her royal lover, but a catholic collection of guests including Diaghilev, Tchaikovsky and Chaliapin who sang the Tsar's role at the premiere of *Boris Godunov*. Invitations to these special *kapoustniki** were prized, apéritifs were served by a dwarf, and a balalaika orchestra of the Empress's Lancers played through these long, romantic 'White Nights'. These bohemian soirées were jealously seen as precious jewels for an elite where even the reticent Tsarevich sang Caucasian folk songs and joined in charades. The heir to one of the most powerful empires in the world once put a basket over his arm and a handkerchief on his head as a bonnet to do a fair but hilarious imitation of Kschessinska as Little Red Riding Hood in the *Sleeping Beauty*.

Little K always knew that one day Nicholas would make a dynastic marriage, but, with the blind optimism of a woman in love, blithely hoped that this might never happen. Their first long parting came in August 1893, when Nicholas and his father left for Europe, but the real body blow was the announcement the following year of his engagement to Princess Alix of Hesse-Darmstadt. Nicholas had always spoken honestly to Mathilde about his feelings for Alix, and once the engagement had been made public he stopped visiting the little ballet dancer.

Nicholas, in a farewell note, assured Mathilde that 'whatever happens to my life, my days spent with you will ever remain the happiest memories of my youth'.[8] He insisted also that Kschessinska should keep the house and, being pragmatic, she sensibly accepted the gift, saying, 'he gave it to me as a present . . . the house where we had spent so many unforgettable hours together'. Their last meeting was at a deserted barn off the Volkhonsky Highway outside the city.

Nicholas told her that whatever happened she could always turn to him. He never signed his letters to her as Nicholas, but as 'Niki', and she could always use the familiar form when addressing him. Now he asked one of her admirers, Grand Duke Sergei Michaelovich, to keep an eye on her, and soon she was living under his devoted patronage.

Over the years, Kschessinska watched Nicholas become fêted as Tsar, father of four appealing daughters and at last a longed-for heir. She used to stand on the illuminated balcony of her house in the

---

*   Intimate theatre suppers.

hope of catching a glimpse of the Tsar on his way to carry out official engagements. Her electricity bills were enormous, but sadly it was the Police Chief who often passed by.

As she was St Petersburg's prima ballerina assoluta, she appeared before Nicholas on grand occasions. In 1911, the Tsar and Tsarina and most of the imperial family came to see Kschessinska dance the Tsar's favourite role in *Fiammetta*. 'When he left the theatre, after the performance,' she remembered, 'he looked up at my dressing-room window, the very one where twenty years before, as a young girl, I had waited for the Tsarevich, who has since become the Emperor of the most powerful country in the world!'

After Nicholas's abdication and the Revolution, Kschessinska was forced to flee; there was no influential Tsar who could save her now. On 3 April 1917, Lenin, wearing his short jacket, trademark baggy trousers and cap, occupied her house and made his famous 'Bread to the Workers' speech from the balcony which Kschessinska had designed and where she often stood wistfully, hoping for a glimpse of Nicholas.

When the revolutionaries first seized the house the cry was 'Come in! Come in! The bird has flown!' Contemptuously, they threw old cigarette ends and bits of paper into the bath, the carpets were stained and the Bechstein piano hurled into the garden.

Today, Kschessinska's house, with its beautiful French door handles and fittings all vandalised by the Bolsheviks, with its exposed electric wires, still has remnants of the comrades' Kafka-esque style. Balletomanes, expecting to see flouncy tutus, old theatre programmes, mouth-watering menus or photographs of Anna Pavlova, Isadora Duncan and Nijinsky, are faced instead with a huge red portrait of Lenin and a slogan saying 'Power to the Soviets'.

The house was first opened to the public in 1957 as a Museum of Revolution. Many of the old Soviets attended the opening ceremony, not because they loved ballet, but because it was associated with Lenin's April Physicists Declaration. Then, with the introduction of perestroika by Gorbachev, it was recognised as the home of the great ballet dancer, and some of the rooms were restored as part of the museum; but mostly it was still kept as a shrine to heroes of the 1917 Revolution. It was reopened in 1991.

Today the custodian is Andrei Pavlovich, a harassed, chunky figure frantically pointing to posters of revolutionary leaders. The Bolsheviks so hated the Tsar, his bosses warned him that any reference to the imperial family must be kept to a minimum. More than one mention of Nicholas II and he would be fired instantly. He has kept his job for thirty years but seems not to appreciate that there has been a change of mood in Russia. He nervously insists in showing a cartoon of a degraded last Tsar in fancy dress, on his knees, handing over his crown. Proudly he points to a collection in a glass case, the minutiae of the great proletarian revolution, Kosygin's calculator, spectacles and watch. On the first floor the room used as a study by Lenin, in which can be seen his typewriter, a wind-up telephone and the fading flags of party committees, has a grim utilitarian air and none of the gossamer delicacy created by the ballerina.

The constant rumble of the underground shakes the dust from a couple of the Kschessinska tutus, now greying, which look desolate on a wooden barre. Pavlovich points to the candelabras, which he refers to as 'bras', and says the revolutionaries shot at them trying to get rid of the decorative swans.

Eventually, Kschessinska settled in the south of France, escaping 'the horrors of war, the Revolution and Bolshevism', she once said miserably, adding, 'in a single day we had become penniless'. Not quite. On one occasion at the Savoy in London, she was wearing lustrous jewellery of such obvious value that the management of the hotel insisted on two security men being seated nearby in the dining room.

Adored by Grand Dukes – one called her 'Douchka', which means 'Little Darling' – she married Nicholas's cousin Grand Duke Andrei Vladmirovich in 1921, and a year later they had a son, Vova. It was a serene marriage, and they settled at Cap d'Ail, surrounded by cats, where she helped Russian émigrés and set up a ballet school. When her husband, a dignified exile, died aged seventy-seven on 31 October 1956, Mathilde always clung to his title, a last remnant of her link to the imperial dynasty.

SIX

'Dearest Pussy'

As the younger son not in direct succession, George was enjoying life as a naval officer in the clubbable but respectful atmosphere of the wardroom; although prone to quick outbursts of temper, yet with his breezy style, bracing humour and lack of snobbery he was popular. When he was promoted to Commander in the Royal Navy in August 1891, he seemed to be without a care in the world.

He had learned to be a good mixer, he could enjoy all the perks of being a royal prince without too much responsibility, leaving him free to go racing in *Britannia*, to shoot at Sandringham or on the Scottish moors. He was not asked by his father to carry out onerous public duties. The burden of kingship would fall squarely on the willowy shoulders of the hapless Prince Eddy.

George's naval career was thriving, and he relished being Acting Captain of the cruiser HMS *Melampus*.[1] Then he caught typhoid in November 1891 after a visit to Dublin to see Prince Eddy, who was celebrating his engagement to Princess May of Teck.

There had been an attempt to get Prince Eddy through Cambridge before he went into the army, but one of his tutors commented acerbically, 'He hardly knows the meaning of the words "to read"', and his tutor Dalton thought him too attracted to things 'of a dissolute nature'. His father took him away from university to join the 10th Hussars, where these character flaws were not a drawback. In the regiment, Eddy was considered ineffectual, but he was popular with other officers. He did not impress the generals, but he described one of them as a 'lunatic'.[2]

Prince Eddy was tall. He appeared presentable but somehow was not an altogether impressive sight as he wandered about with an arm draped around his mother's neck. Queen Victoria was thwarted in her unlikely scheme to marry young Alix off to Prince Eddy, which would have made her granddaughter a sacrificial lamb on the altar of the British monarchy: Alix could not bring herself to contemplate life with this squeaky-voiced Prince, who not only was a bit deaf but also dull. While Queen Victoria might get an empire to do her bidding, she had less success with her Hesse granddaughter.

Alix rejected Eddy's overtures and, before leaving for Darmstadt in May 1890, sent him a letter sweetly explaining that it 'pained her to pain him', and how she would always think of him affectionately as 'her dear cousin'. The Queen was bitterly disappointed and wrote miserably, 'Alix is a real sorrow to us . . . she refuses the greatest position there is', but she still retained 'a faint lingering hope'[3] that her granddaughter might, in time, be persuaded to change her mind.

Queen Victoria was not happy. Still left with the problem of finding a suitable bride for Prince Eddy her eye now lit upon Princess May of Teck, who was summoned to Balmoral for a bleak November stay. The Queen thought her 'very plain', and the young Princess did not help herself by wearing her hair in an unbecoming style with a tight little curly fringe.[4] But with her composure and cultivated taste she passed the test and was soon pronounced suitable as a wife for the heir to the throne.

Princess 'May', born at Kensington Palace on 26 May 1867, always upright and imperturbable, was a great-granddaughter of the excitable George III.*

Her father, Francis, Duke of Teck,† was from a well-connected but impecunious German family who were often in humiliating financial straits. Coming from this small principality had the advantage of instilling in May an understanding of European court life.[5] Her mother, the jolly and excessively plump Mary Adelaide, Duchess of Cambridge,‡ was a cousin of Queen Victoria. Fair-haired, with a pleasant expression, she was famous for her appetite. Her 'coquette' act was tiresome, yet she remained a favourite at the British court.

Her husband had been found for her by the Prince of Wales. Queen Victoria approved; she had a weakness for good-looking men and was happy that Francis should marry 'Fat Mary', as his unfortunate, chronically unpunctual wife was known in the royal family.

---

*   The Duke of Cambridge had been the seventh son of George III.
†   His father was barred from the succession in Württemberg because of his morganatic marriage to a Hungarian countess, Claudia Rhedèy.
‡   Mary Adelaide's mother, the Duchess of Cambridge, who died in 1889, was Queen Victoria's aunt.

The Tecks had four children, a daughter and three sons.* Mary's brother Francis was a particular embarrassment: expelled from Wellington College for throwing the headmaster over a hedge, he had little ambition except gambling.

A French governess, Mademoiselle Hélène Bricka, who wore a toupée, steered May's literary tastes, encouraging her to read Carlisle and George Eliot. When she married, she complained that her husband read 'the most awful rubbish', while she herself was enjoying Tennyson, Dickens and Tolstoy.

May grew up on the fringes of the royal merry-go-round, awkwardly aware that she was the poor relation. Once asked for her autograph, she said shyly, 'Aren't you mistaking me for one of my cousins of Wales? I am only May of Teck.'[6] Her future husband's family, close-knit and super-confident, never lost sight of their royal position, and often teased the shy and correct May, pointing out her plumpish 'Württemberg hands'[7] and laughing at her mother's size.

In 1883, when she was sixteen, she became familiar with the attentions of the bailiffs, the situation so pressing that the whole family had to flee into exile in Florence. But this was not a cultural hardship for the young Princess. Queen Victoria, fond of her blousy, sociable cousin Mary, eased their plight and lent the Tecks a grace-and-favour house in Richmond Park. This was elegant White Lodge, now the Royal Ballet School, where Nelson drew his plan for the battle of Trafalgar by dipping his finger in his glass of port.[8]

As a child, May had been given the unlikely pet name 'Dearest Pussy' by her father Prince Francis, the Duke of Teck.[9] They were devoted and, whenever he was away, she sent him pressed primroses, violets and other flowers she found in Richmond Park.

The Queen had made up her mind: May would marry Eddy. Told by his grandmother when he should propose, he put the question at a weekend house party at Luton Hoo in Bedfordshire. Blithely unaware of the secret side of his life and his forays into unsavoury areas of London, including male brothels, May confided excitedly in her diary after the proposal that she danced around in her bedroom, singing 'Fancy it being poor little me!' She was mesmerised by the royal family and now could hardly believe her luck. The wedding would take place on 27 February 1892 at St George's Chapel, Windsor.

* May, 1867; Adolphus 'Dolly', 1868; Francis, 1870; and Alexander 'Alge', 1874.

Once engaged, she found it disconcerting that the Prince of Wales seemed to have such scant regard for his heir. He often told her how she must make sure she was keeping 'Eddy up to the mark', and instructed her, saying, 'May, please see that Eddy does this or that.'[10] On one occasion, when Princess May complained to her mother about this pressure, wondering if she should really marry into the royal family, Mary Adelaide replied, 'If I could put up with your father for twenty-five years you can handle the heir presumptive of Great Britain.'[11]

Then Queen Victoria's best-laid plans went miserably awry: Prince Eddy was at Sandringham, where he caught influenza and became delirious, shouting abuse and using stable-yard language not often heard by his mother and sisters as they stood anxiously by the bedside.[12] He died of pneumonia at Sandringham at 9.35 on the morning of 14 January 1892.

The fortunes of his younger brother George, known as 'Our Sailor Prince', now altered dramatically. He had been enjoying happy, fulfilling years in the Royal Navy. He never wanted to be anything other than a naval officer. Now he had to give up the life he loved to be groomed as heir to the throne, and face what Walter Bagehot, the Victorian constitutionalist, once described 'as the intolerable honour of monarchy'.

A disappointed royal bride-to-be, Princess May followed Prince Eddy's coffin in a carriage with the blinds down. The Queen thought she looked like a 'crushed flower'. A wreath, in the form of a harp with broken strings, was sent by the ladies of Ireland. Almost before Prince Eddy's body was buried, the grieving royals heard the Duke of Teck frantically buttonholing people, saying his daughter must be married off speedily to the new Prince of Wales, otherwise he would be financially ruined.

The Teck family was now invited to Osborne, where Princess May was presented with a beautiful *rivière* of diamonds, which had been the intended wedding present for her marriage from the Prince and Princess of Wales. With her fondness for jewellery, this small token went some way to comfort May in her disappointment.

The Queen was aware that George, this 'dear & amiable' grandson, was showing no signs of wanting to marry, and now he was heir to the throne she was no longer giving him subtle nudges but asked him directly what he intended to do about getting himself a wife. Victoria feared that 'something dreadful will happen if he does not marry'. Irked by this pressure George complained in a letter to 'Motherdear', as he always called the Princess of Wales, that he wished Queen Victoria would stop nagging him about getting married. 'I am in no hurry at all,' he declared solemnly, and said he thought it was 'very bad for men to marry too young'. Part of the problem was that Alexandra was also in no hurry to lose her darling son in marriage. But Queen Victoria persisted, asking George if he had thought any more about his late brother's fiancée. George, who was not seriously involved with any woman at this time, had never given May a moment's romantic thought, regarding her always as his brother's preserve.

When it was suggested to the Queen that it was a mite insensitive to propel George towards May so indecently quickly, her reply was pragmatic: 'Well, you know May never was in love with Eddy.'[13] The strength of the royal family has often been an ability never to let ordinary human feelings obstruct continuity. May's uncle, the Duke of Cambridge, thought that the whole idea of his niece marrying someone with whom she had not been in love was 'unseemly and unfeeling and horrible'.

But a meeting was arranged in the relaxed ambience of the south of France. A note with an invitation to a quiet supper was sent to May and signed by her 'loving old cousin, Georgie'. He was feeling particularly vulnerable, still recovering from typhoid, during which he had lost a lot of weight: he was now down to nine stone three pounds. He was also emotionally low as he grieved for 'his darling boy', as he called his older brother;[14] he was filled with exaggerated feelings of loyalty towards Eddy and still could only think of May platonically. A prop to his self-esteem that same year was when his father made him Duke of York, Earl of Inverness and Baron Killarney.

Medieval it may have been, but this perfectly acceptable spare fiancée, 24-year-old Princess May, was seen as ideal for George. 'She is the reverse of *oberflächlich* [superficial],' Queen Victoria wrote approvingly in German, praising her sensible qualities, adding that 'she has no frivolous tastes'. May had adopted England whole-heartedly, once saying 'I am British through and through', ignoring her Württemberg ancestry. Princess May's potential had also been spotted by Queen Olga of the Hellenes,* much loved by George,

---

* Formerly Olga Constantinovna, Grand Duchess of Russia and niece of Tsar Alexander III.

who thought of her as a 'second mother'.[15] When he went to stay with Olga in Athens in 1893, she encouraged him to think seriously about marrying May. 'I'm sure, Tootsums,' she said, using her pet name for the future King, 'she . . . will make you happy; they say she has such a sweet disposition.' More importantly, Olga liked the way May always appeared 'so *equal*, and *that* in itself' she thought 'a great blessing, because nothing can be more disagreeable in everyday life than a person who is in high spirits today and low tomorrow'.

He listened. Soon afterwards, on 3 May 1893, he took May to tea with his sister Princess Louise at her home, East Sheen Lodge near Richmond Park. This racy sister, known as 'Loosy', who enjoyed a bohemian lifestyle and married the Duke of Fife, nudged her seafaring brother. 'Now, Georgie,' she urged. 'Don't you think you ought to take May into the garden to look at the frogs in the pond?'[16] Prince George was more comfortable inspecting the gun turrets than making sweet talk, but in this amphibious ambience he proposed. 'The darling girl,' he later told Loosy, 'consented to be my wife; I am so happy.' They never held hands and there were no intimate jokes, even though they were engaged; instead they played bezique and discussed the weather.

George was twenty-eight when he was married at St James's Palace on 6 July 1893. Nicholas, a valued guest at the wedding, was fascinated by the infinite patience of the crowd waiting outside Buckingham Palace for a glimpse of Queen Victoria leading the procession of twelve open state landaus, which were drawn by cream-coloured horses.

'They waited, hour after hour, and at last a little black carriage came out of the palace-gates,' he marvelled, adding, 'Very few of the people in the crowd could see the Queen, but they knew that she was there, and they went away satisfied. One day', he said with ill-placed confidence, 'it will be like that in Russia.'[17]

Nicholas and George looked so alike it became a mischievous joke they both enjoyed. A diplomat, thinking George was the Tsarevich, asked him if he had come over especially for the wedding, and, assuming he was on lackadaisical Russian time, urged him not to be late for the ceremony. George, to the mortification of the embarrassed envoy, replied, 'I am the Duke of York and I suppose I should attend my own wedding.'[18] Even *The Times* commented on the Tsarevich 'whose extraordinary likeness to the Duke of York may have contributed to secure for him some additional cheers'.[19]

Nicholas made little impression when he visited the House of Commons, where he was viewed by some MPs as a 'decidedly delicate-looking stripling', unlike his father, a 'giant who could twist tin plates in the hollow of one of his brawny hands'; this superficial assessment not giving Nicholas much credit for any intellectual ability.[20]

The bride, in her dress of white satin embroidered with silver roses, shamrocks and thistles, Queen Victoria thought 'so pretty, quiet and dignified'. On her head she wore a chaplet of orange flowers and white heather over her mother's lace veil, which was held by a diamond rose of York. The Queen was less approving of the Chapel Royal, which she considered 'ugly'. May's going-away outfit for a Sandringham honeymoon was a golden bonnet trimmed with ostrich plumes and white rosebuds; her husband was in black morning coat. They caught a train from Liverpool Street, in London, for the 100-mile journey to Wolferton near Sandringham.

They were met by a coachman and carriage, and cantered off in style for their honeymoon. But soon, black dust thrown up by the hooves of the horses of the Loyal Suffolk Hussars escorting them covered them from head to foot, so that they looked like a couple of startled chimney sweeps. The bride's outfit was ruined. This did not please the bridegroom, who was obsessional about appearance. But he cheered up when he saw his wedding present, little York Cottage, formerly the old 'Bachelors' Cottage', the unpretentious home where they would enjoy many of their happiest years as a married couple.

As a husband, George was never demonstrative or openly affectionate, yet he remained devoted to his 'May', this modest, serious girl, who was to become an exemplary consort.

SEVEN

Carefree in Coburg

'I'm Sunny,' Alix said to Nicholas when they met in one of the romantic allées in the gardens at Peterhof. It was the spring of 1884 and she had come to Russia for the first time for the wedding of her twenty-year-old sister Ella to Nicholas's uncle, Grand Duke Sergei Alexandrovich. 'I know,' the Tsarevich said, smiling in the way that later on would charm even some of the Bolsheviks.

'I sat next to little twelve-year-old Alix who I really liked a lot,' he recalled in his diary on 27 May 1884, when the Hesse children were staying with the Romanovs after the wedding. The young couple scratched their names with a ring on a window of the Italian House. Nicholas, in his diary, said simply, 'we love each other'.

Ella's marriage was full of disappointment. Her husband was cruelly domineering, and was never physically in love with his decorative wife, preferring the company of young guards officers.

Locked in an arid marriage and missing her family, she invited Alix to come and keep her company, knowing that Nicholas had found her younger sister attractive. The sisters, aware of the need for discretion, always referred to Nicholas as Pelly.[1] Queen Victoria suspected Ella's scheming and sent her a stern message, insisting that 'No marriage for Alicky in Russia would be allowed.' The Queen always blamed Ella, the great beauty of the Hesse family, for leading little sister 'Alicky', who was nine years younger, astray in Russia, 'that horrid corrupt country'. She was outspoken about what she saw as the 'very bad state of society' in Russia and 'its total want of principle, from the Grand Dukes downwards'.

But, whatever her grandmother wished, Alix was soon back in Russia in 1889 at Ella's country estate at Ilinskoe, not far from Moscow. It took three days by train from Darmstadt trundling past endless birch forests, occasionally seeing a tiny village with distinctive blue domed churches dotted with stars.

Alix spent six weeks at her brother-in-law's country home, a simple enough brown wood lodge in a forest by the banks of the

Moskva. Here she enjoyed skating parties and, in the evenings, dancing in a long white dress with diamonds and a white corsage.

Alix and Nicholas fell in love in the hedonistic flamboyance of the Russian court, outshining gilded Versailles with its epicurean banquets and jewel-studded menus. Soon everyone knew about the budding romance and waited for the inevitable strengthening of ties between the two powerful Russian and English dynasties.

Alix fell hopelessly and passionately in love with Nicholas, and they talked of marriage; there was nothing he wanted more. But it was out of the question. Alix could not bear the idea of changing her Lutheran religion to Russian Orthodox, which was essential as the future wife of a Tsar. Religion, she told Ella severely, was not a pair of gloves to be changed at random; the long services, chanting, candles and incense of the Orthodox religion were so unlike the unemotional services she attended at Darmstadt. Besides, she had promised her father on his deathbed that she would never convert.[2]

Too gentle a suitor, Nicholas was not persistent enough. Instead he agonised in his diary, '21 December 1890 . . . Have loved her for a long time . . . the only obstacle or gap between her and me is the matter of religion'.[3] He had given her one of his mother's diamond brooches, but Alix primly rejected it, finding it improper to accept such a valuable piece of jewellery; blushingly, she gave it back to him.

There was a letter of rebuke from Nicholas's sister Xenia, telling Alix that by refusing to marry him she was 'ruining Nicky's life'. Stung by this accusation, Alix accused her future sister-in-law of cruelty and replied sternly that whatever happened 'it NEVER can be'.[4]

Rejected, Nicholas was comforted by his mistress, Little K, although he really only wanted his 'dear beloved Alix'. It was not until her brother Grand Duke Ernst's wedding at Coburg on 7 April 1894 that the couple met again and were now more seriously in love than ever.

Queen Victoria, with her inveterate passion for matchmaking, was pleased about the marriage she had arranged between her grand-daughter, Princess Victoria Melita of Saxe-Coburg, or 'Ducky' as she was known, and her grandson Ernst, Alix's witty, artistic brother, who had succeeded to the ducal title in 1892. It also provided another excuse for a grand family reunion. Carriages trundling through the cobbled streets of Coburg would suddenly stop as 'the Royal Mob',[5] as Alix's father described them, recognising each other, got out and 'started kissing in the middle of the road'.[6]

When Nicholas set eyes again on Alix in Coburg, he found she had 'grown remarkably more beautiful'. He very nearly had not come to Coburg, but thought he would try once more to persuade her to change her mind; instead he met more steely resistance and disconcerting floods of tears.

But then the wedding ceremony worked its magic. Young girls pelted the newly-weds in their open carriage with armfuls of roses, carnations and lilac, and in that romantic aura Alix felt even more intensely attracted to the Tsarevich.

It was the unlikely figure of the Kaiser who finally persuaded her to marry and convert to Orthodoxy. He always boasted later that he had helped to fix Alix's engagement by propelling a hesitant Nicholas forward with a bunch of flowers, telling him it was time to propose. To his surprise, Nicholas now found her reservations had melted away; the spark of love was reignited. On 20 April 1894 in Coburg Alix finally succumbed, with 'heart brimming', and accepted Nicholas's proposal. They both wept at such unexpected joy. Their language of love was English.

Alix had captured the heart of an emperor. He loved her to the end and always understood that, behind the often unsmiling, glacial façade, there was a highly strung, sensual woman. Things were never on an even keel: her mood could change like quicksilver from 'bright sunshine to pitch black night'.

'God, what a mountain has fallen from my shoulders,' Nicholas wrote, adding, 'with what joy have I been able to delight dear Papa and Mama!' Naively, he had been unaware of his parents' misgivings about Alix, or that his mother had complained about her 'English stiffness'.

Nicholas now gave Alix the diamond brooch she had once miserably returned to him, which ever since had been in the care of Xenia, her future sister-in-law. She would wear her pink diamond engagement ring and the matching necklace for the rest of her life. Alix cried a lot but was extraordinarily happy.

On anniversaries of their engagement, she always wore the brooch given to her by Nicholas. In case, like most men, he had not noticed, she reminded him twenty-one years later that she still had the Princess's grey dress she had worn on the morning he proposed. Even more romantically, years later she told him, 'I feel still your grey suit, the smell of it by the window in the Coburg Schloss.'[7]

Queen Victoria was 'thunderstruck' when told of the engagement. Secretly distraught by the news given to her after breakfast in the Palace in Coburg, she softened when she saw the happiness of this favourite granddaughter, and Nicholas's pride. This three-generation family celebration ought to have fulfilled her wildest dynastic dreams, but she could not help but feel uneasy. She worried about this sheltered granddaughter and 'the awful insecurity to which the sweet child will be exposed'; while she liked the future Tsar, she thought he lacked moral fibre. But Nicholas acquitted himself well enough in the drawing room, exchanging banalities about the weather and about the number of heavy stags bagged. 'Nicky' was 'nice enough'; it was his country the Queen deplored.

Carefree in Coburg – without the restrictions of home for either of them – they had shy tête-à-têtes in gardens, under arches of fruit and lilac. The special joy was being allowed to drive in a carriage 'without coachman or servant!' Enthusiastically, they sang operatic arias to each other, such as 'Once again, once again, once again, O Nightingale', and on woodland walks Nicholas kissed the tender, expressive mouth of his 'dearest and incomparable Alix'.

A letter swiftly arrived from York Cottage, Sandringham, from their 'most loving cousin Georgie'. 'My dear, old Nicky! I wish you and dear Alix every possible joy and happiness now and in the future . . . I well know that for some years you have loved Alix and wished to marry her. I am quite certain that she will make you an excellent wife, and she is charming, lovely and accomplished. I am also so glad that your engagement has taken place at Coburg and I know it will have given Grandmama the greatest possible pleasure to be present on this happy occasion. She is very fond of Alix.'[8]

When he became engaged to Alix, Nicholas wisely ingratiated himself with the Queen. In an oleaginous letter, he wrote, 'My dearest Grandmama . . . I thank you so much for all your kindness at Coburg . . . which you showed me . . . there; I shall never forget our breakfasts in your room and the music playing outside . . . Believe me, your most affectionate and devoted (future) grandson.' He never revealed how irritating it was for him, having to 'sit with hands folded and always to wait without end',[9] while the old lady took her time, gathering up her sewing before moving on.

After Nicholas and Alix had to part, he wrote her a love letter describing his lonely journey back to Russia from Coburg by train, dated 'At the frontier 21 April 1894'.[10] When they stopped for luncheon 'at a small station called Konitz', he was charmed to find a photograph of Alix in a glass frame 'with our pink flowers (japonica, I think) all around it',[11] a romantic touch by a railway attendant.

Alix returned to Darmstadt on 2 May 1894, while her grandmother Queen Victoria went back to England with the promise that her newly engaged granddaughter would follow shortly. Love letters continued to fly between the couple. Four hundred of them were found after their death in a black chest at the House of Special Purpose in Siberia, a testament to an exceptional and enduring love.

Staying at Windsor, Alix had much on her mind. Preparing to become a future Tsarina she set about embracing the Orthodox faith. The Queen arranged a meeting with the Bishop of Ripon, Dr Boyd-Carpenter, who explained the subtleties of her new religion. Alix found it galling to have to renounce her beloved Protestant Church, but began to take an academic interest in religious pamphlets. After the death of her father Grand Duke Louis of Hesse on 13 March 1892, she steeped herself by way of comfort in philosophical study, and steeped herself in *Essays and Reviews* by Professor Jowett and *Sermons* by F.W. Robertson.

Learning Russian was almost harder than changing religion. Queen Victoria declared the very thought of her beloved granddaughter speaking that language was distasteful. Crossly, she complained that 'my whole nature rises up against it', and admitted, 'My blood runs cold when I think of her so young most likely placed on that very unsafe throne.'

In Russia Alexander III and his wife accepted their son's choice of wife as a pretty but unexciting, safe addition to the family. But Victoria, with uncanny presentiment, worried about 'Alicky' as a future Empress of Russia. In that vast unruly country, Alix's reserve could easily be misunderstood by the passionate Russians, who always seemed so flamboyant and exotic. When Alix was being showered with diamonds, emerald-studded bracelets and pearl necklaces by her future in-laws, Queen Victoria was concerned that this might all go to her head and warned, 'Now, Alix, do not get too proud.'[12]

The Queen had never taken to Ella's husband, Sergei, though as Governor-General of Moscow he was respected; now Alix was marrying his nephew. Prophetically, she saw her two vulnerable German granddaughters as hothouse flowers, orchids that could perish in the snowy wastes of Russia.

EIGHT

Sweet Kisses

After the tearful excitement of the engagement, Alix went to stay with Queen Victoria, who soon noticed how she always seemed to be tired and complained about pains in her knees and legs. The Queen sent her off to Yorkshire to take the waters in Harrogate, and made it quite plain to Nicholas in a letter from Balmoral, dated 25 May 1894, that her darling granddaughter required 'great quiet and rest'. Enclosed was a copy of a letter from a Harrogate doctor ordering a strict diet and a quiet regime. Almost implying he was responsible for Alix's state of health, the Queen warned Nicholas that he was not to rush her into marriage. It was vital, she insisted that Alix should become strong and well. Anything to delay the wedding.

Meanwhile Alix was sending love notes to Nicky; some were quite short: 'Love-love – what is greater! Kissy kissy. Ta ta!'[1] was typical. How could this frivolous flirtatious creature, who referred to him as 'My sweet *Lausbub* [rascal]', one day turn into a glowering empress?

Dutifully, Alix settled in Harrogate but was happier than she ever expected in this Yorkshire town, which had become increasingly elegant ever since Captain William Slingsby had discovered the celebrated chalybeate and sulphurous springs in 1771. Alix liked the restrained gentility of the spa town but resented being stared at by the locals who knew she was the Queen's granddaughter. In a grumbling note to Nicholas she complained, 'If I were not in the bath chair I should not mind . . . The rude people stand at the corner and stare; I shall stick my tongue out at them another time . . . Ever your own true loving girly, Alix. Many loving kisses.'[2]

Her choice of accommodation was a modest lodging house in Prospect Place near the Stray in Harrogate. Charles Allen, the owner of Cathcart House, was a plumber or, as his 76-year-old grandson Michael prefers to put it, 'a pipe specialist' with a workshop at the back of the three-storey building.

On arrival, the royal party wondered why there was no sign of Allen's wife Emma, until they were told that she was confined to bed. After a panicky 'Anything infectious?'[3] enquiry they were reassured that it was unlikely, as she had just given birth to twins.

Suddenly, Allen realised that his mystery guest, 'Baroness Startenburg', was the future Tsarina of Russia. He was 'tickled pink'[4] but fully expected her to move on to one of the quieter, roomy spa hotels away from crying babies. But Alix told him happily that the twins' arrival was a lucky omen, stayed for a month and started knitting matinee jackets.

Alix helped rock the babies to sleep and discussed the best nursery routine; this unmarried, sheltered Princess told Mrs Allen that, in her opinion, an English upbringing was best. She helped with bedmaking, enjoyed playing at housekeeping and planning meals; Yorkshire pudding was a favourite, shades of sturdy lunches at Osborne.

At Cathcart House they found Alix a 'homely presence, tripping and singing about the house like a happy English girl just home from school.'[5] The novelty of being treated as an ordinary woman was what appealed. Ordinary up to a point, but on her twenty-second birthday the local postman struggled with sackloads of telegrams from the crowned heads of Europe, and from Nicholas there was a signed photograph and jewellery. Thanking her own 'precious Boysy' for the 'glorious bracelet', on 25 May she wrote, 'you naughty monkey, how could you dare to give me such a magnificent thing. You do spoil one.'[6]

Her secretary, Baroness Fabrice, thought one of the reasons for the Princess's high spirits was that, apart from her recent engagement, she was enjoying normal life in this northern town. More used to palatial corridors studded with portraits of severe ancestors, Alix 'had never lived in a house' before.

Highlights included cycle-chair expeditions to beauty spots – Knaresborough, Hampsthwaite and Ripley – as well as many churches. There was always a policeman in the wings, sometimes not very successfully hidden. On one occasion Alix spotted a man leaning on a bridge; when she later discovered he was a plain-clothes policeman, she grumbled good-humouredly, 'Why didn't he push me up that hill?'

During her time in Harrogate, Alix kept her 'darling Grandmama' informed about her spartan regime: 'I send you my very fondest thanks . . . for the nice photo of you and Uncle Bertie, and for the delightful tea basket with which I am quite enchanted'.[7]

Michael Allen, a retired designer now living in Hertfordshire, happily recalls how the future Tsarina of Russia became his father's godmother. 'The Princess asked my grandparents if she could stand sponsor to the twins and said she would like the boy to be called Nicholas and the girl Alix, with the addition of her family name Hesse.'

They agreed and, on 17 June 1894 at St Peter's Church next door to Cathcart House, Alix presented the boy, and the Baroness the girl, for baptism. The christening presents were rather more than the usual spoon and pusher: for little Nicholas, a pair of Fabergé cufflinks in the shape of the Imperial Russian Eagle, and a gold nappy pin; for baby Alix, a gold necklace with a pearl heart and her initials. Modestly, the Princess asked the Allens to accept a signed photograph of herself and the Tsarevich which she hoped they would keep, at least until the children were grown-up, so they could see their namesakes.

Alix left Harrogate in high spirits to meet Nicholas, who would shortly be arriving from Russia. The Allens got a warm letter from her thanking them for their 'various kind services', and telling them how she found the rooms 'very comfortable and the cooking excellent'.[8]

They did not expect to hear from her again, but Alix stayed in touch. When the twins were being confirmed, she sent cufflinks with diamonds and sapphires set in gold for the boy, and for his sister a diamond and sapphire brooch.

During the First World War, when Nicholas Allen was serving with the West Yorkshire Regiment, a brown package arrived on 21 May 1915 from Russia. Enclosed was a gold cross on a chain, inscribed 'Save and Keep', in Cyrillic script, 'With God's Blessing, from the Empress Alexandra of Russia 31 May 1915'. Nicholas Allen took the cross to the trenches and believed it saved his life. 'Well, he came back alive,' says his son.

The legacy of Princess Alix's thoughtfulness on that northern visit can be seen now in Harrogate's Royal Pump Room Museum. The gifts, which include gold cufflinks, a gold chain with scalloped edges and a Mughal-design mustard pot with different shades of blue flowers, are sensitively displayed.

Looking refreshed and well, Alix travelled incognito from Harrogate to meet Nicholas, who had arrived in England on 8 June

1894. His father had lent him his sleek new white yacht, the *Polar Star*, and Nicholas had steamed at eighteen knots across the North Sea to meet his 'sweety'. Queen Victoria gave instructions that the Tsarevich should be given a royal salute and received with all honours.

In London, Alix's older sister, Princess Victoria, who was married to Prince Louis of Battenburg, whisked him off to their house at Walton-on-Thames. This Surrey town became a place of passionate memories for the young couple.

Nicholas, in his diary entry dated 19 June 1894, observing the chasteness expected between royal couples in the nineteenth century, noted that he had 'slept splendidly in my cosy little room', but wrote of the joy he experienced when he woke up and realised that he was staying 'under the same roof as my darling Alix'.

That summer was to be one of the happiest in her life, reunited with her 'Darling Boysy' in this mellow red-brick house. Confident enough about their relationship, he now told her quite frankly about his affair with Kschessinska, who had been mischievously bombarding Alix with letters about the affair. Alix was surprisingly sanguine, reassuring him, saying, 'What is past is past and will never return', and 'I love you even more since you told me that little story',[9] entwining him even more in his besottedness.

Dutifully they went to Windsor, where Nicholas was smothered in what he described 'an orgy of kissing', celebrating the engagement as elderly duchesses proffered powdered cheeks to the good-looking Tsarevich. With his brand of shy charm and habit of calling nearly everyone 'dear', Nicholas was a success at the British court.

He astutely played on the bond between Alix and her grandmother, but privately referred to the great Empress as 'a round ball on shaky legs'. He was appreciative of the Queen's liberal attitude in allowing them to go unchaperoned on sailing trips and picnics, admitting in his diary that he 'never expected that from her'.

This latitude, without duenna, or even servants, close at hand, meant the lovebirds could spend simple days sitting on 'an old rug under the chestnut trees' while Nicholas read Loti's *Matelot* to Alix, who served him tea from her new picnic basket.[10] Although Nicholas spoke English perfectly well, he had been given a badly edited phrase book entitled 'English as she is spoke', which made them laugh as he struggled over unsuitable phrases like 'dress your hairs!' and 'at what o'clock dine him?'[11]

In benign mood, the Queen then took the couple to Osborne; idyllic days for Nicholas, who found Alix so responsive to 'those sweet kisses which I had dreamed of and yearned after'.

When he visited Sandringham, Nicholas found 'Uncle Bertie as funny as usual', but was rather surprised by some of the Prince of Wales's house guests.* His mother, who was anti-Semitic, had always been shocked by the number of Jewish friends in her brother-in-law's circle, which included Sir Thomas Lipton, a grocer, and Sir Edward Cassel, the Jewish financier whose royal links were enhanced when his daughter Edwina married Lord Louis Mountbatten.

After the rare treat of being allowed 'more than a month of heavenly bliss' together,[12] the newly engaged couple had to part. Nicholas boarded the *Polar Star* to sail to St Petersburg for his sister Xenia's wedding. She was marrying her cousin Alexander, a son of Grand Duke Paul and affectionately known within the family as Sandro.

It had all been such a romantic daydream in England that, when he returned to Russia and was asked what he thought of fine buildings like Westminster Abbey, Nicholas looked completely blank. He had to confess that he had not had time to look at them. But he had in fact gone to the Tower of London and in a macabre moment asked if he might stand on the very spot where Anne Boleyn and Lady Jane Grey had been executed.[13]

It was difficult for Nicholas to get back into the old family routine after the heady excitement of being fêted by his English cousins. Writing to Alix from Gatchina, the imperial family palace, the weather was the first topic. 'So warm and lovely we go out for long rows on the lake . . . coming home at half past five for tea. The quantities of strawberries which we then devour is simply shocking, but Xenia certainly might have the first prize for that task . . . after tea at eleven they generally play those detestable patience [sic], while I read *The Times*.'

Nicholas did not need to study the Court Circular to know about George and May's first baby. He had been in England and joined in 'the general happiness and rejoicing' at the birth, at ten o'clock on 23 June 1894, of a son and heir christened Edward, a name 'already borne by six English kings'. Nicholas was one of the future Edward VIII's sponsors.

---

* Like most of the European nobility, Nicholas was distinctly anti-Semitic.

NINE

A Sharp Intake of Breath

'The sun of the Russian land has set down!' Queen Olga of Greece cried when she heard that her first cousin, Alexander III, had died in his chair at 2.15 p.m. on Thursday 20 October 1894 at Livadia. In England, George, shocked by the 49-year-old Emperor's death from kidney failure, declared it 'a terrible calamity for the whole world . . . a more honest, generous and kind-hearted man never lived . . . God help and protect darling Aunt Minny, dear Nicky and Cousins in their sorrow'.[1]

He went to the funeral, where he comforted his 26-year-old cousin, the new Tsar Nicholas II, who talked brokenly about his father, saying it was 'the death of a saint! Lord help us in these terrible days!' Unprepared psychologically, utterly dismayed, Nicholas wrote in his diary, 'My God, my God, what a day! My head is turning round and round.'[2]

Brimming with feelings of inadequacy about succeeding his masterful father, he could not clear his mind of the powerful image of Alexander III on parade, on horseback, as thousands of upturned faces roared, 'Rady staratza, Vashe Imperatoraskoe Velichestvo',* in response to the Emperor's great cry of 'Khorosho, rebiata'.† Nicholas now confided tearfully in Sandro, his brother-in-law, 'What am I going to do, what is going to happen to me, to you, to Xenia, to Alix, to mother, to all of Russia? I am not prepared to be a Tsar. I never wanted to become one. I know nothing of the business of ruling.'[3]

His sister, Grand Duchess Olga, in reflective mood, standing on a verandah, recalled how Nicholas came up to her and put his arms round her shoulders. She said afterwards, 'Everyone in the family knew he was unprepared.' She blamed their father, who had not given him any real training, resenting the intrusion of 'state matters' into an exceptionally happy family life.

---

* 'We are happy to serve Your Majesty.'
† 'Well done, my children.'

Olga, who loved both her late father and her brother, was apprehensive about Nicholas's ability to be effective, and knew his sensitivity and kindness 'on their own were not enough for a sovereign'. Her fear was that Nicholas would prove an inadequate *Batushka Tsar*, or Little Father, to his people. While he had intelligence, 'faith and courage . . . he was wholly ignorant about governmental matters. Nicky had been trained as a soldier' only.[4]

He now became so distraught, he could hardly bear to stay in the death-room as the Orthodox priests intoned prayers for the dead;[5] seeing his distress, Uncle 'Bertie', the Prince of Wales, who had arrived with his wife in the Crimea, took charge of the funeral arrangements. 'I wonder what his tiresome old mother would have said if she had seen everybody accept Uncle Bertie's authority!' Olga mused, adding incredulously, 'In Russia of all places!'[6]

Both families boarded a black-draped train for a painful two-week 1,400-mile journey to a snow-covered St Petersburg, stopping at thirty-nine stations for exhausting obsequies. They were touched by the sight of so many black streamers on lampposts, on trams and black-varnished sleighs.[7] The Emperor's body had been on view first in the Crimea, then in Moscow, and finally at the Cathedral of St Peter and St Paul in St Petersburg.

Alexander lay in state for thirty-six hours in the Kremlin's Archangel Cathedral, attended by constant prayers and doleful chanting. A clutch of sixty-one royals from all over Europe wrinkled their noses at the corpse on such open view in his coffin, clutching a holy picture in his hand. They found it a true test of devotion to have to kiss the late Emperor's 'decaying' face.[8] The Prince of Wales said later, 'It gave me a shock when I saw his dear face so close to mine when I stooped down', and felt decidedly queasy having to kiss the late Emperor on the lips. Lord Carrington, who was in the royal party, thought Alexander III's face 'looked a dreadful colour and the smell was awful'.

During the long-drawn-out requiem, the widowed Empress, close to collapse, was an eye-catching tragic figure as she swayed in the glimmering light of thousands of candles. The Princess of Wales kept a supportive arm round the sister who had always hoped she would die before the husband with whom she had been 'so happy'. Alexandra stayed on for two months to comfort Dagmar; the sisters shared a bed, reverting to carefree childhood days in Copenhagen. Nicholas was so appreciative he gave his aunt a Fabergé crystal flower in a diamond-studded gold bowl to thank her for the support she had given his mother.[9] George, who was a pall-bearer, thought his 'Darling Aunt Minnie . . . so brave', and was full of admiration for the way in which she 'stood the whole time'.[10]

The new Tsar would never have the authority, effortlessly assumed by the late Emperor, or the confidence to drive forward the great tsarist engine, but then few could handle such an inheritance. Russia, a vast unwieldy empire, had always struggled against backwardness, was hard to govern and almost impossible to modernise.

When Nicholas succeeded, the townspeople had a slightly better standard of living than the peasants. In St Petersburg you could tell someone's standing in life by their street; the lowest were known as '*pereúlki*', meaning the 'lanes'. In summer they carried trays on their heads with glass jugs of raspberry purée and ice cream, or else they manned stalls selling old clothes, live fish and blinis. In winter *shiten*, a hot toddy made with honey and spices, was sold with cabbage pie or a piece of gingerbread.

Social disparity was as great as ever. The *belle époque* was vibrant, with the artistic movements of Symbolism and art nouveau flourishing. The aristocracy in St Petersburg sent their daughters to the Smolny Convent, designed by the architect Bartolomeo Rastrelli, and opened in 1748 by Empress Elizabeth, who had flirted with the idea of becoming a nun; but her vocation was short-lived, as her many lovers persuaded her not to take the veil. The principle of the gold-and-blue equivalent of Cheltenham Ladies College was discipline of mind and body. Later, Lenin was delighted to take over this graceful 'School for Daughters of the Nobility', where once its pupils had dressed in lace-trimmed silver taffeta and chinchilla as they arrived for dance lessons with their governesses on exciting newfangled electric trams.

There was a glimpse of Russia's stifling bureaucracy when the trams were first seen in St Petersburg in 1895. A deal had been made with the association of horse-drawn trams, which gave them exclusive rights until 1907, but a lawsuit confirmed that this was only on *terra firma*, so the ingenious electric-tram company laid out its poles and rails each winter on the ice of the frozen River Neva.

The only way the aristocracy knew about the wretchedness of the poor was when they saw it for themselves from the windows of a luxury train, on which they travelled with their own silver ewers and basins to rinse their hands before dinner. When the Trans-Siberian

Railway opened in 1903, running 5,772 miles between Moscow and Vladivostok on the Pacific, it was a triumph for Nicholas, and the key to unlocking Siberia's mineral wealth. The work had been done mainly by hand with saw, shovel or miner's hack, drilling tunnels out of permanently frosted mountainsides, carrying equipment through icy swamps and lakes. This achievement for Russia was as significant as the Great Wall was for China, but it also helped reveal the pitiful plight of many of Nicholas's subjects.

In the remote provinces, across those great stretches of desolate landscape, far from St Petersburg, people were still suffering from the devastating aftermath of famine and loss of livestock. The muzhiks, in their red cotton shirts outside their trousers, their broad leather boots and sheepskin coats, and who had lost their liberty in the Middle Ages, were still not really free, being forbidden even to move from one village to another.

For many travellers, the poverty of the country villages, often made up of one 'long raggling and unpaved street' covered in moss, was startling. But in the poorest wooden hovels there was always an icon with a burning lamp and a brick stove for baking. It disturbed the aristocratic Russians, for whom 'the subject of the peasantry always seemed to send the men . . . into that special mood of earnest self-importance . . . when they discussed a "social question"'.[11] But the serfs who made their estates function would, one day, burn them to the ground and make the owners clean and sweep out the lavatories in prison.

Nicholas inherited the worst characteristics of his father's reign. As a ruler, he was steeped in seventeenth-century autocracy, and he failed to recognise that Russia was on the brink of convulsive change. He made few concessions. The serfs had been liberated by his grandfather, but it never occurred to him that they needed basic human rights. Inevitably, and soon after his accession, a couple of revolutionary parties sprang to life: one was the Social Democrats, and the other the more tolerant 'Land and Liberty' Social Revolutionary Party.

Experienced courtiers became alarmed by the air of uncertainty surrounding their new Tsar, and commented unkindly on Nicholas's 'inconspicuousness'.[12] Dagmar feared her eldest son was emotionally fragile but hoped that marriage a month after his father's death would give him the emotional security to enable him to face his destiny.

There was a brief lull in the elaborate mourning at the Russian court to allow the hurried marriage of the new Tsar to Alix of Hesse on 14 November 1894. His only real love, the German Princess, had overcome her misgivings about converting to Orthodoxy and was given an official Russian name, Alexandra Feodorovna, befitting an alluring Empress with a delicate beauty; but she failed to capture the heart of her new country.

On the morning of his wedding, Nicholas recalled, 'I put on my Hussar uniform at eight o' clock.' He heard the 21-gun salute from the Peter and Paul Fortress as guests gathered in the Arabian Room at the Winter Palace. Even with the excitement of her wedding, Alix still could not resist a little gloom, telling her sister Ella how strange it was 'to be in deep mourning, weeping for a beloved person one day, to get married in fashionable outfits the next'. Afterwards she said, 'Our wedding was like an extension of these funeral rites only they dressed me in white.'

At 10.30 a.m. in the Malachite Drawing Room, attendants put the finishing touches to her russet-blonde hair before putting on a circlet of diamonds and matching necklace. A gold cape and train lined with ermine were gently placed over her silver dress, then she set off to her wedding in a gold coach decorated with sensual Boucher-inspired cherubs and garlands. The coach was lined with gilded velvet, and the procession was 'like a line of living gold'.

As in all traditional Russian wedding ceremonies, crowns were held over the heads of the couple during the *Te Deum*. The newly-weds bowed before the Empress Dowager, who kissed them emotionally. But the Tsar's cousin, Grand Duke Konstantin, noted sourly that the Emperor, at five foot seven inches, was 'just a little shorter than his bride'.[13]

Alix had already been told by her cousin George to make sure she never appeared taller than her husband in public. She thought this was hilarious, and in a letter to Nicholas from Windsor Castle dated 24 April 1894 she mockingly repeated this advice: 'foolish Georgie says that I am to insist upon you wearing high heels and that I am to have quite low ones. May, he says, won't change hers, but he wears much higher ones . . . too absurd, and I am sure you would never do it'.[14] Anyway, Nicholas liked nothing better than wearing military riding boots whenever possible.

George could see for himself that Alix was a head taller than Nicholas; she had not obeyed him, but he was impressed by the wedding. As the newly-weds left the Kazan Cathedral he admired the way in which Nicholas ordered the soldiers to move away so the people could get closer to them in the imperial sleigh. A nicely democratic touch, he thought, after 'a beautiful service but sad', and he watched as they appeared 'at the window and the people gave them a tremendous ovation', adding a little enviously, 'They have got some beautiful presents.' Gifts for the new Tsarina included jewellery, a trousseau with chinchilla, astrakhan, ermine and mink, brocades, silk capes lined with swansdown, 'night-time' accessories, gold fans, Sèvres china, 'an enormous silver swan',[15] and a small palace.

'I do think', George wrote to Queen Victoria, 'that Nicky is a very lucky man to have got such a lovely and charming wife, and I must say I never saw two people more in love with each other or happier than they are.' 'Nicky', he enthused, 'has been kindness itself to me, he is the same dear boy he has always been . . . He does everything so quietly and naturally; everyone is struck by it.'[16]

'Am inexpressibly happy with Alix,' the enraptured Nicholas declared, unable to believe that at last he had won the hand of the Hesse Princess whom he had loved so unwaveringly from the age of sixteen. In keeping with Romanov family tradition, on their wedding night he wore an embroidered silver nightshirt weighing fifteen pounds. 'And so I'm a married man,' he wrote joyfully.[17] 'There are no words capable of describing the bliss it is to be living together.' Below this diary entry there was a loving line added by Alix significantly referring to him as 'my beloved little husband', the diminutive not auguring well.[18] Private happiness failed to help Nicholas satisfy a yearning in Russian hearts for an inspirational leader. He was too destructively inflexible.

The problem for Nicholas and George, both quiet, contained men, was that they could never quite match the bonhomie and exuberance of their ebullient fathers. When Edward VII died on 6 May 1910 at 11.45 p.m. aged sixty-nine, having smoked a large cigar and been given the cheering news that his horse Witch of the Air had won at Kempton Park that day, George, 'stunned' by grief, wrote, 'I have lost my best friend and the best of fathers.'[19]

A black-bordered letter arrived from Nicholas at Tsarskoe Selo, and the tone was one of heartfelt understanding, with echoes of his own earlier grief.[20] Dated 25 April 1910, it read, 'Just a few lines to tell you how *deeply* I feel for you, the terrible loss you and England will have entertained. I know (alas!) by experience what it costs one. There you are with your heart bleeding and aching at the same time [as] duty imposes itself . . . and people and affairs come up and tear you away from your sorrow. How I would have liked to have come now and been near you.'[21]

Representing Nicholas, his younger brother Grand Duke Michael and his mother, Dowager Empress Dagmar, went to London, and with close family they stood with heads bowed in the death chamber while prayers were said over the dead King before he was placed in his coffin.[22]

George V's ascent to the throne coincided with the appearance of Halley's Comet:* that accumulation of rock and ice, orange flame and a white centre, seen blazing across a summer sky on the night of 8 May 1910, was regarded as an encouraging omen.

The difference in character between the two young Emperors is never more apparent than when comparing the way in which the two cousins came to terms with their roles as King and Emperor respectively. George was filled with apprehension, which expressed itself in the first few months of his reign through insomnia, waking at 'about five . . . and making notes',[23] and being plagued by a return of his nervous indigestion. But he was helped by the years of grooming since his brother Eddy, the Duke of Clarence had died in 1892. This enabled him now, at the age of forty-four, to take on his father's mantle and rule a still-great empire.

Behind all the geniality and bonhomie, Edward VII had been an astute, far-sighted father, subtly steering George towards his destiny, ensuring they worked side by side. He showed him state papers, encouraged him to comment and tick anything which needed clarification. George knew about government; he visited the House of Commons, sitting unobtrusively behind the clock listening to debates.

Now he was King George V, in his favourite admiral's uniform, he addressed his Privy Counsellors on 7 May 1910 in the splendour of the Banqueting House. His words were brief and eloquent in their simplicity: 'My heart is too full for me to address you today in more than a few words,' he said, and then spoke of losing not only a father's love but also 'a dear friend and adviser'.[24]

---

* Appears roughly every seventy-six years; its next appearance was in 1986.

He wrote to Nicholas, who understood better than most what he had endured. 'These last three weeks have been terrible,' he told him in a letter dated 14 May 1910. 'My heart has been nearly breaking and at the same time I've had to carry on all my duties . . . and see so many people to arrange about [*sic*] the last sad ceremonies and entertain William, seven Kings and numerous Princes and Representatives from practically all the countries of the world.'[25] But, in spite of his heavy duties as King, he stressed to 'dearest Nicky' how he wanted their friendship to continue. Both men had supported each other during the emotional see-saw of their lives. 'You know I never change,' George wrote, 'and have always been very fond of you.' Not quite fond enough, was the view of the Romanovs.

As George prepared for his coronation on Thursday 22 June 1911, he moved into Buckingham Palace, where he and Queen Mary spent hours rearranging pictures and furniture. This aesthetic idyll was interrupted by a 'cruel and abominable libel', as the King himself described it to Winston Churchill,[26] which could only be resolved by legal action, a desperate and unusual step for a member of the royal family. This was the *Liberator* story about his 'marriage in Malta', which had now been resurrected in a subversive move aimed at destabilising the new reign.

Appearing in court on 1 February 1911, Admiral Culme-Seymour, by now an elderly figure, was an invaluable witness for the prosecution, showing how impossible it was that his daughter Laura could have been in Malta on the dates suggested. Unrepentant, the perpetrator of the rumour, Edward Mylius, tried to have a subpoena served on the King to appear as a witness, but failed. Churchill categorised this to the King's private secretary, Sir Arthur Bigge, as 'a mere piece of impudent buffoonery', which 'should be brushed away with the contempt it deserves'.[27] Mylius was found guilty of libel and jailed for twelve months.

This was not an auspicious start to his reign, and the King, who had remained at Windsor throughout the trial, mulling over the outcome, sunk deep in a red-leather armchair in the room where William IV and the Prince Consort had died,[28] dismissed the libel as 'a damnable lie' which unfortunately had been 'in existence for over 20 years'. He expressed the hope that 'the whole story was now finished'. But Mylius persisted, and issued a pamphlet in America called *The Morganatic Marriage of George V*. Laura Culme-Seymour never married.

In the calmer, sunny days just before his coronation George had valuable time with royal relations, including the Kaiser, who was invited to the ceremony. The two men enjoyed 'a long and friendly conversation on important questions during a walk in the Palace garden'.[29] But peace never lasted long with this German cousin, who airily proposed a pact between England and Germany. 'You'd keep the seas, while we are responsible for the land. With such an alliance not a mouse will stir in Europe.' During this visit the King was presented with the baton of *Feldmarschall* in the German Army, a gift which became an embarrassment during the First World War when the royal family was anxious to shake off its German association.

On the day of the coronation, George and Mary rode from Buckingham Palace to Westminster Abbey in a coronation coach drawn by eight cream-coloured horses, and rulers of Russia, Spain, Norway, Greece and Denmark admired 50,000 troops lining the streets under the command of Lord Kitchener.

The King found the service in the Abbey 'most beautiful and impressive' but admitted it was 'a terrible ordeal'. He thought it 'grand, yet simple and most dignified',[30] which could have been a description of his own style as monarch. He later complained of a splitting headache from the weight of the crown, which he had worn for three and a half hours.

His description of the day went into his diary, which was more like 'a naval log' but 'spattered with tears'.[31] Naturally, the weather was mentioned, but there was also fulsome praise for his 'Darling May', who had looked pleasing in subtle shades of silver, gold and white, which she had chosen personally. In the King's eyes she 'looked lovely', but did not appear as serene as she might have wished to others. One onlooker, Alexander Murray, The Master of Elibank,* thought unsympathetically how 'pale and strained' Mary looked when she arrived at the Abbey, and woundingly observed that she appeared 'a great lady but *not* a Queen'. However, he then changed his mind and decided that the placing of the crown on her head seemed miraculously to transform her into an impressive 'Queen of this great Empire'.[32]

The King, who had his differences with his wayward eldest son, was deeply touched when 'dear David came to do homage to me', so

---

* A courtesy title for this eldest son of a Scottish peer, who was a minister in the Liberal Government.

much so, he confessed, 'I nearly broke down'.[33] The next day the newly crowned King and Queen drove through London, 'over seven miles . . . through most beautifully decorated streets . . . which were crowded with people from top to bottom who cheered in a way I have never heard before'.[34]

George had none of his father's jocular, worldly charm or urbanity, and seemed ill-prepared for the task of ruling over a still-impressive British Empire. But he would resolutely steer his people through the trauma of the next quarter of the coming century.

His cousin Nicholas's coronation on 14 May 1896 had begun with the same glamorous fanfare and imperial pageantry. The Tsar rode to the Kremlin on a brilliant, sunny morning on a half-bred English white charger, Norma, with silver nails in its horseshoes.* Escorted by Cossacks, tribes from all over Russia, members of the imperial hunt in silver and gold woven Circassian coats, and the court orchestra, he was greeted by cries of 'Hurrah' as he made his entry into the Assumption Cathedral, where the floor was covered with red velvet edged with gold lace. The Romanov women all wore long dresses of silk *argent*, and on their heads traditional *kokoshniks* [Russian crowns] embroidered with seed pearls and silver thread. As Nicholas was anointed with sacred rose-coloured oil, the ceremony had the magic of a fairy tale stirring the huge responsive heart of the Russian people, who loved their Tsar, the Orthodox faith and their country, this trinity an integral and traditional part of the Russian character.

His new wife knelt before her husband, watched by most of the crowned heads of Europe. Then Nicholas II, the eighteenth Romanov and last Tsar, made Alix the most important woman in Russia by placing the traditional Catherine the Great gold and diamond tiara on her head. The robes were so heavy that afterwards Alix's brother, Grand Duke Ernest of Hesse, reported anxiously that he had seen his sister 'standing motionless and alone . . . unable to move a step!'

The ceremony began at nine o'clock and lasted for five hours. *The Times*[35] judiciously wondered how 'all the pomp and solemn pageantry which human ingenuity can devise and the resources of a great empire can command' must have affected the newly crowned

---

* In her autobiography, *Dancing in St Petersburg*, Kschessinska suggested that the Tsar's horse's shoes and the silver nails were preserved in the Arms Museum.

Tsar, and commented, 'As he descended from the dais yesterday, with the transient sunlight playing upon the diamonds of his crown, Nicholas II must have been more or less than man if he were not deeply moved. He has been called upon by heaven to perhaps the most responsible position in the world.'

But Nicholas seemed dogged by bad luck from the moment he was crowned. For a couple as naturally superstitious and attracted to mystical signals as the Tsar and Tsarina they must have been horrified during the coronation, when the collar of the Order of St Andrew slipped from Nicholas's shoulders,[36] falling to the ground just as he was being anointed and receiving the imperial crown. There was a sharp intake of breath from the congregation at this ill omen.

Nicholas had always been haunted by a tragic sense of regret because of the unfortunate timing of his birth on St Job's Day. 'Had he lived in classic times, the story of his life and death would have been made the subject of some great tragedy by the poets of ancient Greece,' Sir George Buchanan wrote prophetically.[37] He seemed 'one of the most pathetic figures in history'.

After the ceremony, the newly crowned Tsar bowed to his mother, the widowed Empress; she shed tears, but remembered to kiss her daughter-in-law. Her secret anxiety was expressed in a letter to Queen Victoria as she spoke about her worries about 'my poor beloved Nicky', and the burden which had fallen on his shoulders. It was not easy for Alix, newly wed, newly crowned; as she quickly became aware of her mother-in-law's undiminished influence over her husband, secretly she set her mind to breaking that maternal thread.

When Alix and Nicholas showed themselves to the people, appearing on the balcony of the Great Kremlin Palace, bells from Moscow's one hundred and one churches rang out as the new Tsarina was given a bouquet of roses on a golden tray. Moscow appealed, making her feel like a medieval Tsaritsa; it was more solid and Germanic than the baroquely beautiful gold-domed delicacy of St Petersburg.

At the party afterwards, the Tsar entertained 5,000 guests in the Hall of the Facets, which was lit by 2,500 candles. On each table there was sparkling crystal and an orange tree, as centrepiece for the silver and gold plate. Pheasant in aspic was served on Sèvres porcelain, then a 'ceremonial performance' was given by the Bolshoi of the traditional first and last acts of *Life for the Tsar*.

The glamour of this engaging new Tsar and his graceful wife, with whom he was clearly infatuated and whom he had 'so tenderly' anointed earlier that day, attracted poor people who had travelled many *versts** to catch a glimpse of the man they thought of simply as God, their 'Lord and Judge'. The coronation confirmed Nicholas's mystical link as direct ambassador to God for the Russians.

The people now looked forward to a goodwill 'bread and circuses' celebration, with the sure promise of puppet shows, merry-go-rounds and balalaika music. Circuses were always popular, especially Ciniselli's, where a young woman thrilled crowds nightly by putting her head in a crocodile's mouth until the outraged saurian made short work of her.

In this mood of cheerful anticipation, half a million made their way in great good humour with high hopes to the Khodynka Meadow outside Moscow for this 'special coronation fête', this imperial-alms free feast.

---

* Five-eighths of a mile or one kilometre.

TEN

Cup of Sorrows

Gently picking up a battered old enamelled mug from a bookcase in her home in Westminster, Edomé Broughton-Adderley says, 'This is my Cup of Sorrows', and holds out a Khodynka Meadow souvenir in frail hands. Not that, at eighty-five years old, she is in the least bit sorry for herself as she pours another glass of champagne.

The old lady has never forgotten her mother Chloe Philip's account of the horrifying events on 18 May 1896, when she had been out in her carriage along one of the more fashionable boulevards in Moscow. Suddenly the coachman, turning pale, stopped and pulled in to one side to make way for the approaching long stream of peasant carts laden with dead bodies.

This was the cruel end to what should have been a joyful day, when almost half a million people in the patriotic spirit of old Russia had joined in the celebrations marking Nicholas II's coronation. They were to be given free pardons by the new Tsar, free beer and enamelled mugs engraved with the imperial eagle.

The atmosphere in the meadow, an army training area outside Moscow, had been that of a traditional Russian carnival, with a circus, showmen's booths, tin whistles and laughter as the clowns staggered about uneasily. There was usually a childlike enjoyment of these festivals, with their pavilions and sliding-hills, and cheerful stallholders serving spiced drinks and hot pies. On this occasion, the people would dance all night, sing gypsy songs and toast the newly crowned couple, the Tsar and Tsarina.

But then things quite quickly got out of control, as happened so easily in primitive Russia, when a rumour started that there might not be enough souvenir cups to go around. In a panic the mob surged forward, and after a brief moment 'a terrible, long-drawn-out wail' was heard as mothers, children and fathers crashed to the ground in the stampede. Hundreds were trampled to death in the rush to get to the front of the crowd; many were suffocated, while others fell underfoot and into the trenches or were crushed against the revetments of the exercise ground, which became filled with corpses. All for a tin mug.

Survivors remembered the only way to escape was by walking over the faces of the crushed dead. The official death toll was 1,389,[1] all carried away in farm carts hastily requisitioned to make their sad procession into the city. But several thousand were injured, many lying trapped under bodies or trying feebly to crawl through the mud in the fragile hope of being noticed.

The Tsar's sister Olga remembered seeing 'a procession of carts coming nearer . . . Pieces of tarpaulin were thrown rather roughly over them.' Recalling the sight of 'many dangling hands', in a grim, almost comic moment, her first thought was that 'people were waving at us', but then described how her blood froze. 'I felt sick yet I still stared on. Those carts carried the dead, mangled out of all recognition.'

In the aftermath of what should have been a glorious coronation festival, survivors carried away the injured, helpless and despairing in the face of such devastating carnage. There was a suggestion that disruptive forces hostile to the Tsar had orchestrated the panic deliberately to put an indelible stain on the start of his reign. The Khodynka disaster could hardly have happened in England, where people were not so poor that there would have been the same desperate scramble to get hold of a slice of free bread, a herring or a tin mug.

Shaken by the magnitude of the disaster, still Nicholas seemed not to realise it had been such a monumental catastrophe, saying, 'Of course it was all very sad not to have any influence on the festivities held in honour of the coronation.'[2]

Although he and Alix visited the injured in hospital and mourned the mutilated dead, they made a fateful decision to attend a gala ball being given in their honour that night by French Ambassador the Count of Montebello and his wife. They were persuaded to attend by Nicholas's uncle Grand Duke Sergei, who was Governor of Moscow.

The trouble was that Nicholas listened politely to everyone, inscrutable, gently agreeing. 'He takes counsel from everyone: grand-parents, aunts, mummy and anyone else; he is young and accedes to the view of the last person to whom he talks,' an exasperated General Vannovsky, Minister of War, complained.

Nicholas now responded weakly to what was tantamount to an order by his high-handed uncle, who told him that the French Ambassador had spent half a million roubles on the ball and that politically it would be unwise to upset the French. He virtually commanded his compliant nephew to attend. The Grand Duke could therefore claim responsibility for one of the earliest and most damaging public-relations disasters in Nicholas's entire reign.

Showing an extraordinary lack of judgement, Nicholas and Alexandra obeyed and went to the French Embassy ball. The irony was that neither of them enjoyed these extravagant occasions. In this case, 100,000 roses had been brought from the south of France and exquisite tapestries from Versailles had been lent for the evening.

Nothing could have been more insensitive than the appearance of the new Tsar and his haughty Tsarina leading the dancing at the French Embassy, after a dinner of roast duckling and crème brûlée, while their people suffered and counted their dead.

The Dowager Empress, ever the wise *Matoushka*, or mother, to the Russian people, instinctively got things right by tirelessly visiting all the hospitals caring for the injured, while the presence of Nicholas and Alexandra at the ball had created a scar which never quite healed.

ELEVEN

'I Like My Wife'

The marriages of George and Nicholas were precipitated by the deaths of their fathers. One marriage was arranged, the other was a true love match. They were devoted and faithful husbands, and both lived simply.

George took his bride to an unpretentious brownstone house, originally an annexe to Sandringham House built to cope with the overflow of guests in Edward VII's hospitable time. York Cottage was a frightfully 'glum little villa . . . separated by an abrupt rim of lawn from a pond at the edge of which a leaden pelican gazes in dejection upon the water lilies and bamboos'.[1] The enforced cosiness of this small house offered a novel intimacy for a couple who hardly knew each other; it was here they could play at being ordinary newly-weds.

Early in the marriage, Princess May, in a note to her husband, felt she must apologise for her awkward manner, saying, 'I am sorry that I am still so shy with you, I tried not to be the other day, but alas failed, I was angry with myself! It is so stupid to be so stiff together.' Touching in its honesty, this brought an immediate response and, explaining why he too might 'appear shy and cold', George said this was all due to the pressure of becoming Prince of Wales after his brother's death. Princess May became a soothing presence in his life with an ability to calm her highly strung husband in his anxious diligence to duty.

His private secretaries had to work in their bedrooms, drafting speeches and planning visits to the empire. There was so little space, servants had to sleep in estate cottages. When asked once where they all lived, the artless royal supposition was, 'I suppose they live in trees.' The housekeeper, pushed out to an estate cottage, went most reluctantly. Congratulating his comptroller, Sir Francis de Winton, on the successful eviction, George asked how on earth he had managed to 'make [the] housekeeper give up her room? She absolutely refused to do so when I asked her.' The space was so limited, the royal couple's baths had lids which shut down to provide tabletops as in the houses of some of their poverty-stricken subjects.[2]

Watchful about money, he made no secret of his displeasure shortly after he was married that the £900 overflow from a wedding present collection by the navy was to go to charity. In a letter from York Cottage dated 28 November 1894 he wrote, 'They evidently forget that I have a <u>wife</u> at all; a present for her would have been much more appropriate . . . say, an anchor brooch in diamonds and rubies would have been very handsome. But of course it is not for me to make a suggestion. At the same time I think it very mean and shabby of the Committee.'[3]

George bothered about domestic detail, including even the choice of grates, asking Mr Maple of the eponymous furniture store to send 'an intelligent man . . . with a book of designs to Sandringham'. He suggested the 'tall man with a beard' who had been 'very quick and took things in at once'[4] on a previous visit. The Duke and Duchess kept house on £22,000 a year.[5]

George could hardly bear to be away from what he called the 'dear wee house'. Princess May did sometimes resent the appallingly cramped conditions, particularly after she became Queen, and widowed 'Motherdear' still insisted on rattling round the 'Big House' at Sandringham. Squeezed uncomfortably into York Cottage, in a rare outburst of spite May was heard muttering, 'Selfish old woman'.[6]

Having spent much of his life on board ship, George was happy in confined spaces. He used to say, 'I like small rooms, it reminds me of my time at sea.' Even after he became King, he was still reluctant to move to Windsor and give up Marlborough House for Buckingham Palace. He liked to crowd into the York Cottage telephone cubbyhole with the switchboard operators. 'Do you mind if I share your room?' The embarrassed operators readily bowed agreement to an invitation which could hardly be refused.

It was almost impossible to put up visitors at York Cottage but, self-contained, neither George nor May minded. Soon after they were married, they had to entertain the Kaiser at Osborne. 'Fancy me, little me,' May archly told her mother, 'sitting next to William, the place of honour!!! . . . I talked my *best* German', her Württemberg ancestry now a positive asset. They had inherited an enlightened royal chef, Gabriel Tschumi, but unfortunately his skill was not always valued: stewed plums and semolina were appreciated more than a lemon soufflé.

The Yorks never enjoyed the flummery of court social life, or the elaborate banquets, George far preferred dining *en famille*. But he knew how Edward VII used and entertained a valuable network of contacts. George decided to hold dinner parties for forty or fifty high achievers in public life; not that he enjoyed these occasions much but, unlike the Tsar, he realised their value, as a way of keeping *au courant*.

His wife's uncle, the Duke of Cambridge, was a little dismayed when George told him frankly how he could 'not bear London and going out and hates society'.[7] When he became King he realised the value of being seen at Buckingham Palace, though he would have much preferred to hold audiences in his Norfolk country drawing room.[8]

He was not subtle about hiding boredom at court functions, and was once chivvied by Mrs Asquith, 'Sir, your great fault is that you don't enjoy yourself.' In his direct wardroom manner he replied, 'Yes, I know, but you see I don't like society; I like my wife.'[9]

Both Nicholas and George preferred quiet times, tapping their barometers, watching their dear wives on chaise longues with their needlework while they wrote up their diaries each evening. Writing was not a pleasure for George, who found 'the physical act of writing . . . a torture'. Caustically, art historian Kenneth Clark observed that he 'had never seen any man do it so laboriously'.[10]

May enjoyed less time reclining than the Tsarina and only if heavily pregnant would she allow herself the luxury of putting her feet up, decorously covered with a floral-embroidered white silk throw. Educated partly in Florence, she genuinely loved art, enjoyed reading, and also listening to classical music.

The marriage, which had hardly been impetuous, was a surprising success; they were a devoted couple. George was surprisingly good with their first baby, David, the future Edward VIII,* born 23 June 1894 at Princess May's parents' home, White Lodge, Richmond. He liked to preside at his heir's evening bath. 'I make,' he told a lady-in-waiting, 'a very good lap'. Four days after the birth, the Queen arrived with Nicholas and Alexandra in tow and pronounced her great-grandson a 'pretty child', a rare compliment for any newborn baby.

---

*   Succeeded 20 January 1936; abdicated 11 December 1936.

But May hated being pregnant and having babies. After the birth of her second-last child,* she wrote to her aunt Augusta saying, 'I think I have done my duty and may now *stop*, as having babies is highly distasteful to me.'[11] But there was one more child, the frail Prince John, born 12 July 1905. Both May and Alicky gave up wanting children after each had given birth to a delicate son, the Tsarevich born with haemophilia and 'Johnny', who was epileptic.

As he came to terms with the heavy royal responsibilities that imposed themselves on the immediate heir to the throne, George could relax by escaping into his happiest role as a discerning Norfolk country squire: as well as keeping an orderly eye on the stud farm at Sandringham, he ran one of the best shoots in England. He liked to wear a pedometer and sometimes recorded 12 miles out shooting as he tramped across the marshes and salt meadows.[12]

His diary had predictable fixtures, 'stalking in September, driven partridges in October, covert shoots in the winter'.[13] Almost up to Olympic standard with a shotgun, he once famously bagged a record 3,937 pheasants in December 1913.† The King remarked a little sheepishly to the Prince of Wales on one of these shoots that 'Perhaps we overdid it today.'[14]

There was nowhere in his eyes to rival this simple Norfolk home, for him it was always 'Dear old Sandringham', the place where he later died and which he once declared emotionally was simply 'the place I love better than anywhere in the world'.[15]

He disapproved of gambling, but did allow the occasional game of bridge while always remembering his father's painful skirmish in the Tranby Croft scandal,[16] in which he was accused of cheating. George V's love of racing was attractive to the British people and, in common with many of his subjects, he enjoyed a bet discreetly placed by 'Fethers', Major Fred Fetherstonhaugh, his racing manager. His greatest racing success was with Scuttle‡ a bay filly which he bred himself and which in 1928 won the One Thousand Guineas at Newmarket. Afterwards, Fethers received an endearing

---

* Prince George, born 20 December 1902.

† Major Britten, agent to Lord Burnham at Hall Barn, Beaconsfield, reported seeing the King bring down 'thirty-nine birds with thirty-nine consecutive cartridges'.

‡ When put out to grass at the end of her career, Scuttle had won a total of £12,000 in prize-money.

note from the King, hoping he would 'always find that I am reasonable and have plenty of patience and as a rule [this] brings its own reward'.[17]

He liked playing the role of genial, Norfolk landowner, and being 'Farmer George', winning prizes for his shire horses and admiration for his Aberdeen Angus cattle in Scotland.

There was something cleverly ordinary about his hobbies; like the Queen's interest in racing pigeons, nothing George did seemed unattainable to the ordinary man. In common with many pensioners, he enjoyed keeping budgerigars. If one fell off its perch, it was soon replaced with an exotic bird from the colonies.

Complaining to Mrs Beatie Fetherstonhaugh, his racing manager's wife, in a note to her at the Midland Hotel Manchester, written by hand on 29 November 1930, he told her mournfully, 'three of my Budgerigars (all blue cobalt) have died'.[18]

Soon 'Mrs Fethers' was being thanked for 'the two charming china birds' which she had sent as consolation. The King told her he had put them in the Chinese Room at Sandringham, 'where they will look so nice'; they were obviously not quite suitable to be alongside the Sèvres and Meissen in Buckingham Palace.

George and May rarely wrote to each other because they were seldom apart. May later described how on one occasion when they were staying with the King and Queen of Belgium in individual suites in separate wings of the palace, she heard her bedroom door being opened in the middle of the night and spotted the 'dear little sad face' of her husband, the snub nose and familiar beard appearing round the door.[19] 'Oh, it's only you,' she said. Not that she was expecting some handsome admirer.

The marriage of Nicholas and Alix on the other hand was loving and intense, and he even put up with his wife's passion for nibbling English biscuits in bed. He indulged her: for instance, he loved dancing but she hated it, so they would go home early. 'Alix is very imperious and will always insist on having her own way,' her aunt Victoria, Dowager Empress of Germany, had warned. But Nicholas would always support this delicate girl with the desirable figure, classical features and bittersweet expression, and her face always lit up whenever he appeared.

At the beginning of their married life, they were like a couple of children as they slid down ice hills and took sledges to the islands. As the horses flew along the icy highway and snowflakes as big as

shamrocks fell on her cheeks, Alix buried her face in her high furry
collar and Nicholas, smiling, felt lucky to have such a 'tenderly
beloved wife'.

It was a love match as conventional as the watercolours of posies
of violets she painted. When they were apart, she sent Nicholas letters
scented with sprigs of lilac and he would tell her, 'often I bury my
nose and press my lips to the paper you have touched'. At military
headquarters an aide-de-camp looking over the Tsar's shoulder
quickly learned to recognise the distinctive handwriting as his
commander-in-chief opened another loving note addressed to 'Huzy'.

Even on their twenty-second wedding anniversary, on 8 April
1916, there was nothing stale about the relationship, although all
around them things were beginning to crumble. Alix wrote to
Nicholas of her longing to be held in his arms, 'tightly clasped, and
to relive our beautiful bridal days'.

Alix never shared Nicholas's love of 10-mile hikes and swimming
naked in the lakes, although she did occasionally, dutifully,
accompany him to shoot bear. Queen Victoria disapproved of this
'mannish pastime'; it only confirmed her misgivings about life in
Russia. However, she had to accept that the marriage was a happy
one, but complained that she missed 'Alicky', grumbling, 'I have a
right to her'.

So Nicholas and Alix came to Britain to pay 'Granny' an official
visit, arriving at Balmoral on 22 September 1896. George warmly
recorded going to Ballater, 'where we received dear Nicky and
Alicky'. As always in the diary there was a meticulous entry about
dress: 'Nicky wore Scots Greys [he was Colonel], Papa in Russian
uniform, I wore a kilt'.

The likeness between the cousins was so startling that one of
Queen Victoria's ladies-in-waiting thought Nicholas, 'Exactly like a
skinny Duke of York – the image of him'.[20] It poured incessantly.
Alix, who had always given the impression she loved Scotland, now
found the rocky horizon depressing and dull while the men went off
stalking and fishing. Her grandmother thought Alix had become
stand-offish and remote and was far too extravagant, wearing
beautiful clothes instead of homely Scottish tweed skirts.[21]

They had brought with them their first baby, Grand Duchess
Olga, and had been to Balmoral to show her off. From the moment
of Olga's birth on 3 November 1895, Nicholas kept the Queen
almost too well informed, telling her that Alix was breastfeeding:

'God, what happiness! . . . For my part,' he said, as if expecting criticism, 'I consider it the most natural thing a mother can do and I think the example an excellent one.'[22] Olga was born with a full head of hair, which Russian midwives said was an omen of good luck. For her christening she was carried to the Catherine Palace Church on a gold cushion under a cover of gold, and put in the care of an English nurse sent out by Queen Victoria.

During their stay in Scotland, Nicholas developed toothache. One of the Queen's doctors, Sir James Reid, looked at his swollen cheek and diagnosed 'an irritation at the stump of a decayed molar', and with his finger applied 'tinct' to the royal gum. The young couple were so grateful, they invited Reid to see the baby at bath time. Watching the Empress playing with her child, the doctor thought how unfair it was of her critics to dismiss her as aloof or cold. Unconquerable shyness was the problem, in his opinion. The Tsar gave the doctor a diamond-studded gold cigarette box; with his usual charm he talked about how much they had enjoyed Balmoral, how Alix had taken him to meet the royal retainer, who had taught her to make scones. The weather, the Tsar said – it was one of his favourite topics – had been awful, cold and wet. He'd had no success on any of the shoots.

The Tsar was popular with the servants, tipping generously. Leaving Scotland, with his usual gentle urbanity he said how much they looked forward to a return visit. It was not to be.

The visit turned a spotlight on the cousins' marriages. Unlike the Tsar and Tsarina's, George and Mary's could never be described as impetuously amorous. While Alix presented a cold face to the world she was a wife passionately in love with her husband, bombarding him with 'I kiss you all over' billets-doux telling 'hubby' how much she longed for his 'caresses'. Nicholas found in Alix a mother substitute who kept him in thrall by an invisible thread. Her girlish submissiveness in syrupy love letters – 'Sweetest Angel, if little wife ever did, if anything [sic] that displeased you or unwilling[ly] grieved or hurt in the past year' – concealed a steely will but appealed to a man who had been dominated by his mother.

On one occasion, when Alix thought the evening had dragged on too long at a hussars' regimental dinner, she called out to Nicholas, 'Now come, my boy, it's time to go to bed!' To the Tsar's fellow officers, it did not sound like a sensual invitation; more a peremptory order to their colonel-in-chief from a bossy nanny.

Stately and impeccable, Mary, who also loved her husband, was incapable of showing any emotion. In her view, even an affectionate glance in her husband's direction could appear improper. She refused to smile for photographs, being convinced that when she showed her teeth she 'looked like a horse'. This rigorous restraint was particularly inhibiting around her children. Once, visiting Prince John, the little boy ran towards her in his awkward, lunging way, but there was no hug. His grim-looking mother, standing outside his cottage, asked severely, 'How long has that ivy been like that?' The bewildered boy had no idea she hated ivy.

When told of the death of her cousin, the Grand Duke of Hesse, just as she was setting off to visit her niece, Lady Cambridge, at Bognor,[23] her response was to express the hope that 'they give us shrimps or one of those nice sea things for tea'. This unyielding calm suited George, who could be volatile and quick-tempered, snappishly rebuking an aide if he so much as mislaid a timetable. He liked the way May appeared so splendid a figure, so dignified in her high toques and long skirts, or striking in diamonds or pearl collar with an elaborate pendant and sapphires. Wearing so much jewellery, she always needed a two-foot space on either side of her at table.

It had not been easy for her being married into a family where hunting and shooting were seen as superior fun. Anything 'eyebrow', as the King used to say until he learned that the word was 'highbrow', was treated with suspicion; books were chosen not for pleasure but because they might be 'improving'. According to the King's librarian, Sir Owen Morshead, George 'was a careful reader' who meticulously made a list of all those books he read from May 1890 onwards. His list was catholic and included very little poetry. Lovably, he read books about himself and other crowned heads; more racily, he tackled *Lady Chatterley's Lover* in 1932 and, although not a keen fisherman, *Silver: the Life Story of an Atlantic Salmon*; towards the end of his life, in 1935, he read Mrs Hwfa Williams's *It Was Such Fun*.

His boyish admiration for the old-fashioned concept of 'derring-do' resulted in an invitation being extended to Charles Lindbergh, the celebrated American flyer, to attend a private audience at Buckingham Palace. The aviator, now a world hero, expected to be asked a few technical questions about the *Spirit of St Louis*, the plane he flew on his solo trip across the Atlantic. Instead, the King told him there was one thing he wanted to know: 'Tell me, Captain

Lindbergh,' he asked, 'how did you pee?' The intrepid pilot urbanely replied that he had used 'an aloominum container' and then dumped the contents over France, a solution which seemed satisfactory to the King.[24]

Another hero, Robert Falcon Scott, later to be known as Scott of the Antarctic, was invited to stay at Balmoral, and the explorer was told to bring any slides he might have 'for the magic-lantern show'. These would have appealed more than some of the films shown, including one with a long-drawn-out kiss which was ruined by George shouting, 'Get on with it, man.'

Surrounded by paintings by Gainsborough, Rubens and Lely at Bukingham Palace, he had no time for the French Impressionists, thinking them far too modern. Seeing a painting by Cézanne, his reaction was one of amused disbelief as he called out, 'Come over here, May. Here's something that will make you laugh.' He wanted to put his walking stick through a painting of nudes by the same artist.

Although knowledgeable about classical music, hearing a performance by Kubelik during celebrations marking Edward VII's sixty-first birthday, he admitted, 'He is quite wonderful but I wish he didn't have long hair.' Innately conservative about dress, appearance was everything, no matter how excellent the music or the play.

'Do my own packing,' the sartorially preoccupied George liked to claim. This was more a happy illusion; far from throwing a few shooting suits and a couple of dinner jackets into a portmanteau, a virtual seance was held in his dressing room; the great cupboard doors of his wardrobes were flung open while his chief valet and two flunkeys stood by as the King pointed to his choice from '140 suits, 500 shirts, 6,000 pairs of socks and stockings and 50 pairs of shoes'.[25]

As a royal wife, the aesthetically minded Mary could afford to indulge her love of rare porcelain, miniatures, Mughal jade and jewellery. She set about cataloguing furniture and paintings in the royal homes; many still today have meticulous labelling in her handwriting. This was pleasure, an enjoyable way of filling lonely days when George was on official engagements, but royal duties increased when Queen Victoria died on 22 January 1901.

Aged eighty-two, it was said that the Queen's dedication to duty had worn her out. There was another more human reason. The

Queen loved her food, ate quickly and afterwards was plagued by indigestion. One of the reasons for her final illness was a love of raspberries and ice cream. Her doctors were worried about her cholesterol, and the Queen told them she would give up raspberries but not ice cream.[26]

When she died, Alix was heartbroken and declared, 'England without the Queen seems impossible.' Pregnant with her fourth child, since Olga she had given birth to two more daughters – Tatiana, born on 29 May 1897,[27] then Maria on 14 June 1899 – which had prompted a supposedly sympathetic note from Queen Victoria: 'I regret the third girl for the country. I know that an heir would be more welcome than a daughter.'[28] Both girls were named after characters in Pushkin's *Eugene Onegin*.

Unable to travel to the funeral, in a letter to her sister, Victoria, Alix said of her grandmother, 'Since one can remember she was in our life, and a dearer, kinder being never was.'

A fourth daughter, Anastasia, was born on 5 June 1901. Nicholas was secretly disappointed it was not a boy, but lovingly gave Alix a Fabergé 'lily of the valley' egg in pink enamel with pearl and diamond set. When she pressed the pearl, the egg opened up to reveal a miniature of 'hubby' and the older 'girlies'. Nicholas would find any excuse to shower her with jewelled love tokens: an enamelled powder box with delicate spatula, a rosebud, a catkin or a wild raspberry.

But they were desperate to have a son. It was small comfort when Nicholas got a letter from George telling him of the birth of another boy to the British King and Queen. This was Prince George, Duke of Kent, born on 20 December 1902. 'Fancy, we now have four sons . . . I wish one of them was yours.'

Not deliberately intending to gloat, George had said, 'I shall soon have a regiment not a family.' Nicholas must have felt he was the inadequate if not poor relation in the family.

TWELVE

'A Charming, Dear, Precious Place'

There is still a small black bust of Nicholas II opposite the fading-cinnamon Alexander Palace; it is surrounded by debris and pieces of corrugated iron. There is such a palpable sadness about Tsarskoe Selo. The derelict Agate Pavilion,* with peeling Corinthian columns in the colonnade where once Catherine the Great walked, bears witness to Nicholas II's humiliation in 1917.

The Park, landscaped for a Tsar and his wife, reeks of neglect. Unkempt, the palace where once 500 men were employed to stoke the fires has an air of profound melancholy, as if grieving for a Tsar who lived there in heedless bliss.

Nicholas was born in the Alexander Palace, and so enjoyed a warm but misguided feeling of continuity, escaping the intrigues of the court in St Petersburg. Today the palace windows are boarded up, the glass is broken, a few raggy curtains are at half mast; the army is still in occupation.

Ten days after their wedding, Nicholas took Alix to Tsarskoe Selo, where she instantly fell in love with the small palace built by Alexander I. He thought it a 'charming, dear, precious place', with its English Park, obelisks, arbours and flower gardens. Across the ornamental water were the pagodas of a Chinese village, where the lucky aides-de-camp were quartered.[1]

Tsarskoe Selo, which literally means 'village of the Tsar', is set in flat country. Now it has been renamed Pushkin, and the cluster of decaying grace-and-favour manor houses near the palace are now mostly abandoned.

Leaving the city for the dreary 14-mile journey to the palace, filthy old cars crawl by in a slow stream, their infinitely patient drivers never sound their horns in complaint. Then the traffic melts away and the road is almost deserted, with an isolated factory and a line of broken-down greenhouses. Inertia is today's crop, but little

---

* This small palace was built by Giacomo Quarenghi for Catherine II.

wayside shrines appear from time to time, as surprising as primroses in snow. A feather of smoke curls up from a pile of burning birch branches; a lone horseman gallops by; a white statue of Pushkin is the milestone for Tsarskoe Selo.

In happier times, the road to Tsarskoe was the best and most exclusive in Russia, embellished with ornamental shrubs for the eyes of the Tsar in his gold- and black-embossed carriage. But Nicholas nearly always preferred to make the journey by royal train, with its eight sky-blue carriages, dining room with seating for sixteen, a sitting room with candelabras, velvet-covered sofas and a piano in a room where the windows were draped like a French salon. All four of Nicholas's daughters loved the royal train, which was mostly used for longer journeys, and, when they went to the Crimea, they 'would lie like lizards in the sun beside the train'[2] whenever it stopped. There was a nursery carriage, and another for the royal doctor and pharmacy, and one for cooks, servants and the luggage. Yet another was used solely for trunkfuls of gold and silver goblets and enamelled, decorative cigarette boxes, in case the Tsar wished to give someone a token of his appreciation. The royal train left from its own Imperial Alexander railway station, a red-brick pseudo-Gothic building, now neglected, but where the ornate carved imperial eagles still look down from the entrance.

Turbanned Abyssinians in scarlet jackets and eastern slippers bowed low, as valets in white gaiters and footmen in red capes with the imperial coat of arms supervised the loading of luggage and hampers. Today two boys are playing football and, behind an ugly, high electric fence round the goods yard, there is desultory barking by a wolflike mongrel watchdog. When Nicholas and his family arrived at the Alexander Palace, major-domo Count Kleinmichael offered bread and salt in traditional greeting to the sound of trumpets and laughter.

Even the weather at Tsarskoe Selo was pleasing. Built on a plateau, like the plains around Warsaw it had a better climate than even nearby Peterhof, which was a much grander palace and more suitable for a tsar. It had been modelled on Versailles, with cascades, terraces scented with orange trees and flower beds that were once studded with semi-precious stones.

Peterhof was too lusciously decadent, and far too sensual, for a Lutheran Tsarina more accustomed to the gloom of her German childhood home. Not for her those bacchanalian cherubs astride eighteenth-century French clocks with cockerels, or gaming tables inlaid with 'Arcadian Shepherds' marquetry. The Peterhof boudoir room, with walls covered in a French silk depicting a partridge in flight through sheaves of ripe corn and ceilings painted with a cavorting Venus and Adonis, was too overtly sensual.

Today, in the autumn, the wooden boxes protecting the statues of gods and goddesses from the harsh winter, stacked upright by the empty fountains, look like coffins. A little girl carries a lilac balloon, the Tsarina's favourite colour.

Instead of the extravagant charms of Peterhof, Alix preferred the dark Alexander Palace, which she turned into a bourgeois home, filling it with lemonwood furniture from Maples in Tottenham Court Road, London. Their private rooms were kept deliberately small. The Chippendale drawing room, with a grey-green colour scheme and potted palms, was in the twentieth-century fashionable northern Moderne style.

True to her upbringing, Alix was determined to create a comfortable English ambience at Tsarskoe. This extended even to the Tsar's dressing gown, which was supplied by Jaeger in London. He was delighted by his wife's improvements to the old palace, and thought the room they slept in 'gay and cosy', with the two tall windows opening out on to a romantic view of the park. The bedroom was filled with hydrangeas, porcelain eggs and near the canopied iron bed with its flowery chintz bedspread, padded headboard and huge white lace pillows there was a screen covered with icons for the eye of the fervently devout Tsarina. The couple never slept apart.

Lilac, freesias and lilies were brought from the south of France; in that cloying scent, the Tsarina's 'darling hubby' was fatally drawn into her seductive web. Alix possessed 'a strong sexual drive' mixed with an 'hysterical *exaltée*'.[3] Her art nouveau, rose oil-scented boudoir left no doubt about her genteel preference. The walls were lined with mauve silk with a lilac frieze, bowls of violets were kept on a dressing table covered in Brussels lace alongside diamond-bowed photograph frames of playful children and broad-shouldered men in greatcoats with epaulettes.

Her chaise longue was indispensable. Here she liked to loll around until midday, a delicately reclining figure in a fine linen lilac kaftan with a grape design. Alix, who disliked silk, told her maid without a hint of irony that exotic lingerie was one of her few indulgences.[4]

Exertion was serving tea in her personal criss-cross gold tête-à-tête china or sitting at the piano playing a little Beethoven, throwing her rings casually on to a sofa. Afterwards, there was panic as servants were summoned to retrieve above all else her precious pink-diamond engagement ring.

The Tsarina's tapestry, wickerwork sewing boxes, drawing materials and white lace shawl, which can still be seen in the room, give the eerie sense of entering her private world. There is the original telephone with chrome bell – for her the instrument of so much unhappy information – and the small clock which marked her countdown to hell.

The Victorian influence was her love of clutter: on every little table there were delicate enamelled boxes decorated with edelweiss in tiny pearls, and porcelain Easter eggs. A popular magazine, *The Capital and the Country Estate 1907–16*, still lies open on her original writing desk, with its wobbly left leg.

Gaudy calendar paintings of the Gulf of Finland share wall space with a portrait of her whisky- and horse-loving father, the Duke of Hesse. Alongside these is a Pre-Raphaelite painting of the Annunciation, the Virgin sweetly asleep, encircled by angels, an idealised vision of family life presented to Alix by Queen Victoria. In a corner there is a prie-dieu for the intensely devout Tsarina.

Alix and Nicholas lived on the ground floor. In the early evening, Nicholas liked to go upstairs to the first floor to the eleven-roomed nursery wing, where a silver bath had been engraved with the children's names, to ask them silly riddles and read them bedtime stories.[5] As their eyes sleepily rested on the butterflies and birds on the yellow and green wallpaper,[6] they fell contentedly asleep and their father made the sign of the cross over them.

Each summer there was a ritual trip on the imperial yacht, the *Standart*, to the coast of Finland, where the children fished for trout and sometimes the Tsar liked to set out in a kayak. In this closed world, Nicholas lived *à la Russe*, and Tsarskoe Selo became particularly precious after the first revolution of 1905, when the Winter Palace was no longer a safe place. From then on, Nicholas, to his detriment, cut himself off.

One cynical courtier thought the Tsar was fatally enveloped in a 'sort of everlasting cosy tea-party', organised by his wife. Alix liked to think of herself as a dedicated hausfrau, with standards of domesticity that had been instilled into her by Queen Victoria, including the blacking of grates. However, this was more than any of her Russian maids were prepared to do. Eventually, a manservant was willing to undertake the task, but, as Alix recalled, 'I had actually to show him how to blacklead a grate *myself*',[7] just like the housewives she had seen in the north of England. Her family menus were unimaginative, as she herself could survive on a monotonous diet of soup and *kotlei*, the same dreary breaded chicken cutlets, day after day; but she did allow the children *kissel*, whipped cranberries; and the Tsar, his favourite roast suckling pig with horseradish,[8] served in the Rosewood Room with a little Madeira or port from the Massandra vineyards in the Crimea.

After lunch, Nicholas retired to his Gothic, green silk-lined 'New Study' with matching curtains, dominated by a bust of Napoleon, whom he admired. Over his desk, a portrait of his father Alexander III seemed so reassuring; a crack in the Romanov dynasty seemed impossible. In this air of good order, reclining on an ottoman – always necessary for a busy emperor – with a billiard table, a pipe and a set of dominoes close by, he might pick up a Conan Doyle novel, or a little light, Molière play. He devoured daily newspapers and made sure he had up-to-date news of his English cousin: 'I always read the *Daily Graphic*,' the Lord of all the Russias told George, 'and therefore follow closely all your movements and all you have to do.' But he most enjoyed studying old manuscripts, and so his reading tended to be esoteric.

Nicholas received ambassadors and ministers in his art nouveau study. When they arrived, it was sometimes to the sound of the Empress's contralto voice singing Bach, or else the Tsar might be busy with his photograph albums, dressed in a crimson silk shirt of the imperial family's fusiliers. Sometimes he asked with a smile, 'Would you like to see my family?' They were his joy and his undoing.

The drawing room, with its Frederick III porcelain vases studded with sixteen gold roses, is dominated by a portrait of a macho-looking Nicholas, as *The Hunter*, by Leon Bakst, and a huge rug on the floor is a polar bear he shot – one of his triumphs. But when you lift a grubby curtain, there is squalor outside: fencing, barbed wire and broken-down observation huts. When the Bolsheviks seized the Palace in 1917 they created a prison. Later Stalin ordered the Soviet military to use the palace as a secret nuclear-missile tracking station. The army has been ordered to leave, but remains a sinister presence today.

The drawing room, with its white china owl lamps on the desk alongside a glass owl inkstand, is where the family huddled together to say goodbye to Nicholas on 17 February 1917 before he left for the Front. It reeks of sadness. The superstitious say owls are harbingers of death. This was the price Nicholas paid for a private life of 'cloudless happiness'.[9]

Nicholas' camera on a stand is touchingly evocative of his carefree family life. His passion for photography was a new fashionable pastime that he shared with other European royals. A technician was permanently in residence to develop the day's photographs. Nicholas inspected these each evening before using special paste from England to place his favourites in Moroccan-bound albums, including one infinitely tender photograph of 'Alicky'. He took many captivating photographs of the children, laughing, solemn, running by the water's edge, on board the yacht, the tsarinas dressed identically in Russian folk dresses or polka-dotted blouses with flared skirts, watching their little brother in a sailor suit lying on the pale wooden deck kicking his legs in the air. The girls had a natural grace, ostrich feathers waving in their Edwardian hats as they hopped off the yacht with a flirtatious skip to join their mother for a picnic. They were happy in this claustrophobic, Victorian atmosphere, where they were taught always to carry decorously a white handkerchief in their left hands.

'The Emperor's daughters were brought up just like English girls, growing up in some big, secluded country house.'[10] But as an upbringing it was far too sheltered, with an overprotective mother and indulgent father; they had few friends.

When Lady Muriel Paget visited Tsarskoe during the First World War, she was struck by the beauty of the Tsar's daughters, as she joined them for what she described as a 'sumptuous meal'. Her main memory was of the girls' laughter, 'as they bombarded each other with cherry stones'[11] from a bowl of cherries on the table. The Tsarina said sadly how disappointing it was 'both to herself and to the nation, that she had so many girls'. Sometimes she was like an older sister playing Halma with them; her 'little lovable weakness' was that 'she never liked to lose!'[12]

Nicholas kept fit using an exercise bar and by swimming in the Moorish-tiled sunken bath, which held 84,000 litres of salt water. He was often joined by the Tsarevich, who would plead, 'Papa, Papa, please may I use the pool?' One of the boy's uniforms is now on show at Tsarskoe Selo, along with the ribboned cushion used for his christening. Another made of dark blue velvet with gold braid, silk river pearls and a monogram of Nicholas II was the boy's ceremonial uniform, and still looks pristine because he was rarely well enough to wear it. Nicholas's private dressing room, filled with wall-to-wall mahogany cupboards, hinged icons, hunting knives and cigarette cases presented to him by military units, is a shrine to his love of the soldier's life. Pride of place is given to a grenadier bearskin, a handsome token; Nicholas was Honorary Colonel of the Royal Scots Greys.

Portraits of this compact, upright figure, whether in the heavily decorated East Siberian Shooters regimental uniform or Circassian red regimentals, show him as every inch the commanding Tsar, his unseeing bright eyes looking straight ahead. The swords and the gold-fringed epaulettes, military medals and court ribbons, the wax seal of his authority: these once-powerful symbols for the Tsar of All the Russias are now in glass cases on display. When he became 'Comrade Romanov' after the Revolution, a handkerchief was his only decoration. The lattice stitching on his hussars red tunic, worn for his wedding, and the fur-trimmed cloak are still pristine.

Nearly a century later, on a grey, misty day that is so predictably Russian, the park is overgrown and open to stray dogs. A couple of young mothers in fur hats wheel their prams near the weedy plot where once Nicholas, in captivity, humbly planted 500 cabbages. The oak trees hold their secrets; the sound of children laughing is haunting.

The Tsarina loved the Englishness of the Winter Garden at the Alexander Palace. Down by the white railings and balustrade leading to the 'Children's Pond', there are still a few crumbling stone steps left, where on balmy, cloudless summer days the tsarinas picked water lilies for their mother, once falling off a raft into the artificial lake. The Tsar, who was a strong swimmer, plunged in to rescue them, joking that he had never before provided the Tsarina with flowers under such difficult conditions. Nicholas liked to lean on one of the two little Monet-style bridges watching his children, moments which brought him the greatest contentment.

A century later a man is studying a tree trunk in the park wondering perhaps if the wood can be used to restore the pull-along ferry to the Children's Island and their blue playhouse. Once a magical place, lovingly created by Nicholas I for his children, it had a drawing room, five rooms with fireplaces, and Empire-style ceilings. There were jewel-coloured carpets, and the children's furniture was covered in embossed leather. They had a toy theatre, and servants to change the scenes and switch on the coloured lights. They had their own telephone link to their parents at the palace.

The island still has a strangely attractive quality, although it is now choked with weeds and the little house is streaked with bird droppings. Today it is used by tramps and drug addicts, who have to step over mangled wires to drop empty vodka bottles. But there are plans to restore the 171-year-old playhouse, which one day will surely attract children of all ages.

The partially restored palace evokes the *gemütlich* flavour of Nicholas and Alexandra's life together. Now open to the public, huge numbers of Russians visit every year. But some say they find it difficult to speak in the Tsarina's room, where they feel overcome by a strong spiritual presence.[13]

THIRTEEN

Learning to Rule

Neither Emperor felt he had been properly trained for his role. George V was a midshipman in a battleship by the age of fifteen. Nicholas, always fascinated by military life, knew little else except the life of a guards officer. When he joined his regiment, he wrote to his mother and said, 'I am now happier than I can say, to have joined the army.'[1] Alexander III had never seriously bothered to prepare him for his destiny. Nicholas often affectionately recalled how 'Dear Papa said *verfluchte Schuldigkeit* – damned duty'.[2]

Learning to rule was a challenge. Both Emperors were restrained and conscientious, each equally devout as they embraced their destiny with their faith in the Divine Right of Kings.

In style, George, in many ways, was the opposite of his father, once described by Lord Northcliffe as 'the greatest monarch we've ever had on a racecourse'. But Edward VII's playboy image disguised his qualities as a knowledgeable, diplomatically skilled monarch. He swept away the heavy physical and psychological pall of Queen Victoria's long reign, especially at 'Windsor where Eastern trophies were found infested with moths and tons of ivory . . . discovered rotting in an attic'.[3]

A sophisticated traveller, Edward VII still took a lofty and insular view of foreigners, suggesting that Portuguese nobility looked like waiters. Perhaps he was not impressed by a book on tuna which King Carlos of Portugal had written only a year before his assassination in 1908.[4] But he recognised the value of cordial relations with other crowned heads and in June 1908 paid a first-ever visit to Russia by a ruling British sovereign. Nicholas was delighted, as the King had made no secret of his disapproval of Russia's war with Japan, and thought the tsarist regime shamefully repressive.

For reasons of personal security, Edward VII could not set foot on Russian soil. Instead the two Emperors – or this royal 'trade union', as the King described the meeting – entertained each other on their yachts,* bobbing about convivially in the Bay of Reval† in the Baltic. They snacked on caviar and kirsch and bestowed lavish honours on each other. The Tsar was made an admiral of the fleet in the Royal Navy. Edward VII, looking like a jovial Romanov in his Kiev Dragoons uniform, greeted the sailors with a 'Good morning, my children' in convincing Russian. Paying tribute to his English ties, Nicholas proudly wore the uniform of the Scots Greys. These kinsmen, 'sovereigns of the two greatest empires under the sun', came together, *The Times* approvingly noted, 'to establish the world's peace'.

Alix basked in the convincing show of mutual warmth between her powerful English uncle and her husband, not knowing 'Uncle Bertie' considered Nicholas 'weak as water'.[5] It also inspired him to take steps to ensure that George would be better informed about the intricacies of monarchy so that he would never appear as embarrassingly inexperienced as Nicholas.

As a result, father and son sat together over cabinet and foreign office papers. George learned how important it was for any monarch to be alert to any serious signs of unrest, which could so easily escalate into revolution. He absorbed Bagehot's‡ dictum that the monarch's role was 'the right to be consulted, the right to encourage, the right to warn'. He was being groomed, but never lost his tendency to be outspoken, often loudly so. As his father was dealing with a new Liberal government in 1908, it was not helpful when George, then Prince of Wales, announced at dinner at Windsor that, while he trusted the new Prime Minister, Herbert Asquith, the trouble was he was 'not quite a gentleman'. Churchill mischievously passed on the Prince of Wales's opinion and, not surprisingly, Asquith never cared for George.[6]

George may not have had a brilliant, academic mind, but he had a retentive memory and was decisive. He was also humble, believing monarchy to be God-given, and insisting that the national anthem should always be played slowly, because in his view it was a prayer.[7]

Admired for his straightforwardness, when first facing duties as Prince of Wales, he told his comptroller, Sir Francis de Winton,[8] 'I hate bazaars', insisting functions should be 'as short as possible'. He

---

*   The *Victoria and Albert*, the Tsar's *Standart* and Dagmar's *Polar Star*.
†   Off Tallinn, which became the capital of Estonia.
‡   Sir Walter Bagehot, Victorian constitutionalist.

did not much like public lunches or dinners but, if forced, would drink a glass of wine. 'I like sparkling Moselle.' George always had a poor tolerance for alcohol, preferring ginger ale or half a glass of wine. 'Addresses' were usually preferable to 'speeches'.

He was blessed with a few dedicated advisers, who steered him through the labyrinthine ways facing any future king. His private secretary, Arthur Bigge,* later Lord Stamfordham, one of a northern parson's twelve children, was not in the mould of the usual aristocratic courtier. When first appointed to the household, he endeared himself to Queen Victoria by singing *The Lost Chord*,[9] an accomplishment for any private secretary almost as important as the ability to shoot, handle a canapé or get the protocol right for a tribal chief's state visit.

When the Queen died, it was expected that Bigge would work for the new King but, in a far-sighted move, Edward VII asked him to look after his son. He stayed with George for thirty years and was valued by three generations of the royal family, especially as he took short holidays and worked on Sundays.

A quiet, meticulous man with a waxed moustache, who shared the King's passion for orderliness, Stamfordham always spoke honestly. Once, having heard disagreeable comments about George appearing dour on a public engagement, he asked him to try and smile more, but this invited the classic 'We sailors never smile on duty' reply. Nevertheless, it was an early lesson for George in the importance of striking a harmonious note in public. Another was a formative tour to Australia in 1901 to attend the opening of the new parliament.

Edward VII had not been keen on George travelling abroad, saying plaintively that 'he had only one son left out of three', but had to agree and bade his heir farewell on the *Ophir* in March 1901. George surprised himself by feeling very upset when he had to part from his children: 'I was very much affected and could hardly speak,' he confessed in his diary. It was a terrible wrench: 'The leave-taking was terrible. I went back with them to the yacht when I said goodbye and

---

* Arthur Bigge first came to Queen Victoria's attention in 1879 when he was in the Royal Artillery. Napoleon III's son, who had been posted to his battery, was killed by Zulu warriors, and Bigge's sensitivity, as he escorted the Empress Eugénie to the spot where her son had died, greatly impressed the Queen; in 1895 she appointed him to her household.

broke down quite.'[10] His father, who enjoyed his grandchildren, teased them, telling them that their parents would return with black skins after so much time in the heat of a tropical sun.[11]

It was a significant and maturing tour. He acquitted himself well and made a good impression in New Zealand, Canada and South Africa. His loud laugh, common sense and approachable style went down well, especially as an heir apparent with an 'Oxford manner' had been expected in the Antipodes.

He got pleasure from keeping a personal log of the tour, which covered five continents, so providing enough statistical detail to keep him happily occupied during his 125 days at sea. He recorded, '45,000 miles of sea steamed, 12,000 miles by rail, 24,855 hands shaken at public receptions alone, 62,000 troops reviewed, 231 days of absence from England.'[12] The King rewarded his son by creating him Prince of Wales on 9 November 1901, a week after his return, as a mark of appreciation 'of the admirable manner' in which he had carried out 'arduous duties in the Colonies'.

When he succeeded, George knew how important it was to be seen at Buckingham Palace, that tangible symbol of the monarchy. Audiences held in the India Room, twinkling with rubies, diamonds, emeralds set in jewelled swords and boxes, chokers and tiaras – all humble offerings from maharajas – always impressed.

As King he organised his days with the punctuality of a good old-fashioned railway timetable. He got up at 6.45 a.m. and, if possible, went for a hack in Rotten Row in Hyde Park, returning for breakfast with his wife at nine o'clock, managing to arrive punctiliously between the chimes of Big Ben.[13] Normally obsessed about etiquette, his pink and grey parrot, Charlotte, was allowed to hop around the breakfast table, putting her beak into the marmalade or a guest's boiled egg. The wise visitor tolerated this feathered interference.[14]

Each morning began with a meeting with Stamfordham, who, as he walked along the silk-lined palace corridors to George's pleasant study, wondered what mood to expect. If fiery, he concentrated on Frith's tranquil watercolour of *Ramsgate Sands*. When they drafted speeches, George always modestly dismissed anything which sounded 'too high-falutin', explaining that 'everyone would know those were not my words'.[15]

In a letter from York Cottage, Sandringham, on Christmas Day 1907 he told his Private Secretary, 'I can hardly write a letter of any importance without your assistance. I fear sometimes I have lost my temper with you and often been very rude, but I am sure you know me well enough by now to know that I did not mean it.'[16]

But woe betide the unfortunate who fell foul of his obsessional attention to grooming. When Sir Derek Keppel*[17] arrived at the palace in a bowler hat during the season the King grumbled, 'You scoundrel, what do you mean coming in here in rat-catcher fashion? You never see me dressing like that in London.'

Keppel replied smoothly, 'Well, sir, you don't have to go about in buses.' These outbursts were not taken too seriously by his household. Keppel was used to being called 'every name under the sun . . . obstinate devil', but often found, just as he was leaving the room after an 'explosion', the King would embark on an anecdote: 'Derek, did you ever hear this story?',[18] his engaging way of making the peace.

Displeasure was aired directly. As courtiers listened they were often aware of his beautifully groomed hands as he thumped the table, rebuking them for some oversight or a less-than-shiny shoe. Ministers and ambassadors were always conscious of the King's strong political opinions and sometimes found irksome his tendency to take over any discussion. He was not given to vacillation or ever overruled. Sir George Clark complained how difficult it had been 'to get a word in edgeways' when he tried to put him in the picture about Turkey's troubles. Exasperated, he found the King did all the talking, 'telling him what he thought about Mustapha Kemal'.[19] Some blamed this steamrollering on an intrinsic feeling of inadequacy. George's formative years had been spent sailing and shooting, without much academic influence guiding him towards any rigorous study of the classics or the great events in history.

In summer, he worked in the palace gardens, appearing a 'slight, upright figure with the slightest of stoops . . . always perfectly dressed . . . the grey coat and hat . . . the white gardenia',[20] cigarette in holder, Charlotte on his wrist. He tested the day's weather; if warm enough, he worked in his tent, where there were telephones and typewriters. Letters were answered on the day of arrival. He liked to be in bed by 11.10 p.m. precisely.

'My father's life was a masterpiece in the art of well-ordered, unostentatious, elegant living,' the Duke of Windsor declared.[21] It

---

* Derek Keppel, a younger son of the 7th Earl of Albemarle, joined the Duke of York's staff in 1892 and became Master of the King's Household in 1913.

was a style unchanged from Edward VII's day except that George
did not follow his father's habit and take a bachelor apartment in
Paris or the Riviera to entertain a mistress, from which the elder
monarch earned his nickname, 'Edward the Caresser';[22] George
wanted only to be with his 'dear May'.

The highlight of every summer was sailing at Cowes, when he
became the 'Sailor King'. As soon as he stepped on deck, barking
orders, feeling the sea spray on his face, he became 'a different
man'.[23] Whatever his cares, they were swept away.

His only indoor pastime was philately. In a room known,
unsurprisingly, as the Stamp Room, he studied with a magnifying
glass the priceless albums inherited from his uncle, Prince Alfred.*

As fixed and inevitable as the changing of the seasons, he was
always at Sandringham at New Year for pheasant shooting, where
he kept the clocks half an hour behind GMT to enable him to have
longer time out shooting. A dedicated list-maker, he proudly logged
a total of 12,109 pheasants personally bagged in a lifetime of game-
shooting. It was Windsor for Easter and Ascot, and Balmoral in the
autumn for the grouse moors, stalking and of course the Highland
Games.

He spoke no foreign languages and hated foreign travel. 'Abroad
is awful,' he declared. 'I know because I've been there.' Of two
Dutch cities, he said, 'Amsterdam, Rotterdam, and all the other
dams! Damned if I'll go.'[24] One trip in 1880, when he was a
princeling, and which did little to alter his misgivings, was to Fiji,
where the old cannibal King Thakumbow was still a forceful
presence. The venerable monarch told Prince Louis of Battenberg,
who was in the royal party, that, although now in retirement, 'he did
miss the odd delicacy',[25] and could not deny that he had occasional
yearnings for babies' legs, which were, he pronounced, 'the best dish
in the world'.

But some of George's misgivings about abroad were almost
allayed when he went to India to preside at the Delhi Durbar on
12 December 1911, becoming the first English monarch to visit the
East since Richard Coeur de Lion.[26] The sight of the Durbar Camp,
with about 40,000 tents with 300,000 loyal subjects living in them,
was gratifying: 'I have now been travelling for some months in

---

* The Queen today owns one of the world's most desirable stamp collections,
  valued at at least £100 million.

India,' he observed, 'and I have never seen a happier-looking people, and I understand the look in the eyes of the Indians.'[27]

Both he and Queen Mary hated aeroplanes, 'nasty horrid things', as she once said when stepping aboard the royal yacht. The King may not have liked world travel, but he was stung by H.G. Wells's opinion of his insularity. In a letter to *The Times*,[28] Wells had dismissed his reign as 'alien and uninspiring'. George responded promptly: 'I may be uninspiring but I'll be damned if I'm an alien.'[29] State visits, he thought, were a waste of money and of no real value. By 1923, his ministers found it almost impossible to cajole him into any official visits overseas.[30]

Nicholas, on the other hand, ruled over a transcontinental empire so vast he had little need to go abroad. Besides, if ever he was away for more than three weeks, in true Russian style he became desperately homesick, yearning for the sight of even a barren steppe. The Tsarina was often not well enough to travel with him, but one successful early trip was to France, arriving in Cherbourg in 1894. In an *'exquise toilette de satin bleu'* she was cheered enthusiastically, and given the privilege, in retrospect a chilling one, of being allowed the use of Marie Antoinette's suite at Versailles.

In common with many shy people, Nicholas never said anything unpalatable directly. The telltale sign which should have alerted ministers was the occasional tug at his moustache.[31] After a pleasant conversation, some were shocked to find later that they had been fired by the 'most polite man in Europe'.[32] Others thought Nicholas was Byzantine in his dealings with courtiers and ministers.

Overhearing a disagreement among two of his advisers, Nicholas shook his head: 'Why are you quarrelling?' he asked, and told them, 'I always agree with everyone about everything and then do things my own way.' But, in spite of this show of apparent self-confidence, his 'faculties were seen as rather superficial, [and] he lacked the ability to analyse separate events carefully'.[33]

Whatever the crisis, whether it was crowds of revolutionaries storming the Winter Palace or the declaration of war on Germany, Nicholas remained at Tsarskoe Selo, taking his walk between ten and eleven, escorted by leaping borzois. George, on the other hand, when there was a crisis, as on the first day of the General Strike in 1926, did not hesitate to respond, on that occasion driving from Balmoral to London. He hoped that his presence in the capital might help defuse a dangerous situation, and show the people that he cared.

Nicholas's attitude to the duties of being Tsar was almost cavalier, even in his choice of using a schoolroom at Tsarskoe Selo as an office. Mistakenly, he never appreciated the opulence of the Winter Palace, with its art treasures and gold-studded doors, where traditionally over the centuries Tsars had held their audiences. Instead, he shared Alexander Herzen's view that it was a 'monstrous barrack . . . where the destinies of Russia were woven, in the gloom of the alcove, in the midst of orgies beyond the reach of informers and police'.

There was no Stamfordham to advise him about the importance of being seen in the imperial city or establishing relations with the new industrialists. Instead Nicholas preferred to surround himself with the old aristocrats, who thought trade despicable. Some 1,500 courtiers sashayed languidly round the imperial court, spreading gossip. He liked to believe he was not surrounded by sycophants and would assert, 'I like to hear the truth'.[34]

Among Nicholas's close advisors was Count Benckendorff, the chief court chamberlain; in his heavy gold-braided coat he had a Ruritanian splendour, and commanded three hundred deputy chamberlains. Count Vladimir Fredericks, minister of the imperial court, was a Swedish aristocrat who looked after protocol and security; an indulgent uncle figure he called the Tsar and Tsarina *'mes enfants'*.[35] These were courtly and elegant men but could hardly be described as incisive, politically minded mandarins.

Worshipped as a god and the father of his people, the poor felt that if only they could touch Nicholas's arm or coat, when he rode out on a black Arab horse and wore a gilded helmet, their troubles would disappear. He himself once said, 'It is my chief preoccupation to discover the needs of the peasants who are so dear to me.'[36] When he filled in a form, he simply signed it 'Master of Russia'.

Studiously he answered letters himself, dealing with the minutiae of a peasant's divorce petition, a scrawled appeal from a serf asking to change his name because it meant 'pig', or from a widow requesting a new cow or a pair of spectacles. This attention to detail, his 'great sense of order in the arrangement of his papers'[37] for an emperor ruling over one sixth of the world's surface, helped him escape the burden of monarchy. The Tsar, with the lives of 150 million people in his hands, was stamping his own envelopes.

But Nicholas had one great asset, and that was a 'conquering personal charm',[38] as evidenced in the skilful way he 'worked a room shaking hands with everyone . . . an English gentleman at home . . . in his country house'. 'His dreamy blue eyes haunted me for years,' historian Dimitri von Mohrenschildt[39] recalled seventy years after their first meeting.

The Tsar spoke German, French and colloquial English. Asking a London banker if he was enjoying his visit to Russia in spite 'of the beastly weather', the visitor exclaimed, 'but that is just our word'. Nicholas replied diplomatically, 'Yes, we are great friends with England now so when you come to us, we must have London weather.'[40] London weather was competing well with Russia in 1891, so bitterly cold that the Serpentine was covered with seven inches of ice but supported 30,000 skaters.

In the early, happy days of their reigns, the two Emperors kept in touch with the rhythm of each other's lives through a warm correspondence which changed in tone only towards the end of Nicholas's troubled life. His letters, in delicate sloping handwriting with fine loops, written on parchment embossed with a gold crown and cross, were more those of a devoted younger brother. They were gossipy and chatty: how he shot bear with the impressive imperial hunt at the royal estates of Białowieza and Spala in Poland, or how in the absence of bear he had to make do with '100 deer, 56 goats, 50 boar, 10 foxes, 27 hares – 243 in eleven days'.

His sense of priority was neatly conveyed in one letter in which he wrote in detail about the 'twenty heavy stags' he had just shot, then casually added the more important news that the Archduke Franz Ferdinand, the heir to the Habsburg throne, was visiting Russia. Nicholas thought the Archduke, who was later assassinated at Sarajevo in 1914, igniting the First World War, 'a most pleasant man [who] takes interest in everything'.

George's letters to Nicholas were affectionate but restrained. He never hesitated to make his wishes known, once advising 'Dearest Nicky' on who he would like to see as the next Russian Ambassador to London, saying,[41] 'If it was possible . . . to select Sazanoff it would give me the greatest pleasure . . . your most devoted cousin and true friend, Georgie.' Unfortunately, the impression Nicholas gave, not only to his English cousin but to the Russian people, was often of a 'paralysis of will'. It was too tempting for George, a strong character, not to take advantage.

Superficially, the cousins grew even more alike over the years. When the President of the French Republic, Raymond Poincaré, first met the King in London in 1913, he was 'struck by his resemblance to his cousin the Tsar of Russia', but thought George V's colour was 'not so pale, his expression less dreamy, his smile less melancholy and his gestures less timid'.[42] In this brief formal meeting Poincaré, who had visited Nicholas in Russia earlier, now recognised the more decisive personality. The perceptive Frenchman had already noticed the hint of tragedy about Nicholas, who had a 'sweet melancholy'.

Outwardly the more glamorous of the two, Nicholas was not in the imperial mould of earlier swashbuckling, boorish, hard-drinking Romanov emperors, but courtly and cultivated, a reader of French classics and English history. He believed that his 'heart was in the hands of God', but he would still be ultimately responsible for the end of the Romanovs, who for three centuries had been one of the most powerful dynasties in the world.

George, on the other hand, may have appeared less charismatic, but he succeeded in shaping the Windsor dynasty, which survived both traumas and political upheavals to remain one of Europe's most successful monarchies. Although he had reason for self-congratulation, George never took any credit for this achievement.

FOURTEEN

Their Wives and Mothers Did Not Compare

The marriages of both Emperors were equally successful. On one occasion at the Winter Palace, a companion of the Tsarina's, Anna Vyrubova, thought she heard a bird singing and asked, 'What kind of bird is that?' Alix, blushing scarlet, as she did so easily, said shyly, 'That is the Sovereign calling for me',[1] and ran swiftly to Nicholas in response to his whistle.

After long years of being married, whenever King George came back from an engagement, he always shouted, 'May, May, it is I'. In a letter from St Petersburg in 1894, when he had to attend Alexander III's funeral, he told her: 'I really think I should get ill if I had to be away from you for a long time.'[2]

Both Emperors loved their severe, unsmiling wives, but they were equally devoted to their mothers, Dagmar and Alexandra, delightful, spirited, socially captivating but manipulative sisters. The trouble was neither of their wives, 'May' or 'Alicky', could even superficially be a patch on their husbands' youthful, confident Danish mothers, who hid any hint of dominance over their sons with their deceptive, easy charm.

George once declared that, although he had grown up in an era of beautiful women, 'the two most beautiful of all' in his opinion were 'Empress Elisabeth of Austria and my own mother'. At the end of her days, Alexandra was still 'an old lady of ghostly and tenuous beauty'; even her deafness had a charm. He adored her.

On a visit to St Petersburg, George laughed indulgently and told his Russian cousins how his mother already owned at least 'half of Fabergé's shop'.* The Russian court jeweller provided the Emperor with exquisite jewelled tokens, miniature lapis lazuli furniture, a perfect snowdrop, or a catkin for mothers and wives. Pandering to

---

* Carl Fabergé's grandson and great-granddaughter are gamely trying to re-create the celebrated gold and porcelain eggs; an original Fabergé imperial egg can fetch millions. Christie's sold the Winter Egg for $5.5 million in Geneva in November 1994.

Alexandra's love of animals and her romantic, skittish streak, she was given a Fabergé duckling flapping its wings, a pair of snuggled rabbits in agate with rose diamonds, and a dormouse with sapphire eyes and gold whiskers. One of her birthday cakes was decorated with live goldfish swimming in crystal bowls, between layers of glistening icing, and underneath each grapeleaf-decorated tier she found Fabergé surprises.

It might have been easier if Dagmar and Alexandra had been perennially mournful widows, eschewing bright colours and jewels. But they enjoyed being admired, their soignée appearance enhanced by court jewellery. They held invisible sway. It was not easy for Alix and May, knowing they were being compared with their attractively assured mothers-in-law.

May was realistic enough to know that she could never erode 'Motherdear's' place in her husband's heart; she knew how as a naval officer he had sent his mother childlike endearments, and how Alexandra often signed her reply, 'With a great big kiss for your lovely little face', slightly different from other officers on the warship, who were receiving restrained 'all the best old chap' letters from home. Some of Alexandra's letters refer to her sailor son as 'my little sprat'[3] and often told him how much she missed his 'dear little turn-up [*sic*] snout'.[4]

Nicholas was a nineteen-year-old army officer when his mother was still addressing him as 'My dear little soul, my boy', and sadly that was the way he remained in her eyes. Dagmar was not clingy, but was still a constant influence. Even in the euphoria of being first married, Nicholas stayed protectively in touch with her, writing, 'Dear Mama . . . I am sad that I am not with you and I cannot embrace you.' He was torn between two determined women in his life.

Smaller and more vivacious than her sister, the widowed Dagmar still maintained the tsarist style at the Anichov Palace, keeping 5,000 servants in their gold-braided black jackets, red trousers, yellow shoes and white turbans. Her daughter, Grand Duchess Olga, remembered her favourite was 'old Jim Hercules', a black American who spent his annual holiday in the USA but 'always brought back jars of guava jelly for the children'.[5] Dagmar's exotically dressed page, Omar, with dancing dark eyes, was exciting to the ladies of the court.

The dowager mothers were so close that great distances never kept them apart, and when they got together it was often to talk about their sons' reticent, prim wives. In Russia, the Dowager

Empress still took precedence. This arrangement suited Dagmar, who hardly considered her daughter-in-law's feelings at all, ousting her to appear on Nicholas's willing arm on grand ceremonial occasions. Dagmar succeeded in what she considered was her chief role at court, simply 'to charm those who came into contact with her . . . and was venerated at court by the great mass of the people'.[5] Alexandra interfered less, being a fluttery yet often pervasive presence in May's life: she had put her stamp so firmly on the 'Big House' at Sandringham that not a plant or sweet-smelling herb could be changed without her permission.

Single-minded, with an inborn Teutonic rectitude, and intolerant of any slapdash behaviour even in her plants, if they were untidy, May often had to bite her lip to avoid showing irritation with her frequently unpunctual, often too frivolous mother-in-law.

As new brides, neither Alix nor May could look for much much support from their husbands' sibling sisters. Grand Duchess Xenia had shown some kindness to her new sister-in-law, who responded by sending affectionate notes to her ally, addressing her as 'my Chicken' and signing herself 'your very loving old Hen'. Alix may have got on well enough with the chickens in the imperial coop, but it was the mother hen whose feathers she ruffled.

May had a less successful relationship with her husband's spinster sister, Princess Victoria, who adored her brother George. Difficult and sometimes cranky, on one occasion when asked to dance her partner was taken aback when she warned him before they took to the floor, 'We do not reverse.' When she was told by a guest that he was going to be sitting next to May at dinner, she smiled sourly, and whispered in a far-from-quiet aside, 'Oh, she is an awful bore.'[6]

Alix had the aura of an Empress. She walked proudly, looked striking in creamy-white satin sculpted evening dresses studded with diamonds, making the most of a slim waist; she could also scene-steal in a seductively simple rose-pink chiffon with emerald and turquoise tiara. She had a decided style, and refused to wear Dagmar's recommended choice of fussy *jeune fille* outfits, but this only served to irritate her fashion-conscious mother-in-law, who ordered her own clothes from Worth and other French couturiers.

Never socially adept, and painfully shy, Alix tended to lurk behind an ostrich fan, while Dagmar, although no longer young, sparkled: she was still a social magnet at the imperial court. Another bone of contention was her reluctance to hand over the crown jewels. On marrying Nicholas, Alix had been given a few lacklustre items of jewellery. Nicholas had to intervene, but Dagmar still managed to keep seventy-seven pieces for herself. 'Without actually clashing, they seemed fundamentally unable . . . to understand one another,' Baroness Buxhoeveden later remarked on the women's incompatibility.

Much to Alix's chagrin, the only person ever allowed to interrupt idyllic holidays with Nicholas was the Dowager Empress Maria Feodorovna, who arrived in style, sailing into Finnish waters on board her own elegant yacht, *Polar Star*. As a doting grandmother, she later felt that she was not welcome at the Alexander Palace and had to content herself with buying presents, determined to spoil the grandchildren. In 1913, she gave the Tsarevich a working, child-sized Mercedes car.

Quick to take offence and imagine slights, Alix became convinced that, even if her dog misbehaved, this got back to the Dowager Empress and reflected badly on her. Homesick for Darmstadt, she had tried to keep the German maids she had brought with her, but was forced to replace them with servants chosen by her mother-in-law.

Gradually, Alix began to appear ungracious and more unsmiling, whether cradling a new baby or greeting an influential grand duke at the Winter Palace, prompting Maurice Paléologue, the French Ambassador, to compare her to 'an angry statue'. Unable to master Russian, which she spoke with a strong English accent, she was incapable, unlike her mother-in-law, of frivolous asides or the invaluable art of well-placed flattery. Disaffected courtiers malevolently watched her discomfort as red spots of shyness slowly spread from her neck upwards. Instead of the agony of making small talk in palace drawing rooms, she would have been happier re-reading Darwin's *On the Origin of Species* or nineteenth-century poetry.

Dagmar was furious when, in one of her reclusive moods, Alix refused to wave to the crowds from the imperial train, keeping the curtains closed. The Dowager Empress remarked, 'If *she* was not there Nicky would be twice as popular. She is a regular German. She thinks the imperial family should be above all that sort of thing . . . how many times have I tried to make it plain to her. And yet how often she complains of the public indifference to her.'[7]

Alix felt there was a conspiracy against her, that she was being cold-shouldered by the brittle society of St Petersburg, believing they mocked her for being a German provincial. But she got her own back later when she curbed extravagance at court. Such conspicuous opulence was anathema to her. The high-living Russian court did not strike her as glamorous but profligate after the privations of a childhood spent in impoverished Darmstadt. Disapprovingly, she now cut down on masked balls and parties, disaffecting the beau monde, who never forgave her. Soon after her marriage Alix wrote to Queen Victoria and complained about the Russian aristocracy. Her attitude was, 'I am the Empress, I am damned if I am going to try and be popular with them, they should try and be popular with me.'

A wise old survivor, the Queen responded cleverly, 'Every day I say to myself, "What can I do to make myself more popular with the people?"', aware that her granddaughter was already showing signs of imperiousness and unwisely treating public appearances as a black duty.

May was much cleverer at masking her feelings. Of course, she missed the art and literature she had so enjoyed in Florence, had little in common with her husband or his family, and hated her mother-in-law's Danish family get-togethers, full of practical jokes and loud laughter, all most undignified. But behind that unsmiling face, there was a wry humour which often helped her enjoy public life. May, unlike Alix, could hide her disapproval and contrive to give the right impression in public, even if secretly fuming. Once outside Bath, passing the School for the Orphan Daughters of Officers, she waved at the children who, unable to believe their eyes as they caught sight of the Queen's upright figure in the back of the royal Sedanca de Ville, just stood staring silently. '*Cheer*, little idiots, can't you?' the Queen muttered, putting her gloved hand back in her lap.[8]

The royal family is well aware that, on public visits, doors are repainted and walls re-emulsioned, but Queen Mary had an unerring talent for finding something not quite right – the broken chair or patched curtain. When Mrs Ronnie Greville heard she was being visited by the Queen for afternoon tea at Polesden Lacey, her home in Surrey, the celebrated socialite dashed to London and bought twenty-four deerskin rugs to cover the threadbare bits in her carpet, but was advised that Queen Mary would 'discover' them anyway, 'with the end of her umbrella' acting as 'a divining rod'.[9]

George and Mary, the plainer pair, without the glamour of Nicholas and Alexandra, attracted less instant, ephemeral public admiration. Towering over her husband – because of her

predilection for high hats and the fur collars muffling her long neck
– Americans joked about 'George and the Dragon'. But the dragon,
unlike the Tsarina, was an asset to her husband in public life. Seen
by satirical commentators as distinctly uninspiring, a poem written
at the time suggested that 'The King is duller than the Queen and
the Queen is duller than the King.'

Behind the scenes as Princess of Wales, and later as Queen, May,
with her acute ear and surprising gift for mimicry, enjoyed retelling
incidents, especially when plans went awry. She impersonated an
official at Brighton Royal Pavilion, who had been testing the
hospitality too diligently, confiding in her that a royal visit was
expected and that the place would be filled with 'ladies in their low
laschivous dresshes [*sic*]'.[10]

On another occasion, George was taken out to sea in a submarine
by the First Sea Lord, Admiral Fisher. May, waiting for longer than
was expected on the quay at Portsmouth, then expressed her
concern, remarking impassively to anxious officials, 'I shall be very
disappointed if George doesn't come up again.'[11]

But she was dutiful, always making a point of bowing to her
husband's wishes. She had little sympathy for the suffragettes, with
their demands for votes for women, and she disapproved of their
hunger strikes and violent protests. When Emily Davidson threw
herself under a horse at the 1913 Derby, she dismissed the
suffragette protester as a 'horrid woman', and much more sympathy
was extended towards 'poor Jones', the jockey, who had been 'much
knocked about'.[12]

When she travelled she was no trouble as a guest, usually bringing
sixty servants and only seventy pieces of personal luggage – no fuss.
In Quebec on one occasion during a tour of Canada, a perspiring
porter carrying the luggage to her suite failed to recognise her,
mistaking May for her maid, and grumbled, 'What are you doing
sitting there, Miss? Can't you give us a 'and?'[13]

Unlike her in-laws, May disliked the country and had very little
appreciation of the slow changing of the agricultural seasons.
Reluctantly, she was forced to spend the war years at Badminton,
where her host was Henry, Duke of Beaufort, traditionally addressed
as 'Master'; it helped that his wife Mary was her niece. Trying to
show an interest in farming, the Queen once asked the Master if
hens had fleas and, on being told, 'Yes, ma'am,' enquired, 'Do they
bite human beings?' The answer was 'Yes', at which intelligence the

Queen recoiled smartly from the innocent fowl going about its ovulatory tasks.[14]

Unlike the Tsarina, May never tried to influence the King in any of his decisions about the children or about policy. Yet, during the war, she missed being part of his daily war summary, and not being allowed to read selected government documents. The Foreign Office was asked to send her a briefing in her own red box on how the war was going. So she was by no means the timid, silent, royal wife, but her interference was subtle.

Like her husband, the Queen was meticulous about correct dress. All female members of the household had to wear or carry gloves at Buckingham Palace. Women, staying for Ascot Week at Windsor Castle, were instructed to bring four new outfits in which they had to parade for the lady of the bedchamber's approval, while their husbands' clothes were inspected by the Master of the Household. This sturdy, race-going squirearchy surrounding George V seemed altogether less glamorous than Nicholas II's grand dukes and travelled aristocrats, with their 150-room summer palaces in the Crimea.

Alix inherited her social conscience from Queen Victoria. Soon she was setting up 'houses of diligence' to help the working classes in Russia, who needed food and shelter more than instruction on the finer points of petit point. May was celebrated for her ten-point stitch, a talent inherited by her eldest son, the Duke of Windsor. Self-mockingly describing his reliance on crochet during the Second World War, he said it was a hobby which required some discretion in the mess, as it 'would hardly have done for the story to get around that a Major-General in the British Army had been seen bowling along the roads behind the Maginot Line crocheting'. May had a close bond with her eldest son.

Alix was growing more troubled and introspective and she began to resent the demands of public life. In 1911, she wrote from Peterhof to her governess, 'Darling Madgie, we long for rest, my husband has been working like a nigger [*sic*] for seven months.'[15] Sir George Buchanan could not help noticing there was about her a creeping 'trace of sourness'. Dagmar thought Alix was not showing sufficient respect to Nicholas with her cosy, 'lovey' Victorian endearments in public. A cold message was sent from the Dowager Empress instructing the Tsarina that in future she must always address Nicholas in public as 'Sir'.[16]

FIFTEEN

A Special Gaiety of Spirit

It would be hard to find a more desolate spot than the ruin of the Lower Dacha at Peterhof, where the Tsarevich was born on 30 July 1904. No child could have been more wanted.

There had been one or two embarrassing false starts, including a phantom pregnancy for the Tsarina, who was so desperate for an heir. On a visit to France in 1901 the susceptible Alix had fallen under the spell of Philippe Vachot, a doctor from Lyons who, when presented to the Empress and her husband, struck both of them with his 'pale blue eyes, that . . . sometimes flared up and gleamed with a strange softness'.

By 1902, Vachot was in residence at the Russian court and he persuaded her that she was pregnant and that the baby she was carrying was a longed-for boy. Alix felt contractions on the night of 31 August 1902, but she was then examined by the court obstetrician, D.O. Ott, who declared that she was not pregnant at all, not even a little bit. The charlatan was sent back to France in disgrace. Afterwards she was bed-bound, suffering from severe anaemia. Increasingly withdrawn, she started her own campaign of religious bombardment. Pinning all her hopes on the recently canonised Serafim of Sarovk,* she went daily to pray at the Cave Church at the St Feodor Cathedral at Tsarskoe Selo. A tiny church, built by the Empress with her own money, it was where she found a mystical repose. On a summer's day in 1903 Alix took the whole family on a pilgrimage to the Serafim shrine, and that night she bathed naked in a pool nearby and prayed for a son.[1]

The Cave Church was ravaged by the Nazis, then condemned by the Soviets because of its connection with the Empress, but is now being restored. It has a whitewashed simplicity, with silver icons twinkling above the myriad stands of melting brown candles.

---

* The reclusive holy man was made a saint in 1903.

The custodian of the Cave Church, a young woman called Olga with radiant eyes and dressed in a crocheted black dress, bridles when asked if it is true that the Tsarina arranged for the heart of Rasputin to be brought to this church. A curious group of elderly village women in flowery woollen kerchiefs crane forward to hear her reply, but she shakes her head and denies any connection with the so-called spiritual leader or *starets*. Two of the old matrons give gap-toothed, approving grins. These local women and their families have donated enough money to restore the church, which says something about the Tsarina. In this poor country, immense trouble is being taken to restore the gold-embroidered altar cloths inlaid with pearls; to find exact 11-metre-high silver icons to fill the wooden frames in the authentic Slavic-style dark-green and red original colours; and to make good the delicate Yaroslav blue and white art-deco ceiling.

Alix thought that her prayers had been answered when the Tsarevich was born at one fifteen in the afternoon, 'weighing 11lb'.[2] There had been a portent of bad luck just before the birth when a heavy mirror fell to the floor and smashed into tiny pieces.[3] Shaken and white-faced, Alix was sure that she would die giving birth. But now the dynasty was secure; 300 cannon shots rang out from the Peter and Paul fortress in St Petersburg.

The Tsarevich was christened at the gold and white royal church of the Holy Apostles Peter and Paul at Peterhof. This most important child was carried on a pillow by the elderly Princess Galitzine; she wore rubber-soled shoes, and the white-satin ribbons round her neck had been stitched firmly to the gilded cushion in case she slipped with the precious bundle.[4]

Those first weeks until the fateful diagnosis were a time of enchantment for Nicholas and Alexandra. 'I don't think you have seen my dear little Tsarevich,' the usually phlegmatic Nicholas would say, holding up the baby during a meeting with some disinterested generals or ministers.

Although there were forty doctors in attendance, it took nearly two months before the telltale signs of haemophilia were evident, when Alexei started bleeding from the navel. Expert physicians realised the boy would be in agony from even the smallest knock, as his blood failed to clot, causing massive bruising; even crawling, he was often covered with dark-blue contusions.

There was no treatment then for the 'royal disease', and children with haemophilia died whose conditions can nowadays be treated successfully with regular injections of Factor VIII, a blood-clotting agent. Queen Victoria was a carrier, as were two of her daughters, Alice and Beatrice. Her youngest son Prince Leopold was killed at the age of thirty-one by this devastating rogue gene.

Another granddaughter, Princess Victoria Eugénie, who was married to King Alfonso XIII of Spain and was known as Queen Ena, passed haemophilia on to three of her four sons. One was born dumb. The trauma was more than the King could bear, and when the couple separated said cruelly, 'My heir has contracted an infirmity, which was carried by my wife's family and not mine'.

Soon there was whispered talk about the 'Hesse disease'. The Russian people were quick to blame the Tsarina, as haemophilia is transmitted through the female line, condemning her, saying she had brought this plague to a Romanov dynasty which had been pure and strong until her arrival.

The boy's frailty raised the question of succession. The Tsar's brother Grand Duke Michael, 'Mischa', had been considered next in line until the arrival of the Tsarevich when he gladly stepped down from this dubious honour. Relieved, he said, 'I am no longer on the active list.'[5] Dagmar always favoured her second son, seeing in him qualities of leadership lacking in the Tsar.

Michael had been sent into exile when Nicholas, who had a strong sense of family, took a high moral tone towards his marriage in 1912 to a divorced commoner, Nathalie Cheremetevskaya, 'Natasha', by whom he had a son. Now he was needed by the family whose pet name for him, 'Darling Floppy', he found distinctly embarrassing.

The Tsarevich, naturally, was spoilt. Yet an English bishop, Herbert Bury,[6] recalled visiting Tsarskoe Selo and, on meeting the Tsar, pulled some puzzles made out of wood and steel from his pocket. Diffidently he offered them, saying that it was a simple present and that he knew the boy must have been given many expensive Christmas gifts. 'Not at all,' Nicholas replied. 'We bring him up very simply, and he loves puzzles. These, I see, are new,' he said, with a disarming smile, leaning forward to accept the little home-made gift.

Charles Sydney Gibbes never forgot his first sight of the four-year-old Tsarevich as he appeared in the schoolroom: 'A little chap in wee white knickerbockers and a Russian shirt trimmed with Ukrainian embroidery of blue and silver'.[7] Gibbes was not to know for several years that Alexei was haemophiliac. When he did finally learn of the boy's condition, his tone became noticeably more compassionate. Until then he had despaired of the boy's 'piggish' eating habits, how in the middle of a lesson he liked to send for a servant, who would return and obsequiously present the child with a chocolate in a glass.

Alexei romped in the grounds with his docile spaniel, Joy, or led his donkey, Vanka, from Ciniselli's Circus, round the English Park, pulling a sleigh. But he was often in pain, crying, 'warm my hands' or 'put up my leg', and his carer, Andrei Derevenko, indulged the boy by lifting him on to his massive shoulders. But it was Clementy Nagorny, another sailor, who was with the child in Siberia to the end, paying for his loyalty with his life.

The boy was highly intelligent, quick-witted, and happiest in Russian peasant dress, playing the balalaika. Of course he was mischievous, even if guests were not amused. At one state banquet he went under the table, deftly removing the shoes of a lady-in-waiting, who shrieked when she felt something cold and wet – it was a large strawberry – against her foot.[8] On another occasion, he scooped out the contents of half a watermelon and, creeping up behind Grand Duke Sergei's chair in the dining room, plopped it straight on to the authoritarian figure's head, so that juice and pulp ran down the face of this self-important Grand Duke. This sort of behaviour would never have been tolerated by King George V or Queen Mary; it was unthinkable that Prince John could empty a bowl of rice pudding over one of his uncles or a courtier.

Sometimes Alexei reduced his father to helpless laughter, on one occasion by ordering one of the sentries to march out to sea. Nicholas liked to say that he 'trembled' at the thought of the future rule of his son, 'Alexei the Terrible'; but he knew in his heart that that could never be.

Alexei had an intuitive way of reaching out to the people he met. When Sir John Hanbury-Williams received the news that his oldest son had been killed in France, he heard a small voice at his side: 'Papa told me to come to sit with you as he thought you would feel lonely tonight.' The boy then climbed on to a chair to sit beside the stricken General.

The Tsar and Tsarina could not help but be indulgent parents. Even though Alexei was the cause of inconsolable agony at times, he also delighted them with a special gaiety of spirit characteristic of a frail child.

For Alix, married life was never quite the same after the arrival of the Tsarevich. There would be no more children, although the Tsarina loved her friends' babies and liked to whistle to them. 'A sense of endless despair now filled her soul.' Pierre Gilliard astutely noted the beginning of this psychological collapse when she suffered heart pains and her teeth hurt. She became even more prone to weepiness, heart flutterings and neurasthenia. She had quite 'lost her health'. The Empress suffered from a sciatic nerve pain resulting from the dislocation of some of her vertebrae in childbirth.⁹ In those days, mothers gave birth without monitoring or long-term medical supervision. Today she might be prescribed Prozac or hormonal treatment, but at that period new mothers relied on a barbiturate called veronal, which made her feel constantly low. This condition, combined with migraines and a naturally mournful Hanoverian temperament, prevented Alix from ever becoming a vibrant, vital Empress.

Nicholas now had to cope with a wife who cried easily and was plagued with headaches. He often made excuses for her: 'The Empress is not feeling good today . . . please understand'. The imperial physician, Dr Botkin, thought she had a condition known as 'progressive hysteria', but Alix had lived with pain nearly all her life.

Dr Botkin, grey-haired and avuncular, everyone's idea of a family doctor and devoted to the Tsar, felt that the Empress was never completely normal. Anything could trigger an emotional outburst. A heart condition had been diagnosed in 1908, and, in any case, according to one observer, 'the Empress was neither a mad one nor a normal one'.¹⁰

In this vulnerable and unstable frame of mind, Alix was receptive to the attentions of the smooth-tongued Prince Alexander Orlov, the commanding officer of her Uhlan Regiment of the Imperial Guard, and an inveterate womaniser. Amusing and informed, he was also one of the few people who could make the normally equable Nicholas furious.

Once asked about her feelings for Orlov, Alix told her good friend Anna Vyrubova, 'It would have been so sweet to have been with him . . . but I was never his mistress. Our love was sad, like everything else. I liked talking to him and singing for him.' A French newspaper, *Le Temps*, wrote a scathing piece about the Tsarina's infatuation with Orlov, how she called him '*Solovushka*', 'gentle nightingale'. The flirtation was the talk of court circles in St Petersburg.

Questioning his wife about whether she planned to go on seeing Orlov, Nicholas angrily grabbed her wrists. When she replied 'Yes', he pushed her harshly back into an armchair, muttering, 'I'll send you to a convent', sounding like one of his repressive, medieval ancestors.

Orlov was sent abroad in 1908 on a diplomatic mission but died in mysterious circumstances. Malicious whispers suggested he had been murdered in Odessa on his way to Egypt. Every year, on the anniversary of his death, the Tsarina placed forget-me-nots on his grave.*

The remains of the saint to whom Alix prayed for a son have been reinterred; they had been dumped in a sack at the Museum of Atheism.

---

* Years later Anna Vyrubova was imprisoned by the Bolsheviks and afterwards fled to Finland, where she died in 1964. During the Second World War in a hospital in Stockholm she confided to one of the nurses that 'she was still sad about the Orlov affair', but whether this was on her own account or the Tsarina's is a mystery.

SIXTEEN

'Get That Damned Child Away from Me'

When Edward VII visited St Petersburg in 1908 he was appalled by the imperial children's Scottish accents. They spoke English to their mother, but Russian to their father. One of their tutors was the Tsarina's former governess, Miss 'Madgie' Jackson, who had guided her towards reading Trollope, Thackeray and Carlyle, inspiring her with a love of English writers. Another tutor was John Epps, who had come to Russia from Scotland, originally to teach the children of textile workers. He was a perfectly 'nice man' who dropped his Gs and Hs.

Alix now had to bear with 'Uncle Bertie's' strong criticism of the educational regime she had devised for her children, which seemed limited to reading *Mother Goose* and the *Golliwog's Circus Book*.

Epps, who was then sixty and had been at Tsarskoe for three years, was shocked to be summarily dismissed by the Tsarina. His superior replacement, Charles Sydney Gibbes, described him as being 'completely uneducated'.[1]

Gibbes, who at first was employed only to teach the young tsarinas English, wore evening dress throughout the day. He thought the royal children were out of control by English standards, that they 'generally behaved like young savages'.

Nicholas encouraged his children to read and listen to music, but he was strict about family entertainment, distrusting the bohemian influence of films; but he did allow one or two not very exciting titles, including *A Fish Factory in Astrakhan*, and *The Grasshopper and the Ant*, a 1911 puppet film.[2] He was keen on fresh air, but often found himself pushing his wife around the royal gardens in a bath chair, gallantly making it appear as if this was a great pleasure; the children were often around on these occasions, Olga walking with her parents, Tatiana and Maria in a miniature carriage drawn by two goats, and Anastasia in a basket on board a docile donkey led by a liveried footman.

The tsarinas all kept diaries bound with gold, often not recording anything more momentous than 'we played tiddly-winks' or 'pressed flowers from the Park'. Their pleasures were simple, their world innocent and protected. A high point of the day was racing in for tea in glasses in silver holders and in the evenings playing cards, billiards or dominoes.

Happy in their close-knit circle, the sisters, who wore matching frocks, were divided into the 'Big Ones', Olga and Tatiana, and the 'Little Ones', Anastasia and Maria. The princesses signed their letters OTMA, an acronym of the first letters of each of their Christian names. 'Even when the two eldest became young women one might hear them talking like little girls of ten or twelve.'[3] Alexander Mossolov of the Imperial Chancellery thought the sisters were decidedly immature.

Alix dreaded launching her deliberately sheltered 'girlies' into the 'dissolute milieu' of St Petersburg. Olga was a striking blonde with a retroussé nose and, most like her mother, she was grave and kind-hearted. The beauty of the family was Tatiana, who could be imperious, prompting her siblings to call her 'the Governess'. But she was her mother's favourite. Always solicitous, she often sent little notes hoping 'Darling Mama . . . won't be today very tired and that you can get up to dinner. I am always so awfully sorry when you are tired and when you can't get up.' If the Tsarina tended towards melancholy, it never altered her children's adoration, and there was never any hint of resentment towards their ailing mother.

Maria, with her ready smile, was her father's favourite and liked to flirt with the officers on board the royal yacht, but did not take kindly to being called 'Fat Little Bow-wow' by her slimmer sisters. Anastasia was mischievous and not above tripping up a servant carrying a tray of pink Sèvres family porcelain. Known in the family as 'our good, fat Tutu', she was the daughter who amused her father most. Her letters to him – 'My brilliant Daddy! . . . a million times kiss your feet and hands . . . loving you, your faithful daughter, 13-year-old lass' [sic] – showed their easy, happy relationship. Nicholas liked to instil in them all an appreciation of Russia's Silver Age, taking the older girls to the ballet and the opera.

There were moves to marry off Olga to a suitable European prince; Crown Prince Carol of Romania was on the list. Independently minded, she declared that she wanted only a home-grown husband – 'I am Russian, and I wish to remain Russian' – and cleverly insinuated that 'Papa has promised not to make me, and I don't want to, leave Russia.'

Unlike many European royals jogging along in dull or arranged marriages, Nicholas and George remained intensely happy with their wives. More emotionally secure, Nicholas, who liked to think he managed to be 'at once Emperor, father, and comrade', was able to express his love for his children, who were his joy.

George, on the other hand, although a kind man, was emotionally complex, inhibited and proud of his ability to frighten his children. He believed that princes should be brought up to be frightened of their fathers.[4] As a parent, George's maxim was, 'My father was frightened of his mother, I was frightened of my father', which is perhaps a strange remark when to the world Edward VII seemed such a benign figure. 'Tum-Tum', with his 48-inch waist and willingness to allow his mistresses' children to jump on his knee, hardly ever terrified his sons, though he could be short-tempered. George declared early on, 'I am damned well going to see to it that my children are frightened of me.' He succeeded.

Devoted in his fashion, he surprisingly remembered all his children's birthdays but was incapable of any outward show of emotion. He was better when they were very young and they gathered round him, dressed in blue serge suits, to listen to him reading William Allingham's poem 'Up the airy mountain, Down the rushy glen, We daren't go a-hunting for fear of little men', and another of his own childhood favourites, Charles Kingsley's magical *Water Babies*.[5]

But as they began to grow up, George found his sons, or 'my boys' as he called them, could be irritating, especially when they appeared slow at handling a muzzle-loading gun, without the same assurance he had shown at their age. He was more indulgent later with his grandchildren, especially Princess Elizabeth and Princess Margaret; it helped that they were nice to Charlotte, his parrot.

The two men could not have been more different in their approach to fatherhood. George and Mary had five children in fairly quick succession, all born prematurely. Queen Mary was not naturally tactile, and distanced herself even more than most royals from the royal nursery; children's games or horseplay made her distinctly uneasy. In her high, buttoned-up long frocks, she did not immediately offer an inviting lap for boisterous small children as her mother-in-law Queen Alexandra did instinctively with warm hugs and laughter.

Nicholas, as a loving father himself, could only imagine how pleased George must have been to be back home after a long voyage in 1902: 'What a happiness it must be to see all the sweet children round one after such a long separation!' Replying somewhat testily, his cousin, expressing irritation at the prospect of 'a lot of tiresome functions' ahead, was thankful, he said, that his children were away in Sandringham. 'They are,' he told Nicholas, 'much happier in the country, as we still have fogs here in London.' Fog was not the only reason the royal children were away from their parents. They led a typical Edwardian, upper-class childhood behind a green-baize door, dependent on the kindness of nannies, some of whom could be sadistic.

For three years George and Mary were unaware that their eldest child, David, was being bullied by Mary Peters, a mentally disturbed nurse, who deliberately inflicted pain by pinching him, so that he screamed when presented to his parents, who hated any show of bad manners. They found it tiresome he appeared so 'jumpy' in their company; it was distinctly unflattering.

It was not until 1897 that May, who by then was expecting her third child, realised that the nurse was unwell and dismissed her. No longer were there bellows of 'Can't you stop that child from crying' from George. Another nanny was appointed, Mrs 'Lala' Bill, who became the protective star in Prince John's life.

Lord Harewood, son of the King's only daughter, Princess Mary, the Princess Royal, remembers being terrified on one occasion when he sneezed in his grandfather's presence; George had shouted, 'Get that damned child away from me.'[6] Later, Harewood had his nose cauterised to help stop his sneezing.

Some of George V's impatience with his sons was due to his own exacting years in the navy; having been forced to abandon a life at sea, the next best thing was to insist on nautical precision in the home. The walls of his study, where he summoned his children, were lined with the same dark-red flannel fabric used for French soldiers' trousers. The children stared apprehensively at 'No use crying over spilt milk', and 'If at first you don't succeed' slogans on the walls, as they stood to attention waiting for their father's 'At ease' command. They called him 'Papa' in private and 'Sir' in public.

An intimidating figure with a sea captain's bearing, marine-blue eyes and full beard, George treated them as if they were unpromising ratings on a new destroyer. Sometimes he thought his sons disappointingly wimpish. Their young lives were ruled by a vast preponderance of 'don'ts'. Subconsciously, he thought of his sons as young sailors who needed to be drilled and inspected. This harshness with his children often puzzled members of the royal household, who knew how kind-hearted the King could be and that he never shouted at the servants.

'Get it out,' he would say impatiently to Prince Albert, as he stammered, struggling to get his recalcitrant tongue round a word. His second son, who later became King George VI, was born left-handed; but his father believed that there was 'no such thing as a first-class shot who shoots left-handed',[7] and he forced the boy to use his right hand, with damaging psychological consequences.

If the boys inadvertently put their hands in their pockets during a meeting in the library, they were rebuked, and instructions were given to housekeeping to sew up all the pockets of their suits. Sir Owen Morshead, Royal Librarian at Windsor Castle, once sagely remarked that, in his opinion, 'The House of Hanover, like ducks, produces bad parents. They trample on their young.'[8]

The sibling missing from these grooming classes for future monarchs was Prince John. George and Mary suppressed their anxiety about their brain-damaged youngest son, making sure he was never part of the royal household. This impaired boy, who had been unable to sit up even when he was eleven months old, had developed epilepsy; he was immensely lovable, but was hidden away from the world. Having a disadvantaged child whose behaviour could be so unpredictable was mortifying for May. She bottled up her feelings and refused to let 'Johnnie' dominate her life or interfere with royal routine.

He was never allowed to be with his siblings and certainly not his parents when they were entertaining guests at Windsor or Buckingham Palace. However, on one occasion, hiding behind shutters on a staircase he caught a glimpse of a royal guest and asked, in his refreshingly open way, who was the man 'with the huge head'; at which he was hushed and told it was the Prime Minister.[9]

When he was three, he was moved to a Sandringham estate cottage called Wood Farm, which the palace smoothly suggested was for his own safety. Virtually confined to Norfolk, he was a lonely figure in a sailor's suit who could sometimes be seen wandering on the beach at Snettisham, where he enjoyed saluting any officer he met on these solitary rambles.

From his den, the Prince laboriously wrote letters to Queen Alexandra, thanking her for presents, once sending her a card of a toad sheltering from the rain under a toadstool, with the motto 'No place like home'. He was drawn instinctively to his grandmother, who had all the qualities lacking in his mother. Like the children of many Edwardian aristocratic homes, Prince John also found comfort in the unselfish love of a good nanny.

He made hesitant attempts to break through the invisible barrier surrounding his parents and, interestingly, sent more letters to his father than his mother. Whatever her feelings, Mary could not help but appear tensely distant, often taken aback by the boy's sudden bursts of high spirits. George, on the other hand, for all his abrasiveness appeared the softer, more approachable parent. Enclosing flowers from the woods at Sandringham, Prince John, in childish hand, wrote to him, 'Dear Papa, I am sending a box of snowdrops for you which I have picked . . . best love from your devoted son Johnnie.' He loved his small garden plot and often sent his parents flowers pressed into notes.

This challenged child, a daydreamer, became increasingly lonely; only his brother, Prince George, Duke of Kent paid him much attention. He was always interested in his fair-haired, clumsy brother, always tender and kind, but eventually they were parted when George was sent away to the Royal Naval College. He pleaded with his father, asking if instead he could study music. The thought of one of his sons in the arts and not the armed services triggered an exceptionally high-voltage explosion. 'You will spend your whole life in the navy,' George roared at this artistic son, adding, 'You may even die in the navy.' Artistic interests have often been viewed by the royal family as rather strange: 'It's very odd about George and music,' Edward VIII once said of his cousin Lord Lascelles, who was keenly interested in opera. 'You know, his parents were quite normal – liked horses and dogs and the country.'

Prince George, who was not at all hearty, hated his time at Osborne. The mornings began, even when the grounds were covered in snow, with a plunge into ice-cold water, because it was commonly believed that this strengthened the immune system.

When John died on 18 January 1919 the royal family was not entirely surprised, or too distraught. In a letter to his mistress Freda Dudley Ward,[10] the Prince of Wales admitted that the boy had been 'practically shut up for the last two years anyhow, so no one had ever seen him except the family and then only once or twice a year'; his brother's death had come as 'the greatest relief imaginable and what we've always silently prayed for . . . this poor boy had become more of an animal than anything else and was only a brother in the flesh.'[11]

It is difficult to know what Queen Mary's feelings were, unlike those of the Tsarina, who brimmed with emotional outpourings about the Tsarevich's vulnerability. Mary had been woken by a telephone call at half-past five in the morning telling her that 13-year-old Prince John was dead, and with some relief she said, 'I cannot say how grateful we feel to God for having taken him . . . the poor little troubled soul which had been a great anxiety to us . . . ever since he was four years old.' Arriving at Wood Farm she was painfully embarrassed by the sobs shaking the devastated 'Lala', who had been like a mother to the boy. Even at this agonising moment, Mary could show no outward sign of grief for the loss of this hugely lovable child.

The King and Queen asked especially that the funeral should be of 'the simplest possible character'; Prince John's coffin was made from oak from the Sandringham estate, where the boy loved to roam, and was carried gently by farm workers to the chapel, with its famous silver altar. Canon Dalton led the service and the choir sang two of Prince John's favourite hymns: 'Now the Day is Over' and 'Peace, Perfect Peace'. There was a cross of orchids, arum lilies and white chrysanthemums from 'Poor old Grannie', which read: 'In remembrance of my darling little Johnnie, Grannie's precious grandson, whose memory will never fade.' Alexandra was heartbroken.

SEVENTEEN

Seeds of Unrest

Nicholas had a fairy-tale picture of the Russian people, seeing them as a band of happy peasants, working all hours in the mines and fields with unquestioning devotion to an emperor who shared their belief in *sudba*.* But they were living in unremitting squalor with little chance of ever rising out of the peasant class.

In 1897, only a year after Nicholas's coronation, as unrest increased, the secret police cracked down on protest groups. Lenin, a rebel leader, was sent to Siberia for three years and used his time to foment discontent and work on his successful strategy for the people's uprising.

Sustained by the certainty that he was 'master of the Russian land' and thus answerable to God alone, Nicholas seemed impervious to increasing acts of political terrorism. Not by nature aggressive, he now felt that the Russian Empire needed to extend eastwards, and territory must be seized from China and Korea. Confidently, he sent off thousands of troops on the new Trans-Siberian Railway on this mission of aggrandisement. In addition, forty-five ships from the Baltic fleet moved to the Far East in a journey lasting ten months, as they sailed round the world, fighting disease, in particular, scurvy. Nicholas's blinkered self-assurance created a misplaced confidence; typically, he believed that 'little Japan would never dare' to attack the might of the massive Russian Army.

Exhausted, when the Russians eventually arrived at the Pacific coast, anchoring off Port Arthur, the Japanese, all fresh and vigorous, were waiting. Two-thirds of the Russian fleet was destroyed on 26 January 1904 by the Empire of the Rising Sun's torpedo boats. It was one of the major tragedies of Nicholas's reign. The disastrous 1904/5 war between Russia and Japan sapped Russia's lifeblood and irrevocably damaged his image.

---

* Fatalistic acceptance of misfortune.

Still reluctant to surround himself with good advisers, he appeared immune in the face of an approaching catastrophe. He seemed unaware of the blistering poverty in the countryside, where cattle shared indoor space with nursing mothers and children, in cramped conditions which were breeding grounds for dysentery and tuberculosis; workers in mines and factories, who were underpaid and starving, became increasingly rebellious and resentful.

The reality of life for the masses in Russia was captured by a French aristocrat, the 49-year-old Marquis de Custine,[1] whose father had been guillotined during the French Revolution. Visiting Russia in 1839, he was shocked by the plight of the serfs. He thought the average 'Russian of the lower class' was treated abominably and accepted 'being beaten as . . . often as saluted'.

In a touching vignette of the life of two droshky drivers in St Petersburg, de Custine recalled how on one occasion at the end of a journey, as they struggled to control their shaggy ponies, they courteously raised their hats to each other, and sometimes 'if acquainted would . . . lift their hand to their mouth with an amicable smile, and kiss it'. But he witnessed one of these gentlemanly exchanges being brought to an abrupt end when one of the Tsar's aides brutally dragged one of the coachmen from his seat and, 'because he had not made sufficient haste', struck him 'until he had covered his face with blood'. A silent crowd watched as 'the coachman submitted to the torture like a real lamb'. Then, battered and bruised, he got to his feet, brushed himself down, wiped away the blood on his cheeks, remounted his seat, and began his 'bows and salutations' as if nothing had happened. Submissiveness, de Custine suggested, was the only way the poor could survive in Russia. After several centuries of degradation, the people still remained loyal to the Tsar, but change to an imperialist rule which allowed such indignities was now inevitable.

A band of militants, writers, doctors, artists, lawyers and students, the zemstvos,* now called on the Tsar to act. It was typical of Nicholas that he should dwell on their sartorial correctness, rather than their message. They arrived, he noted approvingly, 'in

---

*   Members of elected local-government assemblies first established in the mid-nineteenth century. These campaigned for social reform, but came to support revolutionary activities when their original efforts were habitually frustrated by central government.

ceremonial dress and wearing white gloves', to ask for a proper elected government. Nicholas, with his inbuilt inflexibility, dismissed this modest request for fuller representation as nothing more than 'a senseless dream'.

Seeing that the Tsar had no intention of acceding to any demands concerning the running of the country, militants now began to set up oak barricades and to tear down portraits of the Tsar. Sailors on board the cruiser *Potemkin*, part of the Black Sea fleet in Odessa, mutinied.

In St Petersburg, seeds of unrest blossomed on Sunday 9 January 1905. The mood had begun cheerfully enough as a crowd of 150,000 unarmed workers gathered, carrying icons, crosses and flattering photographs of the Tsar. In a spirit of goodwill, these well-behaved protesters made their way to the Winter Palace.

They were led by a charismatic 32-year-old Orthodox priest, Father George Gapon, a secret policeman who was later murdered.[2] He was also a gambler, once spotted coming out of a casino disguised as a Romanian bishop.[3] All the protesters wanted was to see the Tsar, to present him with a petition for long-overdue human rights. 'We are beggars, we are oppressed and overburdened . . . we are not regarded as human beings but are treated as slaves.' The mood was not one of anger or resentment against the Tsar, more an appeal to his humanity. 'Your Majesty . . . we have the appearance of human beings,' they pleaded, 'but in fact we have no human rights at all, not even the right to speak . . . we are turned into slaves by your officials.' One said, 'We would like a republic but we must have a good Tsar at the head.'

But their 'good Tsar' was not at the head in St Petersburg or anywhere else except Tsarskoe Selo, as usual. He had been on the verge of going to the Winter Palace to receive the petition until the Tsarina insisted he must never 'capitulate to a mob'. Her baleful influence is captured in a telling photograph in which she is perched on his gold-embossed desk wearing a beautiful flower-trimmed hat. Nicholas is looking downcast and writing earnestly, as if being given dictation. When Edward VII, who was at Balmoral, was told that Alix had not allowed the Emperor to meet his people outside the Winter Palace, he said, 'I am afraid her influence is not always a good one.'[4]

The Tsar, responding to his wife's advice as he always did, now reached for the telephone and gave orders for Prince Vassiltchikov to galvanise a cavalry division to surround the Winter Palace. As the peaceable crowd moved slowly forward to the Winter Palace Square, they were peppered with bullets by the Cossack cavalry. In an incident almost as insensitive as Brigadier Dyer's at Jallianwallah Bagh,* 150 protestors were killed and hundreds more wounded.

Painful memories endured of 'every child's hat, mitten, a woman's headscarf, lying pitifully abandoned on the St Petersburg snow that day'.[5] It would forever be known as 'Bloody Sunday'. Nicholas, no longer the people's benign Little Father, would damagingly be known as Bloody Nicholas after this, one of the more disreputable incidents in Russian history. It gave Lenin quiet satisfaction; he was convinced that it was merely a 'dress rehearsal' for the Bolshevik revolution that would ultimately destroy the Tsar.[6]

The New Year had begun with an omen of bad luck. On 6 January 1905, during the ceremony to blessing the waters of the Neva, just as the great gold cross was being forged through the ice, a shell exploded at Nicholas's feet. Two spectators were killed and a royal bodyguard was shot, his blood a livid red, smearing the snow in futuristic daubs.

As the rounds whizzed over his head from the Peter and Paul Fortress, Nicholas knew they were meant for him, but, with his own quiet sense of *sudba*, he was sanguine. 'I just crossed myself,' he said, 'what else could I do? . . . I knew that somebody was trying to kill me.'[7]

He seemed to show the same inscrutable detachment when his uncle, who was also his brother-in-law, Grand Duke Sergei Alexandrovich, Moscow's hardline autocratic Governor-General, was murdered a month later, on 4 February 1905, on his way to church. Hearing the bomb explode, his wife Ella, the Tsarina's sister, ran out towards the Spassky Gate, and, distraught, tried to pick up the gory remnants of clothing from her husband's shattered body, saying, 'Sergei hated blood and mess so much.' Some years earlier a

---

* Brigadier-General R.E.H. Dyer ordered 50 troops to open fire on an unarmed gathering of 10,000 Indians on 13 April 1919 at Amritsar in the Punjab. Unable to flee because Dyer's soldiers were at the only exit from the *bagh* (garden), 400 were killed and 1,200 wounded by the 1,650 rounds fired in ten minutes. Dyer was court-martialled on his return to England and acquitted; indeed, a public subscription raised several thousand pounds, and he was presented with a sword inscribed 'Saviour of the Punjab'.

fortune-teller had predicted his sudden death, telling the swash-buckling Sergei, 'You have little to laugh about, one day your head will go crack.' Nicholas seemed strangely impervious to the news of his uncle's murder: soon after he was told, he shocked courtiers by continuing to try playfully to nudge his cousin Sandro off a sofa.[8] Ella then became a nun, setting up a religious order, emulating the example of Lazarus's two sisters.* Always keen on style, she ordered worldly designer nuns' habits in pale grey with soft, white lawn wimples.

Nicholas blithely continued to believe that all was well and irrationally blamed his Jewish subjects for creating unrest. His ministers were dismissed as 'a lot of frightened hens'[9] for being concerned. He felt invulnerable because of his sacred inheritance. But gradually he had to accept that concessions had to be made and, against his own instincts, he reluctantly signed the Manifesto of 17 October 1905, agreeing to a Duma, a proper assembly representing the people, giving them freedom of speech and civil rights. It was the brainchild of Prime Minister Count Witte, remarkable for its time but still deeply conservative. Nicholas felt a sting of shame at the thought of how his father would have handled these impertinent demands for democracy. Reluctantly, on 27 April 1906, he presided over the inauguration of this first state Duma, with two chambers, one of which was the state council, which consisted of men who enjoyed the trust of the court. In the stately Tauride Palace, dressed formally in military uniform and sash, Nicholas stood woodenly by the throne staring fixedly ahead. Behind him the gold imperial coat of arms embroidered on red velvet, would soon be a shredded symbol of the Tsar's shattered authority.

The whole occasion, celebrating the birth of Russia's first elected parliament, struck ambassadors, nobility and courtiers as strangely sinister. One minister believed that the walls of the throne room had 'never before witnessed such a scene',[10] and he was not referring to the royal women in their sable-trimmed capes and embroidered gold dresses, but to a peasant mob in rough wool shirts and high boots who had crowded in, ostensibly for the declaration, but really for a chance to glare at the Tsar.

'What wicked faces!' Count Fredericks, Minister of the Court, observed. To him, the mob that had assembled was nothing more

---

* The Order was called the Convent of St Martha and St Mary.

than 'a gang of criminals . . . only waiting for the signal to throw themselves upon the Ministers and cut their throats'.[11]

Nicholas hated the relaxation of censorship and the very idea of a Duma. The word means 'constitution', and the idea went against his indoctrination as an autocrat directly appointed by God. He thought he had been generous and liberal, but now he was shocked by the malevolent look on many of the faces in the crowd. His sister Olga and his mother wondered why some seemed 'to reflect an incomprehensible hatred for all of us'.[12] It had been a fairly bloodless revolution – a small step forward, with the granting of a parliament and some political concessions.

Nicholas had disaffected the aristocracy, who thoroughly disapproved of the liberation of the serfs and believed the new constitution was simply a charter for insurrection. They now preferred to take themselves off to cavort around European casinos or to live elegantly in Florence, Madrid or Paris. Nicholas held the liberals and the intelligentsia responsible for the prevalent discontent. He was isolated. Communications were limited, so he had little idea of the unrest in other parts of his vast empire. In Russia, newspapers and political magazines did not dare to express controversial views or even constructive criticism of the Tsar.

In England, George had no idea the situation in Russia was serious as the calm, pedestrian tone of the letters between the cousins was unchanged. Besides, he was being sent to India with his wife on a goodwill mission by his father. He arrived in October 1905 on board the *Renown* for the start of a tour of the empire that would last four months and two weeks. Stunned by the exotic and sometimes mystical experience of travelling through India, he was charmed by the welcome shown by his father's 300 million subjects in the subcontinent. He had no reason to doubt their loyalty until told about the silent revolution in India, aimed at independence.

George challenged the congress leader Gopal Gokhale, who had been campaigning for the Indians to have the right to run their country, looked him in the eye and asked, 'Would the peoples of India be happier if you ran the country?' Gokhale replied with dignity that they might not be happier but would have 'more self-respect'.[13]

George, unlike Nicholas, was a realist. He hated the inevitable parting of the 'Mother Country and her Indian Empire'. In a letter to one of his advisers, Lord Esher,[14] he suggested the solution to the unrest in India was, 'We must either trust the Natives more and give them a greater share in the Government . . . or else double the Civil Service', which he felt had been overworked and had become out of touch with the grass-roots feelings in the villages. Unlike Nicholas he did not close his mind to change; he listened to the people.

He knew from his father how badly Nicholas had handled events leading to Bloody Sunday, but would have been even more shocked by the rapid social deterioration in Russia. By December 1905, the people were enduring the worst ever shortages of fuel and food, leading to continuing strikes on the railways and in factories such as the vast Putilov metalworks. Landowners were being terrorised, workers conducted violent protests in the cities, and some of the people were so desperate they were reduced to eating snow.

The enlightened Prime Minister Count Sergei Witte resigned on 13 April 1906. Nicholas was relieved, blaming him secretly for the concessions he had so reluctantly been forced to make six months earlier. In May 1906, when more radical reforms were demanded, the Tsar refused to listen. One of Nicholas's more visionary advisers was Piotr Stolypin, his new Prime Minister, who tried to persuade him at least to talk to representatives of the Duma. But Nicholas refused, later making the fatal admission, 'I believe in no one but my wife.' Then, in a high-handed move, Nicholas dissolved the first of four Dumas. It had lasted for only seventy-three days.

Stolypin did manage to push through reforms over the next five years, attempting to improve this vast, wayward empire, where murder and criminal behaviour had long been tolerated. But Nicholas was decidedly apathetic about his Prime Minister's zeal for a better, brighter Russia, which thanks to Stolypin was enjoying a rare prosperity after one of the best grain harvests ever.

He abolished the stifling village communes and encouraged the nine million farming serfs to have a say in their own destiny. If ever they had enough roubles, they could now buy a piece of land, and they were given the freedom to move between villages, which previously had been forbidden. But those with an agenda of sedition and a plan to overthrow the imperialist regime did not welcome this social reform. In 1906, Stolypin cracked down on the newly formed and subversive St Petersburg Soviet Party, executing some 400 rebels.

Bravely, he tried to talk to Nicholas about Rasputin's malign influence at court, producing written evidence that, far from being a man of God, the corrupt Siberian peasant was a scoundrel and former horse-thief.* Coldly, Nicholas responded, 'Perhaps everything you are telling me is the truth, but I ask you never to speak to me again about Rasputin. There is nothing that I can do anyway.' Clearly embarrassed, he was unable to admit that he had no influence over his wife's dependence on the unsavoury monk.

Stolypin paid heavily for his dream of trying to create a 'great Russia'. His dacha on St Petersburg Island was blown up on 12 August 1906, killing thirty-two people and injuring his fourteen-year-old daughter.

His enemies finally killed him on 14 September 1911 during celebrations to mark the unveiling of a monument to Alexander II. He was shot twice sitting in the front row of the stalls at the Kiev Opera House, during an interval in a gala performance of Rimsky-Korsakov's *The Legend of Tsar Sultan*. Worming his way into the theatre, pretending to be one of the secret police protecting the Prime Minister, a revolutionary called Mordko Bogrov[15] pierced Stolypin's liver with one shot. As blood flowed from his white jacket Stolypin managed to stagger to his feet and in a dying heroic gesture turned towards the royal box for a last glimpse of his Emperor.

'Women were shrieking,' Nicholas told his mother in a letter. He had been drinking tea with his daughters Olga and Tatiana outside the royal box because it was so hot, when suddenly he became aware, he said, of 'two sounds, as if something had been dropped. I thought that an opera glass might have fallen on somebody's head and ran back into the box to look.' It never occurred to him that he might have been the real target.

Stolypin survived for five days. Nicholas went to his dying minister's bedside in Kiev but as usual was cavalier about the fate of one of his close circle of advisers. 'The Emperor did not even take the trouble to disturb any of his arrangements to attend the funeral,' Sir Bernard Pares† noted disapprovingly.

However, the British Ambassador's daughter, Meriel Buchanan, heard that 'the tsarinas had been so very upset and shaken'. Their mother insisted they go to Livadia at once. She 'would not hear of

---

* Rasputin, who called himself a monk, claimed miraculous powers and had an alarming amount of influence over the Tsarina because of his ability to stem the haemophiliac Tsarevich's bleeding.

† An academic, an expert on Russia and 'official correspondent' for the Foreign Office.

the Emperor remaining behind in Kief' [*sic*] for the funeral 'and fearing to excite her to an outburst of hysteria he yielded to her entreaties.'[16] Bogrov was hanged. Count Kokovtsov* became Prime Minister until he fell out with the Tsar, resigning over his unavailing attempts to stem corruption, and Rasputin's dissolute political influence at court.

Two years later, in March 1913, good order seemed to have been restored for the celebrations marking 300 years of Romanov rule. *Te Deums* were sung in all the churches, and jewelled icons glittered on the altar in the Cathedral of Our Lady of Kazan during the great Thanksgiving Mass. The Tsar was on his throne and all was well. Afterwards, with Alix in billowing hat with parasol, her arm through the arm of God's representative on Earth, the couple gave the impression of being an invincible Emperor and Empress. The throne seemed secure, celebrated with all those imperial displays, dazzling receptions, military parades and fireworks, and then the emotional surge of patriotic feeling, hearing Chaliapin on his knees, singing the national anthem to his Tsar.

Serenely, Nicholas set off on a romantic Easter journey through old Russian towns, tracing the footsteps of the first Romanov Tsar, three centuries earlier. Serfs came out during his pilgrimage, holding icons and prostrating themselves before him as he inspected treasures in the old churches, confirming his belief in the devotion and loyalty of his poor, simple people. More than ever, they saw him as *tishaishii* – their gentle Tsar.

In this mood of optimism, two months later, in May 1913, Nicholas was in Berlin with King George and his wife's cousin Kaiser Wilhelm II. This was the last occasion when the three Emperors, 'Nicky', 'Willy' and 'Georgie', were together and in real harmony. Although the German Emperor was in good spirits, rejoicing in the wedding of his only daughter Princess Victoria Louise of Prussia,† he was still watchful, jealous of the bond between George and Nicholas, who were the bride's supporters. Her father made sure they were kept busy proposing toasts, and hoped they could not find time to have any real private conversation together. Whenever he was talking to the Tsar, George always felt uneasy, convinced that the Kaiser 'had his eye at the keyhole'.

---

*   Died in exile in Paris in 1942.
†   She married Duke Ernst August of Brunswick-Lüneberg.

To the Tsar the idea of a war being started by the Kaiser was pre-posterous. However, King George knew better than his unworldly Russian cousin. In one letter,[17] epitomising this naivety, Nicholas wrote that he thought the Kaiser had been 'in excellent spirits, calm and comfortable'. George, on the other hand, seldom found Wilhelm II calm and was always wary with him. War with Germany was now inevitable, yet the cousins were still on affectionate 'Willy', 'Nicky 'and 'Georgie' terms.

EIGHTEEN

Hollowness and Vodka

After just four years on the throne, in the long hot summer of 1914 George was facing his first real crisis. Usually he looked forward to sailing at Cowes and racing at Goodwood, but now, with the threat of a world war, his routine was being disagreeably disrupted. Earlier problems dealing with the Empire and the suffragettes, who had chained themselves to Downing Street railings, seemed enviably easy as he realised peace between his cousins, the Kaiser and the Tsar, was now nothing more than an optimistic dream.

Outwardly, the social calendar had not changed. His aunt Dagmar, the Dowager Empress, was visiting, staying in Marlborough House,[1] while cousin Xenia was at the Piccadilly Hotel. Both were so enjoying their stay in London, they ignored warnings that Europe was about to be pitched into turmoil. Eventually, persuaded to return to Russia, they were taunted in Germany, as angry crowds tried to break down the windows and doors of their carriage,[2] shouting at them and shaking their fists.

During the weeks of apprehension, with Germany and Russia hovering on the brink of war, Nicholas still found time to play tennis, have tea with the family and take his daughters out in a canoe. George on the other hand was seriously alarmed by the volatile situation.

Outwardly calm, Nicholas was also a little anxious, confiding in his trusted cousin in a letter from Peterhof dated 16/29 July 1914, 'Dearest George . . . I am writing to you at a most serious moment. I do not know what might happen in a few days. Austria has gone off upon a reckless war . . . It is awful!' Germany had sided with the Austro-Hungarians, declaring war on Serbia and its ally Russia. 'We've tried to be patient and have tried to question Austria but of no avail. If a general war broke out I know we shall have France and England's full support . . . Alix and I have so much thought of you all [at] this trying time.'

George tried to dissuade Nicholas from entering the war, but the Tsar had been swayed by the deceptive potency of his massive army, which already numbered a reassuring 1.4 million men, and after the call-up totalled 4.5 million.[3] As a concerned fellow – an emperor but also as a hard-headed realist – George saw the fearful consequences; unlike his unworldly cousin, who felt invincible, fired by Russia's enthusiastic response to mobilisation.

Aware of the inevitable and horrifying approach of war, George's diary entry on 29 July 1914 began, 'Austria has declared war on Servia [*sic*]. Where will it end? . . . These are very anxious days for me to live in.'[4] He was holding endless meetings with naval and military leaders and dealing with a daily bombardment of foreign telegrams. Reluctantly, he gave up on a favourite July fixture, his annual visit to Goodwood races which he loved so much. He admitted being exhausted during these long worrying days, yet they always started punctually at 6.45 a.m. He gratefully recorded in his diary entry of 31 July 1914 that he was getting to 'Bed at 11.30',[5] only to be woken an hour and a quarter later by the Prime Minister, Herbert Asquith, who had arrived for an emergency meeting. The entry continues, 'I got up and saw him in the Audience Room and he showed me a draft telegram he wanted me to send to Nicky as a last resort to try and prevent War, which of course I did. Went to bed again at 1.40.'[6]

Both men were in a state of shock, and now knew they had underestimated the real threat of war. George wondered, 'Whether we shall be dragged into it God only knows . . . France is begging us to come to their assistance. At this moment public opinion is dead against our joining in the War, but I think it will be impossible to keep out of it as we cannot allow France to be smashed.'

On 1 August 1914, Nicholas was unusually late for dinner at the Alexander Palace. Sensing something was seriously wrong the Tsarina sent Tatiana to find her father. He then suddenly appeared, white-faced, and told the family, emotionally, that war with Germany had been declared. He tried to explain to the children how it had been provoked by the assassination of Austrian Archduke Franz Ferdinand on a visit to the Serbian capital Sarajevo, when his chauffeur took a wrong turn and the assassins were waiting. The Empress burst into tears, and, seeing their mother's distress, the children also began to cry.

Later, whispering on the telephone to a friend, Baroness Sophie Buxhoeveden, the Tsarina told her, 'War is declared'. The lady-in-

waiting replied, 'Good Heavens! So Austria has done it!', thinking it
a reprisal for the murder of the heir to the Austro-Hungarian
Empire. But Alix replied, 'No, no. Germany. It is ghastly, terrible,
but God will help and will save Russia.'

The actual declaration of hostilities on 1 August 1914 was tersely
described by the King in his diary for the momentous day; he wrote,
'I held a Council at 10.45 to declare war with Germany', and added,
'May and I with David went onto the balcony, the cheering was
terrific.' Sounding a more sombre, personal note as a father, he was
apprehensive about his second son, Prince Albert, a serving officer
on HMS *Collingwood*. After one of the most traumatic days of his
reign, he ended his diary with a plea, 'Please God, it may soon be
over and that He will protect dear Bertie's life.'

That evening, Sir Edward Grey, Foreign Secretary, said
emotionally, 'The lights are going out all over Europe. We shall not
see them lit again in our lifetime', a phrase which has endured,
capturing the sad futility of the First World War.*

Typically, George began his 4 August 1915 diary with a
pedestrian weather report: 'warm . . . showers and windy'. It was
just an ordinary day except for the fact that he had just declared
war. Whatever their circumstances, no matter how trying, the two
Emperors hardly ever let a day go by without a mention of the
weather; whether they were about to be married, crowned or, in the
Tsar's case, murdered, there was usually an attentive eye to any
change in climate.

Nicholas was jubilant; to him the good news was that 'England
has declared war on Germany'. He and cousin George, the two
powerful Emperors, were now pitted against the Kaiser who, even
when Germany had declared war on Russia, sent Nicholas a
telegram saying, 'It is not I who will bear the responsibility for the
terrible disaster which now threatens the civilised world. You and
you alone can still avert it', an outrageous suggestion by the
aggressor to the mildest and least aggressive of men.[7]

On 2 August 1914,† three days after Russia had declared war,
Nicholas appeared on the rarely used ceremonial balcony above the
Grand Entrance of the Winter Palace. Never had he been more loved

---

*   At the time Lord Grey was actually watching the gas street lights being dimmed
    in Downing Street.
†   20 July according to the Russian calendar.

by the Russian people as they cried out '*Batiushka*', Little Father, with such feeling it was almost an act of worship. Carrying icons and portraits of their Tsar, fired by patriotism, thousands fell to their knees in the Palace Square, moved by the soaring notes of the Russian national anthem, '*Bózhe Tsaryá Khraní*', meaning God save the Tsar. Nicholas, who believed it was 'a righteous war',[8] now spoke movingly to his people, and told them, 'From this place, the very heart of Russia, I send my soul's greetings to my valiant troops.' Hearing this great crowd singing 'Save us, Lord', and seeing them thronging to catch a glimpse of him, his eyes filled with tears and humbly he crossed himself. A Cossack carried the Tsarevich in his arms. It was the last time that the Tsarina, with her 'hard tragic face', would be cheered so warmly.

In England George's leadership qualities were positively enhanced by the war. He showed an ability to take command, and his quick grasp of military strategy impressed ministers and senior officers.

Morally brave, still he could never take official visits to the Front in his stride, and actually had to force himself to visit wounded soldiers. He watched operations in field and base hospitals. Hating the sight of blood and bandages, he later confessed to 'a lady of the Court',[9] 'You can't conceive what I suffered going round those hospitals during the war.' On one visit to the Front in March 1918, a soldier, spotting a familiar, bearded figure dressed in khaki pounding down the ward towards him could only squawk, 'Gawd, the *King*', and fell back on his pillows.[10] As a gesture to the serving soldiers, throughout the war the King was always seen in uniform.

George kept a meticulous record of the 300 hospitals he visited during four years of hostilities, the 50,000 decorations he personally conferred and the 450 inspections he held.[11] During one inspection in France in October 1915, his horse became frightened by the three cheers given by the troops. It reared straight up and fell back on top of the King, resulting in, as he put it himself, 'An . . . infernal bad fall which completely knocked the wind out of me'. Unusually, this diary entry for 28 October 1915 was not in his own handwriting. He never completely recovered from this fall but liked to joke that it had permanently cured his indigestion.[12] However, he was not as strong physically as he liked to appear; he had been weakened by typhoid fever as a young man. Never robust, he was slight, and his 10 stone 5 pound weight never changed.

After each of the five visits he paid to France during the war, George always returned to the compulsory task of clearing the 'boxes' which had accumulated during his absence, a task he sometimes found almost too much to bear. He liked to be kept up to date, and a salon at Buckingham Palace was converted into a war room, one wall covered with a thirty-foot-long map marking the positions of the troops, the trenches, the Dreadnoughts.[13] The Tsar on the other hand relied on the wireless.

As part of his own war effort, alcohol was banned at the palace, although it was not unusual for the King to slip away after dinner for a little unfinished 'business', which seemed to revolve neatly around a glass of port. Balmoral was shut down, and the royal gardens were turned over to vegetables, mainly potatoes. The heating in the palaces was switched off for the duration of the war. He also gave up shooting, which was a real hardship. One of the few wartime pleasures left was checking his stamp collection; the sight of so many beautiful and costly stamps in meticulous order kept a tense King fairly calm.

For Nicholas, giving the order for mobilisation and the start of the war, which Alix hated, was almost the fulfilment of a boyish dream. While he may have had a romantic view of life as a soldier, it was not something shared by most of his subjects. They knew it was a life sentence rather than an opportunity to dress up in a handsome uniform taking, or in their case giving, salutes. Military service was so hated in Russia that during his father's and grandfather's reigns men facing call-up would often amputate the index trigger finger of the right hand.[14] Conviction for this offence could mean life imprisonment, but, for those conscripted, the alternative was equally dismal. Even in relatively peaceful times, whenever a peasant received his papers he went to confession, received absolution, then a wake was held, for the villagers knew he would never be seen again.

Nicholas desperately wanted to lead his soldiers himself; he was proud of the colonel's epaulettes conferred on him by Alexander III for his army service as a young man. His few wise advisers successfully persuaded him to appoint his cousin, Grand Duke Nicholas, as Commander-in-Chief of the Russian Armies; he not only looked the part but was held in high regard by the military.

Deprived of command, Nicholas did the next best thing and travelled over 50,000 miles on the royal train during the first two years of the war. He visited dugouts and hospitals, climbed over destroyed ramparts and ventured into the danger zones, or as near as his cousin would allow. Dressed in a coarse khaki shirt and the same style of greatcoat as an ordinary recruit, the Tsar strode around the celebrated training camp at Krasnoye Selo, where horse races described by Tolstoy in *Anna Karenina* had once been held during the festive season.

Nicholas's escapist reading on his journeys to and from army headquarters was not always the great Russian writers. In a childlike note to his wife, he told her how moved he had been by 'a charming tale about Little Boy Blue!', confessing, 'I had to resort to my handkerchief several times.'

At the beginning of the war, the Russian First and Second Armies powered forward into Poland but found their sabres and lances were hopelessly inadequate against the Germans' sophisticated machine guns and artillery, which scythed down Russian cavalrymen in the gloomy forests of Tannenberg. Nor did the infantry fare much better; despite its vast manpower the Russian military planning was wholly inadequate for a twentieth-century war, and support systems were virtually non-existent. When an infantry soldier's ammunition bandolier was exhausted he had no means of fighting back under enemy fire. They 'were absolutely unarmed'. Soldiers had been trained with sticks instead of rifles, and were 'actually sent into the trenches with no equipment'.[15] As there were not enough weapons to go round, the young recruit often had to wait for another soldier to be killed before he could lay hands on a rifle.

In the first five months of the war, by the end of 1914, the Russians had lost a million men. Still Nicholas never wavered in his commitment to war, reassuring army personnel and telling them how Russia's enemies 'together with their allies shall pay for all we have spent'.[16]

The following year began more encouragingly, with a Russian advance that overran the Austrians, capturing their major fortress at Przemsyl and occupying most of the territory through the Carpathian Mountains. But directly the German heavy artillery came into action, pounding the Russian trenches, there were 15,000 casualties in just four hours.

News of Russia's early success prompted what turned out to be an untimely letter of congratulation, dated 13 July 1915, from Buckingham Palace: 'I am overjoyed,' the King wrote, 'at the splendid advance your gallant troops are making in Galicia and in your Western Provinces.' He could not resist a tongue-in-cheek dig at the Kaiser. 'William's speech at Kiel about the great Naval victory of the German fleet made me laugh . . . am quite convinced that they lost more ships and more men than we did and we drove them back into their ports'.

These successes notwithstanding, Russia was facing military failure. Grand dukes and generals racked their brains, wondering why things were going so dismally wrong, remembering wistfully the great parades on the Field of Mars, when the country's man-power, at these spectacular military pageants, 'filled every Russian heart with pride and the feeling of invincibility'.

Judged by appearances, the Tsar's generals should have commanded the world with ease, magnificent in their grey astrakhan hats, made from the wool of newborn lambs, and tall in Cossack leather boots and long-waisted Circassian greatcoats. But, sadly, much of it was show; many of the grand dukes looked commanding, but, all the same, behind 'an admirable face' there was often 'nothing, green eyes, broad shoulders, fine hands . . . they drink just not to be afraid'. This was designer Coco Chanel's bitter view years later, after she had been jilted by Grand Duke Dmitri. 'Tall, handsome, superb these Russians are,' she said, 'but behind that is nothing – hollowness and vodka.'

The Tsar's cousin Grand Duke Nicholas was the exception. He not only looked imposing but was able to hold the Tsar's armies together, even in the face of defeat. By the autumn of 1915 Russian casualties numbered 1.4 million, and almost a million more would be taken prisoner. The hard truth was that for every 100 tsarist soldiers who fell in battle, 300 surrendered.[17]

The Kaiser's troops were storming relentlessly ahead across the Polish border towards the Baltic, and the fear was they would soon seize Petrograd, as St Petersburg had been renamed at the beginning of the war. The Tsarina was now urging her husband to be more 'like Ivan the Terrible',[18] telling him that he must now take personal charge of the army. Above all, she insisted, he must get rid of Grand Duke Nicholas, who was becoming a more authoritative figure than the Tsar. In fact it was Alix herself who was fulfilling that role, as Rasputin, her malevolent 'other voice', urged her to act as regent in the Tsar's absence. She listened to her 'mountebank confidant',[19] but kept sending messages to Nicholas at military headquarters, including one telling him to 'Remember to comb your hair before all difficult talks and decisions'. An English upbringing should have taught Alix how a constitutional monarch should behave; but under Rasputin's spell any hopes that she could be an enlightened influence on the Tsar evaporated in a poisonous atmosphere.

In the late summer of 1915, Warsaw fell, a catastrophic blow to Russian morale that enabled the Tsarina to have her way. On 5 August Nicholas made the calamitous decision to remove his cousin as Commander-in-Chief. This was the moment when this unworldly autocrat put his signature to his own death warrant; taking control of the army was the worst decision of his life. He was now Supreme Commander, even though he had never fought on a battlefield.[20]

Nevertheless, the Tsar believed he had made the right decision. He later told the King enthusiastically in a letter from headquarters dated 7 September 1915, 'In this serious time my country is going through, I decided to take over the leadership of my Armies in my own hands. In announcing to you this fact I once more express my conviction that with God's help and through the combined efforts of the Allies then . . . victory will crown this bloody war. Love to you and May.'

His impressive 6-foot-5 cousin, humiliated by the Tsar, dismissed from his post as Head of the Russian Army, behaved impeccably. He was given the fine-sounding title of Viceroy and Commander-in-Chief in the Caucasus. When a crisis developed, the Tsar begged him to take command again on the Russo-German Front, but it was too late. Physically declining, he preferred to indulge his passion for porcelain, English etchings and hunting scenes. In 1929, aged seventy-two, he died of pneumonia in France, still being spoken of as 'the ablest royal soldier since Frederick the Great'.

The Dowager Empress instinctively felt that Nicholas was now moving towards 'inevitable ruin', and she blamed her daughter-in-law. Like many a doting mother, she said of her son, 'It was not my dear boy who did this!' And she was right. Her great fear, which proved horribly true, was that Nicholas could now be held responsible for everything that went wrong in Russia, and blamed for the millions of war dead.

In the spring of 1916 the Tsar and Tsarina toured southern Russia. While he reviewed troops, Alix and her daughters inspected hospitals, going about in heavy mackintoshes and tucking up their skirts because of the torrential rain. Tatiana was a great favourite with the soldiers: they called her *lanye*, meaning 'a doe'.

In wartime the Tsarina, calling herself 'a sister of charity', helped oversee the setting up of eighty-five hospitals, including one Red Cross Hospital with Lady Sybil Grey and Lady Dorothy Paget. Being gentle with the wounded soldiers, she was seen as human and caring. Alix proved herself surprisingly capable, explaining, 'I learnt to do useful things in England . . . I've never forgotten what I owe to my English upbringing.'[21] She assisted doctors during primitive operations without anaesthetic, 'taking amputated legs and arms from the surgeons' hands . . . breathing in all the stench and viewing all the horror'. Afterwards she said it had been the only time in her life when she felt a true sense of pride, satisfying her Victorian desire to do good.

In spite of her solicitude for the wounded, in her own circle Alix's image was still often one of disapproval. Mrs Marina Bowater, whose mother had nursed alongside the Empress at Tsarskoe Selo, said later: 'I heard from my mother, known as Sister Paltova, about her chilliness. During those three years of the war, she never once saw her smile. She was always morose and withdrawn.' But her mother also told her that the Empress, 'who always seemed to emanate sadness and quiet but not tranquillity', did occasionally cry out with the pain of sciatica.[22]

In her Cotswold-stone house in Cirencester, frail but still possessing an *ancien régime* elegance, her hands covered with rings, and wearing huge pearl earrings, Mrs Bowater's china-doll blue eyes were quietly expressive when she spoke of the Tsarina who was unpopular and 'dismissive of people at court, contemptuously calling someone a "real muzhik"', but the Tsar, she said, was 'utterly charming'. Pointing to four signed photographs of the imperial family in antique silver frames, she explained, 'These were given to my mother by Grand Duchess Tatiana, whom my mother adored . . . but her memories of the Empress were not happy'.

As Commander-in-Chief, in the company of his fellow officers, assured of their loyalty, Nicholas still felt confident. He brought the Tsarevich to the front in December 1915, took him for walks through meadows and beech forests with his English setters bounding ahead after rabbits. Man and boy enjoyed playing at being real soldiers. Father and 'Sunbeam' – his parents' pet name for Alexei – wrapped in Caucasian mufflers, shared the soldierly life and ate cabbage soup and kasha.* In spite of this calorific diet, people were

---

* A mush of buckwheat groats.

shaken by the change in the Emperor's appearance. By 1916 he 'had greatly aged and his cheeks were sunken'. Count Constantine Benckendorff told the Tsar's doctor that he thought Nicholas had become 'quite apathetic', going through his 'daily routine like an automaton, paying more attention to the hour set for his meals than to affairs of state'. The Tsar, he thought, was 'a changed man', unable to rule Russia or command his army.

Anxious about the Tsar's state of mind, his wife was haunted by the memory of his 'lonely, pale face with big sad eyes' when he left for GHQ. Writing home to her like a schoolboy, he told her how useful he was finding his hanging trapeze. 'I swung on it many times and climbed up it before meals. It is really an excellent thing for the train, it stirs up the blood and the whole organism.' The trapeze was one of the few things he was allowed to take with him to Ekaterinburg in 1917.

The mood of despair on the battlefields was spreading. By 1916 the army on the Eastern Front had begun to rebel, the troops were disaffected and there was open discontent. The constant roll-calls of the dead prompted vicious anti-German feelings in the cities. St Petersburg had already lost its charming but Germanic name in 1914 at the beginning of the war, when Nicholas decided that his capital should sound more Russian and thus patriotically renamed it Petrograd. In 1916, a mood of hopelessness and despair, with 1.2 million men lost in the summer of that year,[23] provoked a wave of hostile whispering against the Tsarina, blaming her for her German ancestry. The same mood infected Britain, with the result that in 1917 her brother-in-law, Princess Victoria's husband, Lord Louis of Battenberg, was dismissed as First Lord of the Admiralty. Feelings of xenophobia were running very high. The King, always sensitive to mood – he had already changed his own family name of Saxe-Coburg to Windsor – thought it expedient to oblige the Battenbergs to become Mountbattens in order to sound more English.

In a concerned letter to the Dowager Empress dated 28 October 1917, Xenia could not help wondering, 'What would have happened if dear Papa was still alive? Would there have been war, disorder, intellectual ferment, dissents . . . I think not.' Both women were appalled at the way in which Alix had seized control as unofficial regent while Nicholas was away at the front. Although this was permissible under the Russian constitution, it gave her enemies enough ammunition to hold her responsible for the disasters still to come, which led ultimately to the collapse of the monarchy.

An apocryphal story about the Tsarevich was now doing the rounds in St Petersburg. The boy was seen weeping in a corner when the war was at its height. When asked why he was so sad, he replied, 'Well, when the Russians are beaten, my father cries. When the Germans lose a battle, my mother cries', whereupon he tearfully enquired, 'When am I to cry?'[24]

The seedlings of revolution were sprouting. The suffering masses were taking to the streets to protest about food shortages, and lack of the barest essentials needed to sustain life. The Tsar's divine authority suddenly seemed futile when a child was dying of malnutrition in its mother's arms, and there was bitter talk about 'the incapable Tsar'. With uncanny foresight, philosophically Nicholas assumed 'I mean to be the victim', quietly accepting his fate as the scapegoat needed to save Russia.

The war lasted for four years, three months and ten days. Russia lost nearly two million men, twice as many as Britain, and was utterly devastated. Nicholas, his army defeated, was still at the 'head of Europe's largest war-machine'[25] in February 1917, but for only one more year.

After the Armistice was signed on 11 November 1918 the King, reviewing 30,000 wounded servicemen on horseback in Hyde Park, was almost mobbed by a surge of soldiers and sailors. Normally there would have been a gruff rebuke, but, deeply moved, on this occasion he found it difficult to speak. Instead he made sure that each man was sent a personal copy of his speech, in which he told them how glad he had been to have had the chance to look 'into the faces of those who for the defence of Home and the Empire were ready to give up their all, and have sacrificed limbs, sight, hearing and health'.[26]

With the war finally over, the King's firm leadership was being applauded; although a huge number of widows and mothers were mourning husbands and sons, the nation still appreciated that George had taken the right line against the Kaiser. It may have sounded disloyal of the King, but he said of his German relatives during the war, 'They are my kinsmen but I am ashamed of them.' Now, driving with Queen Mary in triumph through the streets of London, he felt indebted to his people.

NINETEEN

Sparkling Cyanide

The Tsarina, distraught with sadness about her son, began to be attracted to zealots who claimed mystic powers. These holy men roaming around Russia, convinced God was speaking through them, were known as holy fools. The most infamous of these was Rasputin. The self-proclaimed monk could ease the Tsarevich's pain even from miles away and, with his beautiful hands and wild, 'coldly piercing' eyes,[1] he would captivate and destroy the Tsarina.

Two exotic Montenegrins were always blamed for introducing the impressionable Empress to Rasputin: Grand Duchess Melitza, wife of Grand Duke Peter, and her sister Stana. Known as the 'Black Crows' at the imperial court, they had convinced her that the true spirit of Russia could only be found in the simple, good peasant. To the emotionally needy Alix, the magnetic, semi-literate *starets*, who was so vain, 'he had dark red snow-nets on his sleigh to match his beard', enthralled her with his hysterical, hypnotic spirituality and compelling personality.

Once he became a court favourite, Melitza's grandson, Prince Nicholas Romanov,[2] says, 'He changed from being a simple holy man from the backwoods of Russia to become thoroughly corrupt, whoring in Moscow and St Petersburg, seducing stupid ladies who believed in his magic ideas, advising the Emperor on military matters, and unfortunately the Empress on who to choose to run the country.'

In defence of his grandmother and her sister, he points out that they quickly detached themselves from Rasputin when they realised his malign influence, but the Tsarina never forgave them and cut them coldly out of her circle. Alexandra, like many a mother of a sick child, fell under the spell of Rasputin if only because he seemed to ease the Tsarevich's suffering.

An intriguing figure in St Petersburg, although he smelt, Rasputin was mesmeric. He symbolised society's 'bit of rough'. Fyodor Dostoevsky always claimed that in the simple uneducated peasant a simple truth could be found. The trouble was that this could hardly be said of Rasputin, the former horse-thief. Nobody ever knew if he would sink to his knees in a religious ecstasy or set fire to a dacha.

Claiming to be a monk, embracing an austere way of life, Rasputin travelled round the holy places of Russia, visited Jerusalem, prepared a book of *Meditations* and was often seen in a prayer-induced ecstasy. Socialites, abandoning their brocade and pearl-studded dresses for peasant smocks, followed him to Siberian villages, gladly cavorting through meadows and into the bathhouse, captivated by a rascally pied piper. He could dance for hours, attend an orgy and then be seen attending matins.

During one particularly harsh winter he went outside the city, dug a hole in the snow and, jumping in, announced, 'I will live as an ascetic and you throw me rich herrings!' Far from having to rely on the humble oily fish, he was brought baskets of delicious titbits by St Petersburg's fashionable women, who not only hand-fed the holy man but jumped into the freezing trench beside him.

Such was his power at court that Alix suggested to Nicholas that she should bring Rasputin to Stavka, the site of Russian military headquarters. To a man, the soldiers objected; they did not want the phoney monk's blessing. This refusal of an imperial request was unprecedented. Rasputin had once in 1905 asked if he could come to Stavka to bless an icon. Grand Duke Nicholas had replied, 'Yes, do come and I'll hang you.'[3] Now, for once, Nicholas was firm, and forbade Alix to bring Rasputin; so she arrived alone, although the wives were not allowed at military headquarters.

At the Alexander Palace, governesses and nursery-maids began to notice how often the monk liked to appear suddenly at the girls' bath time, taking the opportunity to tuck them up afterwards in bed. Outraged by this familiarity, when Sophie Tiutcheva, a lady-in-waiting, reported these slightly prurient encounters to the Tsarina, she was fired instantly.

Rasputin dealt in drugs and prescribed strange Tibetan and Chinese concoctions for the Tsar, who had an incipient heart condition, the result of stress. Soon the knives were out for Rasputin who was nevertheless a convenient excuse for those forces hostile to the Tsarina that were baying for the blood of the long-lashed *Nemka* [German woman]. Gossips claimed he was having sexual relations with her; even if Alix had publicly appeared on the balcony of the

Winter Palace announcing that Rasputin was being banished to Siberia, they would not have been satisfied. There was now serious alarm among advisers close to the Tsar about his wife's reliance on the 'mad monk'.

'My poor daughter-in-law does not perceive that she is ruining both the dynasty and herself.' The Dowager Empress was close to tears as she mournfully discussed Rasputin's malevolent influence at the imperial court. 'She sincerely believes in the holiness of an adventurer,' she said, and added prophetically, 'We are powerless to ward off the misfortune which is sure to come.'[4]

Steps were now being put in motion to rid the court of Rasputin; even the British secret service was allegedly involved.* In the end the task, which proved macabrely difficult to complete, was taken up by one of St Petersburg's gilded noblemen, Prince Felix Yussopov, son of the richest woman in Russia.[5]

He was married to Xenia's compellingly attractive daughter Irina, a favourite niece of the Tsar, who gave them a bag of twenty-nine diamonds as a wedding present. In St Petersburg and Moscow she held legendary soirées fussing over artists, including the prima ballerina Pavlova, who danced in the Yussopov private rococo theatre.

Felix, because of his close ties to the imperial family, felt that something now had to be done about Rasputin. Suave, effete, rich and spoilt, Yussopov seemed an unlikely candidate to be a murderer, although he did have accomplices. He really was happier cross-dressing, once looking so fetching he hoodwinked a bedazzled King Edward VII. With a group of friends, he liked to dress up in his mother's clothes and jewellery, then, 'muffled in fur-lined, velvet pelisses',[6] they sashayed out along Nevsky Prospekt. Sometimes, after too much champagne, Felix enjoyed lassooing other guests in restaurants with a long string of real pearls.

---

* *Timewatch: Who Killed Rasputin?*, BBC2, 1 October 2004. John Scale, a British secret service agent, met Rasputin and had never before known anyone 'with such an aura of evil', according to his 91-year-old daughter Muriel Harding Newman. Her father, who died in 1947, was away with the Tsar on the night of the murder. Another British agent, Oswald Rayner, who had been up at Oxford with Yussopov, was apparently in the palace that night but destroyed all his papers. The question remains unresolved of who put the third bullet into Rasputin.

The cousins. *Left:* Nicholas aged three, a touchingly confident-looking future Tsar of All the Russias. *Right:* George, also three, fetching in a frothy confection.

A family group at Cowes, 1909. Back row, left to right: Prince Edward, future Duke of Windsor; the Tsar's aunt, Queen Alexandra; Princess Mary; Princess Victoria; Grand Duchesses Olga and Tatiana. Sitting: the Duchess of York, later Queen Mary; Nicholas II of Russia; Edward VII; the Tsarina; the Duke of York, later King George V, with a protective arm round Grand Duchess Marie. Seated in front: the Tsarevich; Grand Duchess Anastasia.

Left: Prince John painstakingly autographed this photograph for one of the housekeepers at York Cottage, Sandringham. *Right:* The sisters Queen Alexandra (left) and Dowager Marie Feodorovna of Russia, in 1911, in the cluttered conservatory at Hvidøre in Denmark.

A formal imperial family group in 1914 before the devastation of the war and Nicholas's forced abdication. Standing: Marie; the Tsarina; Anastasia. Seated: Olga; the Tsar; the Tsarevich; Tatiana.

The coronation procession of Tsar Nicholas II of Russia, May 1896.

The coronation of King George V of Great Britain at Westminster Abbey, 22 June 1911.

Left: Nicholas II and George with their heirs Prince Edward and the Tsarevich at Cowes, 1909. The two men liked to emphasise their resemblance by dressing alike. *Right:* Nicholas and the Duke of Connaught at Balmoral, September 1896.

A pensive British royal family group at Balmoral, 1905. Left to right standing: Princess Mary; Queen Alexandra with her ubiquitous Pekinese; Princess Louise, next to her brother, later George V; Alexander Duff, Duke of Fife, in a tweed cap unusual for a royal indoor occasion; Prince Edward alongside his statuesque aunt Princess Victoria. Seated: the daughters of the Duke and Duchess of Fife; at their feet, Prince Albert, later George VI; the Duchess of York with Prince George, Duke of Kent and Prince Henry, Duke of Gloucester.

Nicholas II inspecting Russian troops at the Great Palace, Peterhof, an unlikely setting for a military parade, 1910.

Left: George V made several visits to the Western Front during the First World War, his insistence on getting close to the action necessitating a tin hat. *Right:* Nicholas II with George V in Berlin for the wedding of Kaiser Wilhelm II's favourite daughter Princess Victoria Louise of Prussia, May 1913.

A confident Kaiser with Tsar Nicholas II, superficially in harmony, on their way to Princess Victoria Louise's wedding in Berlin.

Below, left: Sir George Buchanan, 1912. To many Russians he was almost a caricature of the perfect British diplomat. *Right:* Royal family group at the wedding of the Duke of York to Lady Elizabeth Bowes-Lyon, 26 April 1923. Back row, left to right: Prince of Wales; Prince Henry, Duke of Gloucester; George V; the bridegroom, Duke of York; Prince George, Duke of Kent. In front are the Princess Royal and her mother Queen Mary.

Above: A courageous attempt at a smile by Nicholas and three of his daughters under house arrest and the prurient gaze of their captors.

Right: The bald headline, 'Ex-Tsar Shot', in *The Times*, 22 July 1918, confirms the worst.

Below: The end. Nicholas after his abdication sitting on the stump of a tree he had cut down himself. Once a mighty Tsar and autocrat, he is now plain Citizen Romanov. Mourning the downfall of his empire his simple dignified pose has a certain grace.

EX-TSAR SHOT.
OFFICIAL APPROVAL OF CRIME.

The following news is transmitted through the wireless stations of the Russian Government :—

" At the first session of the Central Executive Committee elected by the Fifth Congress of the Councils a message was made public, received by direct wire from the Ural Regional Council, concerning the shooting of the ex-Tsar, Nicholas Romanoff.

" Recently Ekaterinburg, the capital of the Red Ural, was seriously threatened by the approach of the Czecho-Slovak bands. At the same time a counter-revolutionary conspiracy was discovered, having for its object the wresting of the tyrant from the hands of the Council's authority by armed force.

" In view of this fact the Presidium of the Ural Regional Council decided to shoot the ex-Tsar, Nicholas Romanoff. This decision was carried out on July 16.

" The wife and son of Romanoff have been sent to a place of security. Documents concerning the conspiracy which was discovered have been forwarded to Moscow by a special messenger.

" It had been recently decided to bring the ex-Tsar before a tribunal, to be tried for his crimes against the people, and only later occurrences led to delay in adopting this course. The Presidency of the Central Executive Committee, after having discussed the circumstances which compelled the Ural Regional Council to take the decision to shoot Nicholas Romanoff, decided as follows :—' The Russian Central Executive Committee, in the persons of the Presidium, accept the decision of the Ural Regional Council as being regular.'

" The Central Executive Committee has now at its disposal extremely important material and documents concerning the Nicholas Romanoff affair ; his own diaries, which he kept almost to the last days ; the diaries of his wife and children ; his correspondence, amongst which are letters by Gregory Rasputin to Romanoff and his family. All these materials will be examined and published in the near future."

An account of the life of the ex-Tsar appears in the preceding page.

ALLIES ON MURMAN COAST.
TROTSKY'S THREAT TO BRITISH AND FRENCH OFFICERS.

The following news is transmitted through the wireless station of the Russian Government :—

The following order has been given by L. Trotsky :—

" In connexion with the landing of English and French detachments on the Murman coast, and the open participation of French officers with the counter-revolutionary mutineers—the paid Czecho-Slovaks—I order all military institutions and soldiers not to support the French and English naval and military officers; not to permit them to go from one town to another ; to watch carefully all their acts as the acts of persons who, it has been proved, are capable within the territories of the Russian Republic of conspiring against the sovereignty of the Russian people. The causes which have compelled me to issue this order will be explained later."

RUSSIAN CHOLERA EPIDEMIC.
HUNDREDS OF CASES IN MOSCOW.
(FROM OUR OWN CORRESPONDENT.)
STOCKHOLM, JULY 20.

In consequence of the cholera epidemic in Petrograd and the discovery of several cases on steamers arriving in Swedish ports from Russia and Finland, vessels are now bound to call at a quarantine station at Fejan to be disinfected and suspicious cases are interned. The number of such infected cases interned during the past week is 13, and two deaths have occurred.

The following news is transmitted through the wireless stations of the Russian Government :—

On July 19 there were registered in Moscow 26 cases with stomach disease, 75 cases suspected to be cholera, and 224 known to be cholera. As far as we know, within the province of Petrograd 120 cholera cases occurred.

It is proposed to take over without delay all good rooms and make them freely available to the occupants of overcrowded and unhealthy rooms in the workmen's quarters. It is also decided to order the mobilization of the *bourgeoisie* for the formation of health detachments for the struggle against cholera and for the cleansing of the city, those between the ages of 18 and 45 years to be so employed.

GERMANS AND MOSCOW.
(FROM OUR SPECIAL CORRESPONDENT.)
THE HAGUE, JULY 21.

The *Cologne Gazette* says the German Government has arranged with the Soviet Government to protect the German Embassy in Moscow by some hundreds of German soldiers who will be sent there for the purpose. They will wear civilian clothes.

Prince Michael of Kent (centre) in Russia at the reburial of his relative Tsar Nicholas II and his family on 17 July 1998, the eightieth anniversary of the executions.

Nicholas II's simple marble tomb in the Cathedral of St Peter and St Paul in St Petersburg.

The Yussopovs owned seven palaces, and one of their thirty-seven estates stretched for 125 miles along the Caspian Sea. On a visit to Italy, one Yussopov who coveted a marble staircase found it was not available, so he bought the palace. They had 3,000 gardeners. When they gave receptions for the Tsar, the 2,000 guests were all served at the same time with hot food in blue Sèvres Marie Antoinette china from gold and silver containers.[7]

The Yussopov Palace on the Moika Canal in St Petersburg, where Rasputin was murdered, had been given to Felix Yussopov's great-great-grandmother by Catherine II. In the palace there were some 4,500 pieces of art, paintings and sculpture. Even after the Bolsheviks had taken their share of Rembrandts, Velázquez and Angelica Kaufmanns, there were still 2,000 paintings left and 1.5 tons of silver. The palace was nationalised and became the headquarters for teachers; today it can be rented out for social occasions. Regrettably, the crystal bowls once filled with real emeralds, opals and uncut sapphires for decoration are now quite empty.

It is a shock to go into the Yussopov Palace and in the blue-walled cellar come face to face with Rasputin, the 'lusting he-goat', as he was once described by Paléologue, the French Ambassador. There is a cold feeling of menace in this waxwork recreation of the poisonous supper party. The monk, with his protruding cold eyes and his dank black hair parted in the middle, is being plied with wine and cakes; his host Prince Felix Yussopov's darkly sensual good looks and high cheekbones reflect his Tartar origins; Grand Duke Dmitri Pavlovich,* a cousin of the Tsar's and one of the Prince's accomplices, is detached-looking, standing beside the table. The figures look horribly lifelike in this reconstruction of the events of the night of 17 December 1916, when Rasputin was murdered at the Yussopov Palace.

In the drawing room upstairs, with its Fragonard-inspired gold *trompe l'œil* ceiling, someone is playing Mozart's *Turkish Rondo* on the piano. The Yussopovs owned at least 120 musical instruments, including a harpsichord and a Stradivarius, all confiscated by the later Bolsheviks. In the oak dining room a photograph of Queen Elizabeth II, who visited the palace in 1994, is prominently displayed.

---

*   In England he studied economics, and one of his tutors was Dr Hugh Dalton, later Chancellor of Exchequer in the Labour government of 1945.

Rasputin had an uncanny awareness of the approach of his own death. Ten days before he was murdered he wrote to the Tsarina, 'I feel that I shall leave life before January 1st,' adding an eerie warning, 'You must know this: if it was your relations who have wrought my death then no one of your family . . . will remain alive for more than two years. They will be killed by the Russian people.'[8]

An inveterate lecher, Rasputin could never resist a beautiful woman and, flattered, responded warmly to an invitation to the Moika Palace, excited by the prospect of meeting or possibly laying hands on Irina, Yussopov's wife. Arriving at the palace, the intemperate 'monk' heard 'Yankee Doodle Dandy' on the phonograph – the Yussopovs were always the first to have the latest fashionable tunes – then he was taken down to the 'little boys only' den in the cellar, which was used for orgies. He enjoyed wine, poisoned hors d'oeuvres, and little cakes glittering with sparkling cyanide crystals. This 'Borgia-like repast'[9] seemed at first to have no effect on the mad monk.

Glass in hand, Yussopov then invited the monk to give an opinion on a Renaissance crystal crucifix. Rasputin leant forward to examine the objet d'art with a pious 'You can't look too often at the image of Our Lord crucified', only to receive the first of several bullets in the back from his wealthy host.

Upstairs, the accomplices heard the shots and were relieved that Rasputin was dead; all they needed to do now was to throw the tiresome monk's body into the Neva. Grand Duke Dmitri Pavlovich, at twenty-six the youngest of the group, was dispatched to fetch his motor car.

But when Yussopov checked again on his handiwork, he was 'frozen with terror' when the starets, lying apparently lifeless on a white bearskin rug, leapt up. 'Foam was coming out of his mouth; a roar filled the room and . . . bellowing horribly, like a wounded beast, he hurled himself' towards Felix. Ripping off one of his epaulettes, his hand clawing the nobleman's shoulder, Rasputin growled, 'You wretch! You'll be hanged tomorrow!' At this Yussopov managed to tear himself loose from the maniacally strong grip of the dying man, and raced upstairs covered with blood. In a frenzy of fear, he shouted, 'He's still alive! He spoke to me . . . quickly, the revolver, quickly, he's still alive!' Even to these worldly men, this seemed a fearful sign that Rasputin perhaps did have extraordinary powers.

Writhing on the stone floor, Rasputin hauled his wounded body across the snowy palace courtyard and into the street, croaking with his dying breath, 'I'll tell the Tsarina everything.'

The third accomplice, Vladimir Purishkevich, a conservative deputy of the Duma Party, fired and missed. After the fourth shot, Rasputin eventually 'dropped like a stone face downwards in the snow with his head twitching . . . I was sure that now his goose was cooked,' Purishkevich said, resorting to homely language to describe the monk's approaching death. Yussopov had now recovered and, anxious to redeem himself, violently smashed the monk's head with a bronze candlestick. The body was thrown into the Neva from the Petrovski Bridge but later emerged through the ice on New Year's Day 1917. It had to be thawed out over two days and nights.[10] The Tsar was in 'especially high spirits' when at Mogilev he heard the news about Rasputin's death, and most of that day he 'whistled and hummed'.

At Tsarskoe Selo the utterly devastated Tsarina, exceeding her rights, claiming it was because the Tsar was away, gave orders for the house arrest of Grand Duke Dmitri and Yussopov. When Nicholas returned, he refused to listen to her demand that the murderers should be brought to trial. He knew Rasputin's death had brought great rejoicing in court circles.

The battered corpse was taken secretly to Tsarskoe Selo for royal burial. On 3 January 1917, Alexandra pinned a note to her mentor's body, before it was interred in a plot of land belonging to Anna Vyrubova. Later Rasputin was buried in the tiny Cathedral of St Sophia; it is believed that his penis was preserved in a velvet box. The Tsar punished Prince Dmitri by deporting him to Persia. Grand Duchess Xenia was appalled by the whole episode, particularly as her son-in-law had stayed in her palace the night he committed the murder.

However, the Yussopovs were now described as 'the saviours of Russia'. *The Times* carried a piece offering 'congratulations to the Russian people, rid of the baleful influence of "dark forces" and a "National Disgrace"'.

Felix and his much-admired wife survived the trauma unscathed, and after the Revolution fled to Europe. On the long voyage, Felix Yussopov did his best to relieve the tedium by playing his balalaika but always seemed encumbered by a large parcel, which he never allowed out of his sight. Another passenger, Prince Roman, son of one of the Black Crows and father of Prince Nicholas Romanov, practically fainted when the parcel was unwrapped and he realised he was looking at two Rembrandts. However, in common with many Russian exiles, Felix Yussopov was not a good businessman: he never got the right price for the two Rembrandt paintings, *Portrait of a Gentleman in a High Hat* and *Portrait of a Lady with an Ostrich Feather*, which can be seen today in Washington's National Gallery.

In London, Felix and his wife had a flat in Belgravia, but, like most Russian émigrés, they preferred to spend time in France, where this elegant couple were often seen strolling along the Paris boulevards. Occasionally he went to his mother Zinaida Yussopov's small Château de Keriolet near Concarneau in Brittany. She had married again, this time to a much younger and impoverished suitor Charles de Chaveau; she bought him a couple of titles and the couple rejoiced in their new family motto *Toujours et Quand Même* (Carry On Regardless). When Zinaida died, her son, no lover of the countryside or the simple Breton pastimes captured by Gauguin, had no compunction about selling off the chapel to the local communist mayor who used the ancient stone to build himself a *bricolage* villa. Yussopov was unrepentant.

The ruin of the chapel is like a gaping wound alongside the partially restored fourteenth-century château where his increasingly deaf mother had created alcoves designed so she could hear echoes of the sea. Felix died in 1967, aged eighty, his beautiful wife three years later. The Yussopovs are both buried in the Russian cemetery of Ste Geneviève-des-Bois outside Paris, alongside ballerinas, choreographers and writers. Nearby is La Maison Russe, an old château set up for the care of frail Russian exiles.

Every Easter as the wind sways the bare branches, petals fall like snowflakes on to the white tombs; the graves are visited by some of these elderly Russians, who take with them a piece of *Paschka* cake filled with cream cheese and crystallised fruit to sit in quiet harmony on a tomb. It is the Orthodox belief that visiting the dead is an important part of living and a cheerful way to spend an afternoon.

TWENTY

Jaded Eau-de-Nil

The view from the old British Embassy is still of the gold spire of the Peter and Paul Fortress. Unchanged, the 20,000-year-old Nile sphinxes are as inscrutable as ever. From the French windows, the 'fairy-like'[1] view of the Neva, where great blocks of ice in winter are swept along from Lake Ladoga, is still inspiring. For political, economic and aesthetic reasons, there has been little modern building in St Petersburg, so the imperial city, with its 150 bridges to the 19 islands, remains virtually unchanged since tsarist times.

But the embassy building in the once dark-red Soltikoff Palace is now a jaded eau-de-Nil, drab, with greying net curtains; the elegant interior, with a graceful ballroom on the first floor, is filled with functional fifties office furniture. There is no longer a red carpet covering the double staircase leading to the chancery, where the ambassador reeled in shock when he heard about the King's decision to refuse the Tsar safe haven in England.

Gone, too, is the fashionable roller-skating rink opposite the embassy, where the ambassador's daughter, Meriel Buchanan, was such an enthusiast in the palmy imperialist days. 'If one did not skate,' she said, 'or at least go and look on at the skating, one simply did not exist in Society.'[2] Grand Duke Kyril's wife once held a famous roller-skating ball on the rink at midnight, where the high point was a roller quadrille.

The ambassador, upright with moustache and monocle, was a foreigner's idea of a typical British diplomat. In one of his short stories, Somerset Maugham's* caricature of him was of someone possessing 'a frigidity that would have sent a shiver down the spine of a polar bear'.[3]

To others he appeared a kindly schoolmaster with a 'baffling simplicity',[4] epitomising 'all that the best of England stood for'. He

---

* Maugham, visiting Russia in 1917, made no secret of his socialist sympathies.

was never at ease with the wild revolutionary ideas circulating in St Petersburg and was criticised for living 'so continuously in conservative and official circles that all parties of the Left, whether Cadets or Social Revolutionaries, seemed to him to be equally dangerous'.[5]

The appointment to St Petersburg, was considered a plum, although during the Revolution it became the 'most difficult diplomatic post in Europe'. The ambassador found he was dealing with a courtly, remote Tsar, and entrée to the Russian court was difficult. But Sir Frank Lascelles, the British Ambassador to Berlin, might have envied such difficulties, as often he was woken by the Kaiser bursting into his bedroom at six in the morning, berating him for not being at his desk.[6] The opposite was true for Buchanan, who complained that he hardly ever saw the Tsar, because 'of his preference for living outside the capital'.[7]

While trying diligently to keep in tune with the wishes of George V, and admiring his attention to detail, Buchanan found the King less inspiring than Edward VII, who had always fully enjoyed foreign affairs.

Visitors to the embassy in St Petersburg found Buchanan's study, hung with portraits of King George V and Queen Mary, reassuring. The Buchanans furnished the embassy state rooms with gold baroque chairs which they had picked up in a market in Naples, a gold chandelier from a castle on the Rhine, an Aubusson carpet, and a decorative writing table which had belonged to Marie Antoinette. So many palaces and houses in Russia had memorabilia from the ill-fated French Queen's collection of objets d'art at Versailles.[8]

The Buchanans were a popular couple. Lady Georgina had been brought up in Gloucestershire in the sylvan setting of Cirencester Park with its grace-and-favour houses nestling round flowery Cicely Hill. She was beautiful, with fair hair and compelling eyes. Her father, Lord Bathurst, had disapproved of Sir George, the younger son of a Scottish baronet, as a suitor, dismissing him as an impecunious fellow without prospects. But the couple were eventually allowed to marry when Georgina 'out of sheer depression and misery' developed jaundice, forcing her father to relent. Their daughter Meriel was born at the Bathurst home.

When the Buchanans arrived in Russia from the Hague in 1910, the British Embassy was still in a state of half-mourning for

Edward VII.* Their first impression of Russia, which they grew to love, was of an indefinable smell, not of exotic candles and incense, but of a concoction of leather sheepskin coats, cabbage soup and sunflower oil. When their train stopped at Wirballen, a Russian Empire frontier town, the imperial waiting rooms were opened specially for them, and a 'wizened little Tartar waiter with a yellow face and a completely bald head' served them memorable 'plates of steaming cabbage soup, and little birds like partridges cooked in sour cream'.[9]

The ambassador, who relied on a small staff, liked to write his own dispatches by hand. 'My first impression was of a typing . . . bureau conducted by old Etonians. British agent Sir Robert Bruce-Lockhart was shocked at the waste. 'Here,' he said scornfully, 'was a collection of young men, all of whom had thousands of pounds spent on their education, who had passed a difficult examination . . . yet . . . were occupied for hours on end in work which could have been performed just as efficiently by a second-division clerk.'[10] The principal attaché, Sir Charles Eliot, was an expert on sea slugs. Apart from an English butler, an Italian chef, a porter, footman, chauffeur and numerous housemaids, it was the muzhiks, or serfs, who kept the embassy whirring and the birch log fires blazing.

Indispensable was William the Chasseur, who always carried a sword and, when the wind whistled round the city, made sure there was a fox-fur rug and hot-water bottle in the coach for the ambassador. Ivan, the bearded coachman with piercing Tartar eyes, in his long 'sapphire-blue coat . . . tied round the waist with a gold belt',[11] drove like a fury with both arms stretched out, the blue reins wound tightly round his fur-gloved hands. The stately ambassador was whisked round the city by Ivan, who would bring the two long-maned greys to an abrupt halt outside the palace or embassy they were visiting, and with a vigorous shout announce their arrival. The Buchanans had also brought an English car and chauffeur to Russia.

Nicknamed 'Fluffy Ruffles'[12] by the Tsarina's brother-in-law, Grand Duke Sergei, the ambassador's daughter chafed against the insistence that she must wear black in mourning for the late King. All around her, women of the court were wearing low-cut evening

---

* At this time full mourning was observed at court for three months after the death of the sovereign.

dresses and imperial two-headed eagle diamond clasps on pale shoulders. Her mother, a forthright woman, considered low necklines worn in the daytime 'vulgar and second rate',[13] forcing her daughter to wear modest English 'Peter Pan' collars.

In St Petersburg, when they were seventeen, young girls put their hair up to show off a delicate neckline, all the better to catch a grand duke and be driven off by him at the wheel of an Hispano-Suiza. Those who were not engaged were chaperoned to a *Bal Blanc*, where white was compulsory. These cygnets, or debutantes, then lined up behind a huge hedge of pink roses before reaching over to take the hand of an unseen partner to dance the cotillion and be given posies of little silver bells tied with velvet ribbon.

For a well-brought-up young Englishwoman, this was thrilling, so unlike a hunt ball in the Vale of the White Horse country. Young Meriel now danced in ballrooms scented with roses and carnations, brought specially from the south of France. Officers in ornate, gold-braided uniforms whisked daughters of the nobility into a final quadrille to the heart-stirring music of Colombo's Band. But the protocol was strict: the Tsar forbade his officers, if in uniform, to dance the tango or the one-step,[14] which were considered too provocative. Outside, coachmen huddled, blowing into their hands in the glittery cold night as they waited to take the dancers home at great speed, when the horses' hooves would throw up crisp slivers of ice.

During the day, the ambassador's wife and daughter liked to take tea at fashionable Conradi's on Nevsky Prospekt, enjoying rose-leaf jam and hot honey cakes before visiting exclusive boutiques. Druce's was the celebrated meeting place for the foreign community, where they bought Floris soap, tweed from Scotland or Atkinson's *eau de toilette*. It was known as the 'Druce habit'[15] at a time when anything English was considered stylish and exclusive. Shops had charmingly painted signs showing their speciality: bales of material and scissors if it was a tailor's, or an umbrella for Tremen, the German weather shop.

The ambassador's idea of relaxation was not bear-shooting but a round of golf at Mourina, a little village 20 miles away on a course created by the English colony. His golf earned him an oblique compliment in the *Hamburger Nachrichten* in 1917. 'Sir George Buchanan', it said, 'had walked round the golf links of Europe for years, until at last he was able to hole out in Petrograd.'[16]

Lady Georgina was keen to marry off her daughter to a suitable young English aristocrat or landowner. Instead, Meriel fell in love with Grand Duke Alexander 'Sandro' Leuchtenberg, an attractive Russian aristocrat who was aide-de-camp to the Tsar. But the romance could not survive once the King cancelled his invitation to the Tsar. This change of heart was seen by the grand duke as a complete betrayal.

After the summer season, when the diplomatic corps went abroad and the nobility to their estates, the Buchanans returned to England. The ambassador kept hinting at his unease about the Emperor's 'diffident and irresolute' personality, though he admired his 'quick intelligence'. He thought that Nicholas, in spite of his cultivated mind, seemed incapable of making decisions or taking command. He was not considered a patch on his father Alexander III and, worse, the ambassador felt that his choice of wife had been 'unfortunate'.

But to Meriel the Tsar was a benign uncle figure. She never felt intimidated by him, even watching him presiding at the great ceremonial occasions at the Winter Palace like the Blessing of the Waters of the Neva, when he was surrounded by an entourage of grand dukes, courtiers, officers, and Cossack life guards in crimson and blue under their magisterial black cloaks. Hearing the chanting of the Gospel by the bearded Patriarch in his gold vestments, and watching Nicholas plunge the great silver cross into the ice three times with saluting cannons, while the pealing bells competed with Tchaikovsky's *1812 Overture*, never failed to stir the emotions of even the most phlegmatic foreign diplomat.

Meriel was not seeing an all-powerful Emperor of all the Russias, but a kindly, reassuring Tsar who had once comforted her as a child. Her mother had taken her to see *Hänsel und Gretel*, and, at the moment when the witch's cottage was blown up, terrified, she had shut her eyes tightly. When she opened them, she saw the Tsar in the royal box smiling at her. He leaned over to Lady Georgina, saying quietly that he quite understood her daughter's panic. 'Please tell her,' he said, 'that I hated it, too.' 'Child though I was,' Meriel later recalled, 'the singular charm of that smile and the softness of the grey-blue eyes stirred me strangely.'[17]

Unfortunately, this gentleness and compassion was not being directed towards a downtrodden people deprived of their human rights. They had no part in the Tsar's official birthday celebrations when the diplomatic corps, after four hours' standing, watching salutations and march pasts, enjoyed a light lunch of lobster salad, chocolate ice cream, fruit salad and champagne.

Russia had become an agitated mass of discontent as a patient people railed against the inertia of a futile Tsar. A palace revolution was being openly spoken of. Buchanan was warned by a Russian friend that things were so bad, it was a mere question of whether both the Emperor and Empress 'or only the latter would be killed'.[18] Nicholas remained obstinately reluctant to make concessions, unaware of the increasing mood of exasperation and subversiveness.

Horrified, Buchanan sent a note to the Foreign Office on 7 January 1917, saying, 'I am ready, if you think it advisable, to make one more attempt to bring home to the Emperor the gravity of the situation, as well as the danger to which the dynasty may be exposed.'[19]

In this mood, he set off on a mission of conscience to Tsarskoe Selo on 12 January 1917. He seemed not to take into account how the Tsar might feel at being lectured by the British Ambassador, who was a guest in Russia, but Buchanan always claimed, 'I am always careful to represent what I say coming from myself personally.'[20]

The ambassador told Bruce-Lockhart that if 'the Emperor received him sitting down all would be well'.[21] But when he arrived he was 'disagreeably surprised', and admitted his heart 'sank' when he was ushered into the audience chamber to find Nicholas in full uniform, emphasising his authority. The Tsar received him coldly. 'On all previous occasions, His Majesty', Buchanan noted miserably, 'received me informally in his study . . . asking me to sit down.'[22] On these previous visits, the two men had talked amiably and smoked cigarettes together.

Now the ambassador realised he was not welcome and quickly tried to explain that his visit was on the grounds of his devotion to the Tsar and Tsarina. He then began pleading with Nicholas, face to face, 'to break down the barrier that separates you from your people and to regain their confidence'.[23] As a good example, he mentioned Lloyd George's inclusion of a Labour representative in his war cabinet, showing, Buchanan said, 'solidarity between all classes of the population'.

Nicholas looked at him icily, stung by the implied criticism, and sarcastically asked why Buchanan was taking such a pessimistic view. 'Do you mean that I am to regain the confidence of my people or that they are to regain *my* confidence?' The ambassador replied, 'Both, sir'. Sensing the increasing chill and relying on all his diplomatic skills, he began to speak with poetic fervour. 'If I were to see a friend,' he said, 'walking through a wood on a dark night along a path which I knew ended in a precipice, would it not be my duty to warn Your Majesty of the abyss that lies ahead of you? You have, sir, come to the parting of the ways, and you have to choose between two paths.'[24]

Nicholas had one thing in common with Lloyd George, and that was his cynical view of diplomacy, believing ambassadors were 'invented merely to waste time', a comment he made to Prince Sixte of Bourbon Parma in 1917 when there was a move to separate Austria from her allies.[25] Both men agreed with Bismarck's definition of an ambassador as 'A man sent to another country to tell lies for the benefit of his own'.[26]

In an awkward silence, Buchanan waited uneasily until the Tsar, with a reproachful look, turned to him, held out his hand and said, 'I thank you, Sir George'. He was told afterwards by Grand Duke Sergei that if he had been a Russian subject he would have been sent to Siberia for his outspokenness.[27] It had been fatal even to hint at the Tsarina's unpopularity, how her political interference was creating a bad impression that was beginning to set in aspic. The Tsarina loathed Buchanan, partly because he always refused to bow down before the 'saint', as Rasputin was known at Alexander Palace.[28] The ambassador thought her altogether too controlling and never forgot one of her steely asides, when she told him sharply, 'The Emperor unfortunately is weak; but I am not, and I intend to be firm.'[29] Buchanan always believed she was the 'chosen instrument' of her husband's ruin. 'Her Majesty', he declared on one occasion, 'was under the impression that it was her mission to save Russia.'[30]

One of the few people sympathetic to the Tsarina was his daughter Meriel, who in a womanly way often spotted the Empress's social distress. Arriving at a ball in St Petersburg in a silver and white couture evening dress with grand diamond necklace and sparkling tiara, Alix seemed outwardly calm and regal. But minutes after her entrance on the Tsar's arm, and while dancing the opening polonaise, her face became 'grave and taut with strain', the expression of her mouth 'most tragic'.[31] Excusing herself, she left almost immediately and outside almost fainted in the Tsar's arms.

In a last bid, Buchanan asked the Tsar's likeable brother, Grand Duke Michael, to use his influence and to 'beseech the Emperor in the name of King George . . . to show himself to his people and to effect a complete reconciliation with them'. But this endeavour met with an equal lack of success. Buchanan was now of the opinion that the Tsar was 'one of the most pathetic figures in history'.[32] Revolution was now inevitable.

TWENTY-ONE

The Crow's Nest

Whenever he felt troubled, Nicholas's thoughts turned to Livadia, the hauntingly beautiful, white-marble palace rising magically above vineyards and cypress groves in the Crimea. Perched above the brilliant blue of the unfairly named Black Sea, far from the ice and snow of St Petersburg, the family always found respite at the place they affectionately called the Crow's Nest.

This summer palace, with its rose gardens and olive groves, had great charm for them, especially as the Tsarevich always seemed healthier in the tingling air from the snowy Jaila Mountains. In spring, the nights were 'incomparable, clear and mild, the air filled with the perfume of flowers'. Count Grabbe recalled the enchantment of looking out at the 'moonlit peaks' from his balcony, and hearing the 'waves breaking on the rocks below'.[1]

The fashionable time of the year for the 'Russian Riviera', as it is known, was the 'Black Sea Season' in September. Yalta was romantic, used by Chekhov in his famous short story 'Lady with a Lapdog'. It was also restorative for patients suffering from tuberculosis, a disease that was so prevalent in Russia in the early part of the twentieth century, and featured by many Russian writers; Chekhov himself died of TB in 1904.

For Nicholas and Alix, summer was the best time to be at Livadia, when the air was scented with rosemary and lavender, and the palace conservatory was filled with pelargoniums and pink camellias. Some 7,000 serfs – the men were called 'souls' – made sure a weed never raised its head in the 800 acres of royal flower beds.

There was some criticism of the Romanovs' huge estates, which had been bought at pitifully low prices from Tartar villagers. They were also accused of failing to leave strips of land near the sea for common use, and of damaging the livelihoods of fishermen, who were frightened to come too close to the shore.[2]

For Nicholas, Livadia was the exotic equivalent of Cowes. Alix loved it because, when the yellow acacias were like 'perfumed clouds',[3] it reminded her of Osborne and childhood holidays with Queen Victoria.

Her first glimpse of Yalta, with its onion domes silvery and shimmering in the autumn sunshine above the old Byzantine port, had been from a train after a punishing journey from Darmstadt in 1894. Emperor Alexander III was dying in Livadia and she had come to be at Nicholas's side in the sickroom.

After they married, she redecorated the old Moorish palace, recapturing some of its Florentine flavour. She also freshened up the little church in the grounds. Greek marble figures found in excavations close by in the Crimea were now strategically placed around the palace gardens and by the fountains.

The imperial servants liked to grumble about the journey from the port along the cornice, it was so precipitous they called it 'the mother-in-law's tongue'. But once at the Crow's Nest they cheerfully carried luggage along the swept paths billowing with oleander, staggered under arches of roses and lilac, past statues of sleepy lions, and cherubs clutching grapes and spouting water on to stone frogs in the fountains.

In the tranquillity and security of Livadia, there were family expeditions meandering through hillside villages past old Tartar graveyards, and on the way home they heard the muezzin as they admired the 'oriental-looking children with stiffly braided hair under high gold caps . . . and the Tartar carts drawn by horses with bright-blue harness'.[4]

Alix became a different person at Livadia: no longer tense but sociable and relaxed, almost playful, as she was privately with her children. She enjoyed entertaining and planning dinner parties, especially for the Emir of Bokhara, whose retinue intrigued her: 'so sweet, with their long red-dyed beards and silky movements gliding round the Palace in silver and gold kaftans'.[5] Prince Yussopov, another guest, lived not far away at Kokos in a sumptuous palace in a Tartar village where toasts were drunk to George V and Queen Mary.

Knowing his wife was content, Nicholas was free to enjoy long hikes, setting off in heavy boots at ten in the morning for 7 to 15 mile walks along mountain paths.[6] Sometimes he met his mother out riding as she stopped to let her horse drink from a waterfall. Her palace at Ai Todor was only a few miles away. Mother and son enjoyed these impromptu moments together, away from Alix's ever-watchful eye knowing she was happy, perhaps playing the white grand piano in the music room, with its handmade china flowers on sky-blue walls, or reclining after her exertions on a lemon-silk chaise longue. They appreciated these few snatched moments when they could talk tenderly but seriously.

Livadia was where the tsarinas swam in the warm salt water and Alexei pottered about on the beach, collecting shells. He always refused to go fishing, saying he preferred to see the fish alive.[7] Carried on the shoulders of his valet, he was taken with his sisters into the old town, past the faded pink-and-sepia houses, where vines covered the rococo carvings above the louvred shutters. Stopping by wooden-fronted bakeries, they cajoled their nurses into allowing them *maroshnaya*, the justly famous Russian ice cream. There was no worry about security.

The subtropical climate of the Crimea was ideal for grapes; early on, Alexander III had spotted its potential. The imperial Massandra vineyard produced 2 million bottles a year; in recent years, some have been found in secret cellars, hidden away after the Revolution, the last cache being auctioned at Sotheby's in London on 3 December 2004.* The only case left of the rare Massandra Madeira, Nicholas's favourite, fetched £4,140.†

Prince Lev Galitzine was the Tsar's winemaker, and a genial and generous host. He liked to dress as a Tartar merchant or a bohemian artist in a smock when he welcomed Nicholas and the family as they disembarked from the *Standart*.[8] The wine cellar on his estate at Novy Svet had been carved out of the side of a mountain, with a dining hall where robust roast lamb[9] was served with saffron rice, baklava and rich sweet wine. Afterwards, in high spirits, the imperial visitors sailed back to the Crow's Nest, relaxing on deck in comfortable wickerwork chairs, well-fed, and ready to watch the sun go down.

A world away from the pillared elegance of the palace, the simplicity of these easy-going family excursions was appreciated by

---

* The total was a modest £150,000, a much lower figure than the hugely successful 1990 sale.
† 'Lot 89, Crone Brothers, from Nicholas II's 1913 collection of favourite sweet, sherry-style wine.'

the children, who loved piling into one of their father's favourite motor cars. When the Head of the Imperial Chancellery, Prince Vladimir Orlov, had arrived at Tsarskoe Selo one day in a 'very smart car', Nicholas asked if he could go for a drive in 'this kerosene thing'. This was the start of his love affair with the French-made Delaunay-Belleville, as synonymous with luxury then as a Rolls-Royce is now. He ordered a fleet of them. In 1908, a pneumatic self-starter was specially fitted to the 11.65-litre model to enable the Tsar to make a quick getaway in case of a terrorist attack; an ironic accessory, given that nothing would save him from the assassin's bullet in 1918.

Today Livadia is open to the public. A babushka in black, the ubiquitous colour for Russian grandmothers, insists on the removal of shoes to protect the marble floors, as she leads the way to the Empire Room where Churchill, Roosevelt and Stalin met in 1945 for the Yalta conference. Sir Winston is the only one of the powerful trio to be given the honour of a room specially named after him at the palace, commemorating the 'Big Three' conference.

The children's names – Olga, Tatiana, Maria, Anastasia and Alexis – are still gracefully entwined over the entrance to the White Palace; it still has a wistful charm, but everywhere there are ghosts. It would have been the perfect safe haven for the besieged Tsar, but the revolutionaries had other plans.

TWENTY-TWO

In a Snowbound Siding

Traditionally, March is a wicked month. It proved as fatal for the Tsar as it had been for Julius Caesar, and just as it had been for Nicholas's ancestors: Emperor Paul was murdered on 1 March 1801; Alexander II was killed by a bomb in March 1881; and now, in March 1917, the Romanov dynasty would be toppled.

Mourning the loss of two million sons, the Russian people were mortified by the defeat of their once mighty army. The economy had collapsed – the rouble was almost worthless – and many were starving.

The destructive and debilitating war still dragged on. During the winter of 1916 food prices escalated, the number of strikes in factories increased, and there was an upsurge in vengeful looting and the burning of manor houses.

Alix was far too involved in the running of the country. 'Ministers were being appointed and dismissed, as quickly as the Tsarina changed her gloves.' Sir Bernard Pares believed that 'the Empress had carried out her purpose of driving out of office practically everyone who could claim . . . to possess the confidence of the country.' But he excused her on the grounds that 'She was fighting with her back to the wall against the Duma for the autocracy of her little boy.'[1]

Rasputin's lingering influence was now seen in the appointment of the sycophantic Protopov, 'with his mad brilliant eyes [and] restless movements', and with his 'his quick staccato voice'.[2] He became Minister of the Interior in September 1916. Alarm was spreading like a flame through court circles, prompting Ella to make the journey to Tsarskoe Selo to warn her imperious sister about Rasputin's damaging influence.[3]

At the mention of the lascivious monk's name, the Tsarina's fury was frightening; she immediately reached for the telephone, as if her sister was an intruder, and called for a car.[4] Sounding like a soothsayer, the departing Ella warned her sister to remember the fate of Louis XVI and Marie Antoinette. Afterwards, crying at the memory of the awful meeting, Ella said, 'She drove me away like a dog . . . Poor Nicky, poor Russia'. Even their brother, Grand Duke Ernst of Hesse-Darmstadt now joined the chorus of lament about his sister: Nicholas, he said, 'was . . . a saint and an angel but . . . did not know how to deal with that woman', meaning his sister.

Malicious suggestions about the Tsarina's involvement with her German relatives during the war readily fanned rumours of treason. But she had embraced Russia beyond any level expected of foreign wives. 'I am English,' Alix once said, 'and not German.'[5] Nevertheless, when Lord Kitchener was drowned on 15 June 1916 on board HMS *Hampshire*, torpedoed on a mission to revitalise the Russian Army, she was blamed. Mischief-makers suggested that Rasputin, through his friendship with the Tsarina, had let the Germans know the course of the British cruiser.

The next envoy who had tried to talk sense to the imperial couple, resolutely holed up in Tsarskoe Selo, was Sandro, the Tsar's brother-in-law, who told Nicholas that a proper parliamentary government was the only sensible way forward.

'All this talk of yours is ridiculous,' Alix said, lying back in a delicate white negligee on the large double bed she shared with Nicholas, stressing unashamedly that 'Nicky is an autocrat'. Rolling her eyes, she enquired, 'How could he share his divine right with a parliament?' This prickly conversation, in English, came to an abrupt end as she told Sandro, as if he was a child, 'Some day, when you are less excited, you will admit that I knew better.'[6]

Alix and Nicholas tended to blame enlightened writers like Tolstoy and Gogol for the disagreeable but accurate picture of a discontented, disabled Russia. In St Petersburg, society continued with its usual hedonistic carnival: Kschessinska was dancing *Giselle*; Chaliapin was singing *Don Quixote*. A spectacular banquet was held for a foreign delegation on 29 January 1917 – at which they dined on *Longe [sic] de veau Marengo*; *Poulets de grains rôtis*; *Salade de concombres*; *Fruits glâcées de Gatchina* and *shampanskaye*[7] – to consider the unfortunate course of the war.

Most of his ministers were painfully aware of the simmering discontent in the capital, yet Nicholas continued to hold bland meetings in his art nouveau state study at Tsarskoe Selo. Nobody seemed able to break through his 'fatal obtuseness'.[8]

The entire country was dissatisfied and on the verge of rebellion. Time and again the dice fell favourably for the Tsar, but he always missed the chance of negotiating or making any concessions. He tended to be influenced by the last person expressing an opinion. Now, mockingly, he was being compared to a feather pillow bearing the impression of the last person to have sat on him.[9]

Even in the final weeks of his reign, his devotion to routine and trivia would seem almost laughable if it had not been so tragic. Apologising to Count Benckendorff for his slow reply to a letter, Nicholas explained he had to order a new uniform for a photograph in which he would wear military medals rather than the normal court ribbons. A month later he would be known as Comrade Romanov, without any honour.

Deaf to entreaties about any form of democratic government, Nicholas was now becoming a hated figure. The slippery Protopov kept reassuring him that there were no food shortages in the city, that 'there is plenty of flour'.[10] After Rasputin's death in December 1916, the minister concentrated on holding seances with the Tsarina, in the hope of getting in touch with the monk, rather than making enlightened gestures towards a troubled people. The Revolution was sparked as much by the inertia of both men as political unrest.

Although Nicholas was hearing disquieting stories about disturbances in the streets of the capital, still he refused to return to the Winter Palace, where he might have altered the course of Russian history. Trotsky was cruelly comparing him to the French King Louis XVI, and, even worse, as 'altogether less intelligent'.

Count Vladimir Kokovtsov, a former prime minister,* who also made a desperate journey out to Tsarskoe Selo, was dismayed by Nicholas's appearance, and even felt 'afraid to ask after his health'. He thought the Tsar's eyes 'seemed faded . . . the whites had yellowed . . . his lips preserved a sad, forced smile'. Events were taking their toll and yet he was unable to act.

As a pale wintry sun tried to filter through the frost-covered windows at Tsarskoe Selo, Alix still urged her husband, 'Lovey, be firm, because the Russians need you to be.'[11] While outwardly supportive, she later confessed in her diary to a feeling of 'such deep sadness and alarm . . . such terrible times for us now'.[12]

---

* In 1911, he had been dismissed for having the temerity to criticise the influence of Rasputin and the corruption of society generally.

Suddenly Nicholas decided his place was at Stavka [military general headquarters] with his staff, peremptorily announcing, 'I'm going to GHQ tomorrow'. 'Cannot you possibly stay with us?' Alix pleaded, telling him the children were running high temperatures. But, for once, her 'weak-willed hubby', as Nicholas once described himself in a letter to her,* was transformed into the Tsar-Commander-in-Chief. He replied briskly, 'No, I must go',[13] hugged his wife and children then went to Mass in the palace chapel. On Wednesday 7 March 1917 he set off for Mogilev, putting himself firmly out of reach of those advisers who could have warned him about the gravity of the situation in the capital.

He was escaping. In his own words, 'My brain is resting here. No Ministers. No troublesome questions demanding thought.'[14] He felt comfortable with fellow officers known for their loyalty to the Tsar as Supreme Commander-in-Chief, and he was relieved to be away from the disapproval of his Romanov relations, who were dismayed by his passive attitude to the new 'Red Dawn'.

This lack of judgement or understanding of the evolving crisis, which propelled him towards GHQ to play 'chequers' with the soldiers, was Nicholas's death knell. Deliberately, he had put himself out of reach of the people who had pleaded with him to authorise acceptable measures for his desperate subjects. Kept below subsistence level for centuries, what they were suffering was now beyond endurance, and they could no longer remain devoted to their Little Father. He had failed them, turning his reign from splendour to wretchedness.

Almost contentedly, living in two rooms in the governor's house at Mogilev, Nicholas discussed strategy with his generals, drove round the countryside in his Delaunay-Belleville saloon, or read history, but he never reacted to the frantically urgent telegrams coming from St Petersburg.

The February Revolution of 1917, which 'came like the death of a friend who had been lying sick for years and years',[15] began quietly enough. On Thursday 8 March 1917, a woman in desperation, living on starvation rations in arctic weather, threw a stone through an empty baker's shop window; an enraged, sympathetic crowd joined her.[16] Soldiers sent to sort out the chaos of these queues of

---

* This was a letter written by the Tsar from Stavka; at the time it was believed that he was having a nervous breakdown.

starving people, seeing them waiting for hours in biting, bone-marrow cold for nothing, now sided with the rebels.

The next day, real violence erupted in St Petersburg; strikers surged through the streets shouting Marxist slogans such as 'The proletarians have nothing to lose but their chains.' They jumped on trams, 'hanging like grape-vines on the steps' to listen to impassioned speeches, as wild-eyed orators railed against an inept, remote Tsar. Every factory came out on strike; worse, the police disappeared; there was anarchy. Revolutionaries stormed the Duma, the Tsar was blamed for the war and for the plight of his 160 million downtrodden, starving subjects.[17]

St Petersburg was in turmoil by Monday morning, by which time 'some 25,000 troops had made common cause with the people'.[18] A rebellious horde now surrounded the Winter Palace, which was no longer being protected by the 1,500 men of two prestigious regiments – the Cossacks of the Emperor's Escort and the *Garde Équipage*.

Officers were being murdered and government buildings set ablaze, but communications were still non-existent between Stavka and the palace at Tsarskoe. The Tsarina dismissed the uprising as 'a hooligan movement, young boys and girls running about and screaming that they have no bread'.[19]

Sitting by a huge log fire in the salon listening to Goulesko's fashionable gypsy orchestra, she gradually began to understand the creeping horror of the situation. Her companion asked, 'Oh, Madame, why are you so sad tonight?' Soulfully, Alix replied, 'Why am I sad? I can't really say, but the music depresses me . . . I think my heart is broken.' A glass of champagne was suggested to help change her mood of introspection, but it was refused: 'No . . . the Emperor hates wine, he can't bear women to drink wine'.[20]

Becoming more introspective, she huddled with her sick children at Tsarskoe Selo, pulling the heavy silk curtains across to shut out daylight and reality. The telephone lines had been either cut or disconnected.

The Cossacks, who usually carried whips to control the crowds in the city, now put them away and joined in singing the Marseillaise, and, like the French Revolutionaries before them, they clamoured insistently for 'Bread! Bread!' Elite regiments founded by Peter the Great, those once impressive warriors who had stood nobly to attention as Nicholas rode past, now sided with a raggle-taggle mob crying 'Down with the Tsar'.

Finally, a message was received by Nicholas at GHQ from the President of the Duma, telling him about these events in the city, that the 'state authority is totally paralysed and utterly unable to reimpose order'.[21] Nicholas held up this telegram and said dismissively, 'That fat [Mikhail] Rodzianko has written all sorts of nonsense to me, to which I shall not even reply.'[22]

Nicholas 'the Procrastinator' could not be persuaded to act until he received a flurry of telegrams from his own generals and a last appeal from Rodzianko, who warned 'the last hour has struck . . . the fate of the dynasty is being decided'. The Tsar then realised there was no future in repressive measures and it was necessary to make some concessions. Perhaps he was also remembering a conversation with Rodzianko some fifteen months earlier. He had been advised then that people were 'turning away from the Tsar' because, as Rodzianko pointed out, 'all they see . . . after all their suffering and bloodshed' are 'fresh trials . . . in store for them'.

'Is it possible that for twenty-two years it has all been a mistake?' Nicholas asked. The President of the Duma replied, a little embarrassed, 'Yes, for twenty-two years you have followed the wrong course.'[23]

King George had no real idea about the momentum of the revolutionary surge in St Petersburg, and fondly he imagined that Nicholas was still in control. His cousin was at military headquarters, Stavka, where sometimes he would not allow himself to be disturbed to be told news that the imperial guards had mutinied, killing their officers, because he was too busy playing chequers.

But when he heard that even the imperial guard protecting his wife and family had gone over to the revolutionaries, Nicholas decided to leave Mogilev. In his diary, he wrote simply, 'It is such a horrible feeling to be so far away and to receive fragments of bad news!'[24] He would return immediately to Tsarskoe Selo, where an apprehensive Empress was praying constantly.

'How hard it must be for poor Alix to live through these events alone! . . . God help us!'[25] Nicholas said as he left Mogilev at dawn on 13 March, believing that once he was back in the capital, peace would be restored by his loyal troops. He was touched by the unlikely sight of half a dozen schoolgirls standing on the platform who began to cry when they saw him. The cold air was piercing, and he tried to persuade them to go home. But when his train left, two hours later, he could not help but be pleased that, 'they were still there. They blessed me, poor children'.[26]

However, stations along the line had been taken over by rebels determined to keep him from reaching Tsarskoe Selo and the baleful influence of Alix.[27] His gold and blue train was diverted to Pskov by railway workers hacking inches of ice off every set of points. Once the northern army headquarters and enclave of White Russia, this unusual city, famous for its beautiful churches and graceful architecture, is now better known as the place where the Romanov dynasty ended.

After two chilly nights on board the train, when the temperature outside reached minus 30°C, Nicholas was at breakfast in the green regency-striped parlour car when a telegram from Rodzianko was handed to him: 'Too late,' it read, and then, chillingly, 'It is now time to abdicate.'[28] This was so shocking, doctors feared that Nicholas would have a heart attack as he read the unbelievable demand. Three days later, during Mass at the Cathedral, Nicholas did experience 'an excruciating pain in the chest . . . I could hardly stand the service out and my forehead was covered in drops of perspiration'.

Two Duma deputies, Alexander Guchkov, the Minister of War, and Vasily Shulgin had arrived with the abdication document. Alix had always found both men 'excessively impertinent', especially Guchkov, with his yellow-goggled glasses. Now the imperial entourage stood in horrified silence, watching as Nicholas, gaunt and pale, made the sign of the cross and then spoke, asking the critical question, 'Are you sure . . . can you promise that my abdication will benefit Russia?' The two delegates told him impassively that the matter was not for discussion, then to their surprise in a rare show of fighting spirit, Nicholas struck the table with his fist and shouted, 'I am going to speak, I *will* speak.' But he was told, 'Your Majesty, it is the only thing to save Russia at the present crisis.'[29] Taken aback, now sunk in thought, Nicholas asked for time to think things over. He consulted the royal doctor, Sergei Feodorov, about his son's health. 'Please tell me frankly,' he asked, 'is Alexis's disease incurable?' The imperial physician replied that 'in his opinion the Tsarevich would not outlive his sixteenth year, and in any case would never be a normal, healthy man'.[30]

As Nicholas absorbed this brutal prognosis, smoking incessantly, he said quietly, almost talking to himself, 'If Alexis cannot be helpful to the motherland, as I wished he could be, we have every right to keep him to ourselves.'[31] However, constitutionalists believe the Tsar had no right to stand down on behalf of his son, and that he was breaking the laws of succession created by Tsar Paul.[32]

But Nicholas had made up his mind. Later that night he told the deputies what they wanted to hear. 'I have taken the decision, Gentlemen, to renounce the throne . . . I am ready to abdicate.' He signed the Act of Abdication at 11.40 p.m. on 15 March 1917. Sadly, he told them, 'until three o'clock today I thought I could abdicate in favour of my son but at that point I changed this decision in favour of my brother Michael'.[33]

Grand Duke Michael felt it was a 'heavy burden'. Technically, Michael was the last Emperor of Russia, if only for a few hours. He wrote of the grim honour which 'devolved . . . upon me by the quill of my brother who has passed on to me the Imperial Russian throne at a time of unprecedented war and popular unrest'.[34]

He had received a hasty telegram from Nicholas, already addressing him formally as 'His Majesty the Emperor Michael', explaining how 'recent events' had forced him 'to decide irrevocably to take this extreme step'. As always, a courteous man, Nicholas apologised: 'Forgive me,' he said, 'if it grieves you and also for no warning – there was no time . . . Your Nicky.'[35] But, unhappy about accepting the crown without the consent of the people, Michael declined the honour. Even so, he was murdered by the Bolsheviks in 1918 for being a Romanov.

After his abdication in a snowbound siding, Nicholas ordered a glass of tea from the samovar. While outwardly calm and resigned, he looked exhausted, with bags under his eyes and his skin jaundiced with distress. In those final days of his reign, he was being prescribed cocaine to ease incipient heart problems.

Even at this stage, George V was still sanguine about events in Russia, although he did blame the Tsar for the uprising, saying, 'I fear Nicky is the cause of it all and Nicky has been weak.' This crushing character dismissal is followed by a more pedestrian 'Bikaner came to luncheon' entry in his diary for the same day.*

* The Maharaja of Bikaner was an urbane, devoted subject of British rule in India, popular with the royal family, and later an Olympic bronze medallist in shooting.

Even when he heard about the abdication, George felt there was still no reason to worry about Nicholas's survival. After all, the new revolutionary liberal-leftish government headed by Prince Lvov, as Prime Minister, was not baying for the Tsar's blood. Lvov was soon succeeded as head of this first provisional government by the hooded-eyed, left-wing lawyer Alexander Kerensky, who also seemed to take a humane view of the Tsar and his family. Nicknamed 'Napoleonchik'[36] because he folded his arm in the same way as the French general, Kerensky was once described by Alix as nothing more than a 'pretentious windbag of a lawyer . . . who must be put in prison'.

In a speech to the Moscow Soviet on 21 March 1917, Kerensky triumphantly announced that the 'former Czar' was now in his hands. It had been a bloodless coup, not vengeful. 'Nicholas II', would, he said, 'be taken to the harbour and from there sent to England by ship'.[37, 38]

At Pskov, in his last minutes as Emperor, Nicholas, with impeccable courtesy, said, 'I hope, Gentlemen' – he was always punctilious about correct forms of address, in this instance treating Guchkov and Shulgin as if were loyal courtiers – 'you will understand a father's feelings',[39] and asked, 'Is my family safe and sound?' He was reassured. His wife and children meant more to him than any abstract concept of being an enlightened ruler.

'Will Your Majesty go to Tsarskoe?' Nicholas was asked, as if nothing had changed and he had the freedom to choose. Ever the dedicated soldier, he replied, 'No, I want to go to Headquarters first to say farewell. And then I would like to see my mother.' Inwardly his spirit was broken. 'Am surrounded by betrayal, cowardice and deceit',[40] he wrote as he left Pskov at 1 a.m., 'with a heavy heart'.

As the train left the station and gathered steam, Nicholas seemed almost relieved to have the burden of monarchy lifted from his shoulders. On the journey, he revealed he had 'read a lot about Julius Caesar', and how 'at 8.20' he had 'arrived in Mogilev'.[41]

Describing his parting from 'the officers and Cossacks of the Convoy and Mixed Regiment', in his diary for 21 March 1917 Nicholas wrote simply 'my heart nearly broke!'[42] As he shook hands with every officer, from distinguished generals to young, raw-faced subalterns, some fell on their knees and bowed their heads before their Commander-in-Chief.

'This is the last time that I shall address you, my well-loved troops.' Nicholas spoke carefully and explained, 'Since I renounce the throne for myself and my son, the supreme power has, on the initiative of the Duma, passed into the hands of the provisional government.'[43] After a few more words, finding it impossible to speak, he raised his hand in a mute gesture of farewell.

He then went to see his mother at midday and, remaining with her on board her own train, 'sat with her until 4.30'. Mother and son played bezique and drank tea. As they parted, the Dowager Empress tenderly hung an icon round her son's neck. It was, she said afterwards, 'one of the most awful days of my life'. A few months earlier she had been apprehensive about Alix's interference in political matters, saying, 'My daughter-in-law does not like me; she thinks that I am jealous of her power . . . yet I see that we are nearing some catastrophe, and the Tsar listens to no one but flatterers, not perceiving or even suspecting what goes on all around him.'[44]

That evening Major-General Sir John Hanbury-Williams, head of the British military mission to Russia since 1914, a charmer celebrated for the lamentable spelling of his dispatches,[45] who always signed himself as 'old soldier' in letters to the Tsar, went to see him at the eerily silent Mogilev governor's mansion. The two men had enjoyed each other's company at Stavka. Now shocked by the sight of 'the lonely figure of the man who had always been surrounded by a crowd of courtiers, the desolation . . . the dust over the great rooms', he noticed how Nicholas kept touching his collar; his left hand, where he held his gloves, kept opening and closing nervously. 'He was very pale, almost livid, haggard with distress.'[46]

At dusk, Nicholas appeared on the railway platform lit with blue lanterns. A lone figure in his Kuban Cossack uniform and silver-lined greatcoat, he later boarded a train already stripped of its embossed imperial crowns. Following were his escorts, four members of the Duma who kept their bowler hats on as they reverently carried the *Manifesto of Abdication of Nikolai II* like a precious jewel.

Looking outside, Nicholas was faced with the dusty, brutalised faces of his former subjects, contorted in grinning triumph; a roisterous crowd wearing red armbands and red hats celebrating the departure of the man they were calling 'Bloody Nicholas'.

But one old woman burst into tears when she saw the ex-Tsar standing palely at the window of the train, as he tried to clear the steamed-up glass with his gloved hand, calling out, 'Don't go away, *Batiushka*'.[47] But the man she was calling 'Little Father' could only smile wanly as she cried, 'You are the glory and hope of our Motherland; you can still lead our men to victory.'

The train* rolled out at 4.45 p.m. for its 25½-hour journey to Tsarskoe Selo. Outwardly impassive, Nicholas wrote in anguish, 'it's miserable, painful and depressing'.[48]

The British Ambassador, who had been on another holiday in Finland, returned to find the streets littered with overturned trams and cars. He was given a low-key account of the traumatic events unfolding in the city; his staff suggested that there had been a 'certain amount of disorder . . . but . . . nothing serious'. The ambassador had been as foolishly complacent as the Tsar himself, but would now see the ancient imperial regime collapse spectacularly.

On 15 March 1917, George had felt impelled to write in his diary, 'I am in despair.'[49] He realised how bad the situation had become in Russia. Seriously apprehensive, he said he doubted that, if Nicholas was 'thrown into the prison of St Peter and St Paul' whether he would 'ever come out alive'. Unlike his father, who always strongly disapproved of Nicholas's unenlightened regime, George V had usually taken a more understanding view. He sent Nicholas a telegram: 'Events of last week have deeply distressed me,' but assured him, 'I shall always remain your true and devoted friend, as you know I have always been in the past.'[50]

At this stage, Nicholas himself was not unduly alarmed. When asked what he would do now he was no longer Tsar, and thinking of his son, he told the Duma delegates, 'We'll settle down in Livadia. The climate is very good for him.' The memory of the sunshine and soft breezes of the Crimea brought light briefly to his tired eyes.

---

*　The carriage used for Nicholas's humiliating journey is now in a museum in Helsinki.

TWENTY-THREE

'The End Is Inevitable'

The King received an alarming message from the ambassador, informing him that the Tsar and Tsarina were now completely isolated and had been deserted, even by the grand dukes.

As revolutionaries gained control, Sir George Buchanan worried about the Tsar, saying, 'I shall not be happy until they are safely out of Russia.'[1] But he lost no time in the emollient offering of formal recognition of the new provisional government on 22 March 1917,[2] believing the new regime would create order and stability. The aristocratic Prince Lvov was a moderate with whom the British government could do business.

The ambassador's daughter Meriel was in the embassy ballroom sorting out bandages and dressings as part of her war effort when Grand Duke Alexander Leuchtenberg arrived. Agitated, he immediately blurted out his concern about the Tsar.

'Does your father know how desperate the Emperor's situation really is?' he asked. An imposing figure in his grey military overcoat with cape and fur collar, he usually reminded her of Eugene Onegin, but now was not the time for any formal niceties or flirtatious exchanges.

Calmly folding another piece of lint, she assured him that her father was well aware that the Tsar was under arrest and on his way back to Tsarskoe Selo, but asked, 'Is there any fresh danger?' Emotionally, the Grand Duke replied, 'The end is inevitable . . . Unless your father arranges for the Emperor's escape within the next few days His Majesty will be murdered! . . . The most urgent thing is to get him and the Empress away while it is still possible for them to go.'[3]

Meriel immediately went to her father, who still appeared unworried. The provisional government's first Foreign Minister, Paul Milyukov, had assured him that special measures were being taken for the protection of the Tsar. But Buchanan was worried enough to send a second telegram to England with the urgent intelligence that extremists would prevent the Emperor from leaving Russia.

At dinner that night he told his wife and daughter, 'I have put things very strongly', hoping to spur the Foreign Office to 'take action'.[4]

The King was at Sandringham when he heard about Nicholas's decision to give up the throne. He immediately summoned Lord Stamfordham, saying, 'He has abdicated and we are agreed that they can come and live here in England', an immediate warm and generous response. The telegram inviting the Tsar to come to England was sent to Sir John Hanbury-Williams, believed to be at military headquarters at Mogilev with the Tsar. This was the protocol.

The contents of the celebrated telegram, dated 23 March 1917, conveyed the King's heartfelt message that 'apprehensive for the safety of his cousin', he 'would be happy to receive him' as soon as possible in England, 'where he and his family would find a sure and peaceful retreat'. A British cruiser would meet them in Murmansk and bring them to safety.

Unfortunately, the Tsar had already left Mogilev for Tsarskoe Selo, and he never received the telegram. It was passed on to the British Ambassador in St Petersburg, who immediately got in touch with Milyukov, who in turn seemed genuinely pleased to hear about the King's invitation. 'It's the last chance of securing these poor unfortunates' freedom,' he said, and then as an afterthought added, 'and perhaps of saving their lives.'[5] Then, with honeyed words, he enquired about the logistics of the rescue, but Buchanan had no answer. Nothing had been set in motion.

Blame for non-delivery of the vital telegram to the beleaguered Tsar hovered over two heads: Buchanan's mainly, but also Milyukov's. Asked later why the Tsar never received the King's invitation, Milyukov, with faux innocence and a devious logic, plausibly suggested that as the telegram had been wrongly addressed to 'the Emperor' it had been returned to the British Embassy as 'Nicholas was no longer Emperor'.[6] In his book *Les Dernières Nouvelles*, he made things worse by claiming that he told the ambassador to withhold the telegram and that Sir George, out of consideration for the provisional government, had agreed to act according to his advice.

During these volatile days, the British government was anxious not to upset the sensibilities of the new regime in Russia. Buchanan was told that he must stress that the English offer of safe haven had been issued only because it was understood to be the wish of the provisional government. But events in Russia had already overtaken any such moderate suggestion; rebellious factions were already demanding that the Tsar should be put on trial for treason,[7] and be thrown into the Fortress of Peter and Paul with the Tsarina to await execution.

Sitting in chancery at the embassy in St Petersburg, the British Ambassador serenely opened a telegram from London. He had fully expected it to be a message in code with final instructions for the Tsar's journey to England. As he started to read, a slight twitch around the nostrils signalled his distress.

Disbelievingly, he looked again at the startling words: 'The residence in this country of the ex-Emperor and Empress . . . would undoubtedly compromise the position of the King'. It was a brisk command from the Foreign Office in London dated 13 April 1917, ordering him to cancel the King's invitation to the Tsar. Standing up, shaking, he hurried to the dining room, flung open the big white doors and collapsed so dramatically into a chair that his wife asked, 'Are you ill?' He shook his head and told her flatly, 'I have had news from England; they refuse to let the Emperor come over!' He threw his hands in the air. 'They are afraid,' he exclaimed. 'That is the truth of it . . . they are afraid!'[8] The invitation was being cancelled, although it had been agreed at a cabinet meeting. Sir Arthur Balfour, the Foreign Secretary, had been told by Stamfordham that the Tsar must not set foot in England, as his presence 'would be strongly resented by the British public'.[9]

Exasperated, Buchanan explained to his wife and daughter that 'the Government are nervous of any interior unrest leading to strikes in the shipyards, the coal-mines or munition factories. There has been a certain amount of revolutionary talk in Hyde Park,' he continued grimly. 'The Labour Party declare that they will make the workmen down tools if the Emperor is allowed to land. They have told me to tell the provisional government to cancel all arrangements.'[10]

Lord Stamfordham, the King's private secretary, made the King's wishes crystal clear in case there was any confusion, writing,[11] 'We must be allowed to withdraw from the consent previously given . . . the presence of the Emperor and Empress . . . in England would be *very* hard on the King and arouse much public comment if not resentment'. The message was endorsed by the Foreign Secretary, who wrote, in a minute to the Prime Minister,[12] that a 'Romanov presence in England would place the King in an awkward position'.

Forgoing elegant courtly exchanges, Lord Hardinge, Permanent Under-secretary and later Head of the Foreign Office, advised that, 'although the King was devoted to the Emperor . . . the Radicals and Socialists in the Country' were 'hot against the Imperial Family coming to England', but added that of course the King, because of his 'relationship and affection for the Emperor . . . would go out of [his] way to be civil to him', which was a comfort.

It is true that there had been growing sympathy in England for the revolutionaries wishing to end the Tsarist regime, this support stemming from a budding Labour Party which had grown from being a fledgling that hardly chirruped in Queen Victoria's day to a vociferous presence with 1.5 million trade-union activists. Dissatisfied British workers who had watched the oppression of the Russian people now cheered the Bolshevik uprising. Royal advisers were alarmed by any insidious criticism of the monarchy, fuelled partly by the aftermath of the war, but also as a result of this idealised view of the Russian Revolution. There was a new spread of class consciousness in Britain, which had been unthinkable in the previous century, when everybody had known his place.

A valued royal adviser, Lord Esher proposed a swift programme for the 'democratisation' of the monarchy. If the King was not to face the same fate as the Tsar, it was vital he should become more approachable and have more appeal to the working class. A document, carefully drawn up by palace mandarins, entitled 'Unrest in the Country', outlined the way in which he might be seen as a more caring, hard-working monarch, delighting in nothing more than meeting his subjects. It helped that George V, ever since his days in the navy, had had no snobbery. Unlike the Tsar, he listened to his advisers, no matter how fat or thin they were or how disagreeable their message.

As a result of the royal campaign,* the King became the first monarch to attend an FA Cup final and was delighted to record in his diary how 'the crowds cheered me',[13] and that it was 'a good match'. In the past, kings had been more familiar sights on the best racecourses. George was alarmed at how easy it was to visualise the Red Flag flying over Buckingham Palace, and imagined Russia's 'anti-monarchical movement' spreading to England like an infection. He did not want to be seen as part of a monarchical mafia of

---

*   It was filed away in the royal archives, unseen until 1999.

emperors sticking together, saving each other's skins. These considerations influenced him in agreeing to the decision to refuse safe haven to the Tsar, although it has always been convenient and fashionable to blame the Prime Minister, Lloyd George.

The King liked the stocky, quick-witted Welshman, with his blazing blue eyes and gift for oratory; he also appreciated his lack of obsequiousness. Born in 1863, brought up in north Wales by an uncle who was a shoemaker, he was no royalist and occasionally referred to the King as 'my little German friend'. He was against large estates, made no secret of his natural affinity with the starving Russian peasants, and hoped the Bolshevik Revolution might unshackle Russia.

He was aware of the King's uneasiness about the threat of revolution, although he thought it unlikely. While the country was no Utopia, being still dominated by class structure and with only rudimentary social welfare, yet a Bolshevik-style uprising among the phlegmatic British people was more a figment of the imagination of an anxious monarch preoccupied with self-preservation.

Lloyd George assumed that the King, as a close relative, would be putting one of his houses at the Tsar's disposal. But that was the problem – there was nowhere available except Balmoral in Scotland. Lord Stamfordham solicitiously pointed out it was 'not a suitable residence at this time of year',[14] being 'far too cold'. The King readily agreed with the wisdom of his private secretary, without apparently questioning its logic. March might be cold in Scotland, but would surely be springlike to most Russians, used to cutting winds sweeping across the steppe from Siberia.

The Tsar was now being discussed like a parcel nobody wanted. In a cruel quirk of fate either because of Russian dilatoriness, Machiavellian intrigue by the provisional government or the ineptitude of the Foreign Office, Nicholas never knew that his 'honorary brother', the King of England, had stretched a helping hand across the sea, albeit only briefly.

The King's anxiety about the plight of the Tsar is not allowed any real expression in his diaries. A typical entry, written at Buckingham Palace when the Russian crisis was at its most volatile, opens with a pedestrian weather report: 'frost, bitterly cold, wind, snowing off & on'. Then almost *en passant*, George adds, 'had a talk with Motherdear about Russia and Nicky, she is very much upset about it'. But then the tone brightens, the weather has improved, 'fine afternoon. Arranged stamps with Bacon* . . . .'[15] This is a perfect example of how routine was essential for the King's equilibrium. In common with many of his subjects, talk of the weather was escapism, in this case enabling George to put Russia out of his mind.

In an almost childlike mood of optimism, Nicholas revealed his hopes, writing in his diary in his elegant hand on 5 April 1917: 'I began to pack the belongings which I shall take with me, if fate wills that I am to go to England.'[16] His two older daughters, Olga and Tatiana, with the hopefulness of youth were seen by one of the household, Sestra Effrossina, their nurse,† busying themselves, making 'everything ready for England'.[17] Having been to stay with the King, they fondly remembered happy family times and noticed now that their mother seemed to dwell constantly on her life with her grandmother in England.

The servants began to pack the Tsar's English uniforms, certain that they would soon be leaving Russia,[18] touchingly imagining his life of military ceremonial would continue in England.

But the Foreign Office began to suggest Denmark, Spain or the south of France 'would be more suitable' for the Tsar and his family. The British Ambassador in France, Sir Francis Bertie, a great favourite with George V, disagreed, saying adamantly, 'I do not think that the ex-Emperor and his family would be welcome in France.'‡ The Empress, he said, 'was not only a Boche by birth but in sentiment', adding harshly, 'She is regarded as a criminal or a criminal lunatic.'[19]

The thought of the Tsar coming to England prompted *The Times* to ask,[20] 'How can we tolerate this friend of Germany in our midst?', referring to a virulent antagonism towards the Tsarina because of her German background. The underlying fear was that the presence of *'la bochesse'*, as the French referred to her disparagingly, might spark off simmering xenophobia.

---

* Sir Edward Bacon, the curator. The King arranged for the weak-chested Bacon to be given a fur-lined coat to protect him as he travelled from Croydon to Buckingham Palace.

† She had been with the children since they were born and now said, 'I could not separate from my dear children whom I saw come into this world.'

‡ When Lloyd George insisted on Bertie being recalled as British Ambassador to France in 1918, the King was not pleased and tried to reward his old favourite by creating him an earl. But he was thwarted by Lloyd George, who insisted Bertie only be made a viscount, and sent Lord Derby to Paris as ambassador. Kenneth Rose, *King George V*, p. 208.

This anti-German feeling was calculated to send a shudder down the royal spine. The King was appalled at a dinner party when Lady Maud Warrender unthinkingly said, 'Oh, sir, the rumour is that you must be pro-German because of your name.' She never forgot how he 'started and went pale'.

Stirred up by the Germans, the Bolsheviks began dropping leaflets describing Buchanan, this mild-mannered, courtly figure, of 'reigning in Russia and drinking Russian blood'. Although privately warned that there was a plan to seize the British Embassy and that his life was in danger, he remained predictably calm, complaining that these upsets were a 'great nuisance'.

In St Petersburg, he was now having to play a duplicitous role trying to placate those in the Tsar's circle who kept reminding him of Russia's great loyalty to Britain during the war against Germany. He knew that no amount of invisible diplomacy could save the doomed Tsar.

He refused to abandon his evening stroll in front of the embassy along the banks of the Neva, crossing over Trinity Bridge towards the legendary ballet dancer Mathilde Kschessinska's little 'toy palace'. But by 3 April 1917 she had gone, and Lenin was installed, looking slightly incongruous writing his angry pamphlets in such frivolously feminine surroundings.

Revolution continued in the humid mosquito-ridden July days. Armed demonstrators swarmed through the streets carrying 'All Power to the Soviets' banners in an attempt to dislodge the moderate government in favour of the hardline Bolsheviks. A British Embassy housemaid saw a revolutionary cutting a sailor's head clean off with a sweep of his sword. This intelligence disrupted dinner at the embassy, where pudding had to be left untasted in the 'slightly undignified rush'[21] to the ambassador's study, which afforded a grandstand view of the rioting from its first-floor window. But the Bolsheviks failed in their bid to overthrow the moderate government, and Lenin crept off to Switzerland.

Taken to a charity ballet at the Mariinskiy Theatre for the widows and orphans of the Revolution, Meriel Buchanan was shocked to see the great imperial gold eagles had been ripped away from the royal box, leaving chipped walls and gaping holes. Even 'the corps de ballet', she wryly noticed, seemed rebellious, 'slow to obey the conductor's baton, whispering in corners, slack and inattentive'.[22] The sons of the Revolution were lolling about in the Tsar's box, spitting out sunflower seeds and leering at her.[23]

After seven years *en poste*, Buchanan could only remember sadly the exotic, privileged St Petersburg he had known years earlier and a Moscow exuding the mystical power of centuries of tsarist rule.

Gone now was the glamorous confidence of the Tsar riding in triumph on a white horse over carpets of roses and orchids; gone the wild cheering, the outriders in scarlet and gold; gone the Empress and the tsarinas following on white satin cushions, smiling under huge hats covered with flowers; gone the *skorohods** with those distinctive yellow and black ostrich feathers in their caps.

Buchanan's feelings were overwhelmingly 'dark depression . . . foreboding and sadness everywhere'. The Tsar was now a prisoner, dressed in shabby army cast-offs, and sawing wood.

---

* Private messengers for the imperial family.

TWENTY-FOUR

A Sad, Bearded Woodcutter

The Empress was at Tsarskoe Selo drinking cafe au lait[1] in the scarlet drawing room surrounded by the children's jigsaws and pieces of half-finished embroidery lying on the red-and-white chintz-covered chairs. A telegram she had sent to Nicholas at Stavka, addressed to 'His Imperial Majesty', had been returned with the bald instruction 'Address of person mentioned unknown'[2] scrawled on the envelope. Telephone lines had suddenly been cut, so that Alix knew nothing about the abdication or the seriousness of the Bolshevik Revolution.

But when Dr Botkin, the family physician, returned from a visit to Petrograd, he told her about 'drunken soldiers without belts and all unbuttoned were running back and forth carrying all they could lay their hands on in the shops . . . bottles of wine and vodka, while some had entwined themselves all over in red silk ribbons'. His daughter Tatiana had heard the resentful crowd outside the Alexander Palace, shouting 'Down with the Empress'.

Alix then asked one of her companions to telephone the Winter Palace, hoping there might be news of the Tsar, only to be told by an alarmed courtier, Prince Retief, 'The mob is even now at the gates of the palace.' Then, with ingrained civility, he asked to be excused: 'Madame, it distresses me to appear discourteous, but I fear I am about to be killed.'[3] These were his last words before the line went dead.

Looking so 'deathly pale she seemed hardly alive', and greatly agitated, the Empress now discovered that loyal troops were deserting. 'My sailors, my own sailors,' she cried. 'I can't believe it.'[4] Outside there was the alarming sound of gunfire, but she was not to know it was only drunken revolutionaries firing desultory shots at the unsuspecting deer in the English Park.

But now Alix had a premonition that it was all over and began to sort out ten boxes of intimate documents, including her white satin-bound diaries holding pressed flowers and photographs of her children in summer meadows. Curiously, some of her most private love letters to the Tsar were not thrown on the drawing-room fire, but correspondence from Rasputin went up in flames. Carefully she folded away her silk stockings and eye-catching couture outfits, and arranged for them to be given in charity to Polish refugees. She kept a few icons, her crystal bottles of verbena cologne, her sapphire cross and favourite English Atkinson's white rose toilet water. A photograph taken of her in the grey dress she wore on the day of her engagement, a favourite bedspread, several watercolours, photographs and a gramophone were packed as precious keepsakes.

The first inkling Alix had about the abdication was when a palace servant came to her and showed her a leaflet saying the Tsar had renounced the throne; the news was then confirmed by a more authoritative source. Unable to believe her eyes or ears, shocked and incredulous, she stumbled towards the writing table between the windows, brokenly repeating, '*Abdiqué!*'[5]

As if 'in deep mourning now sombrely dressed',[6] Alix was then obliged to receive General Kornilov, Commander of the Forces. It was clear this was not a social call: he told her he was arresting her officially on orders from the provisional government.[7] Red-eyed, she said simply, 'Do what you will; I am at your disposal', with a sad, reconciled dignity.

Her arrest, she was assured, was simply 'a precautionary measure'. Shortly, a British ship would be taking the Tsarina, her husband and children to safe haven in England. But from that moment the doors of the palace were locked and the Empress was under armed guard. Aware of the feelings of hatred towards her, she said a few days later to her priest, 'I only wanted to do good.'[8]

The Tsarevich was told about his father's abdication by his Swiss tutor, Pierre Gilliard, who, in an attempt to soften the news explained gently how the Tsar had been burdened with 'many difficulties of late'. The boy looked at him in astonishment and, in that direct way children have, asked, 'In that case, who will be Emperor?' 'Nobody,' he was told. Biting his lip, Alexei asked who was now going to rule Russia.[9] There was no answer.

His father, in a mood of resigned fatalism, arrived back at Tsarskoe Selo.* As he was taken from the royal train, advisers and courtiers mysteriously melted into the background, some showing an unaccustomed athletic alacrity as they leapt down on to the track on

---

* Normally a journey of 450 miles but, because of the diversions, an extra 200 miles was added on.

the wrong side of the carriage. 'His Majesty's suite had gained the platform and taken to their heels, scattering in all directions.'[10]

When Nicholas saw troops occupying Tsarskoe Selo, he was taken aback. 'God, what a difference,' he thought. 'Guards are on the street and inside the park surrounding the palace.'[11] It brought home to him the shaming truth of his situation.

The Emperor and Autocrat of all the Russias had to wait like a *skorod* [messenger] for permission to enter the marital home he had loved for twenty years. A slouching sentry wearing a red badge asked sulkily, 'Who goes there?', and, peering at the Tsar, then shrugged, and muttered, 'Oh, Citizen Romanov', unlocked the gates and let the man through who had once had the power of life and death over his people.

Arriving at the palace sunken-jawed and shockingly pale, Nicholas's footsteps on the polished parquet floors no longer had that confident, resounding ring. Loyal retainers, showing a delicate sensibility, turned away as the Tsarina raced towards him and threw herself into his arms. It was not until they reached their private apartments that they both wept, the ex-Tsar 'like a child'.[12] For once his wife found it impossible to comfort him.

Recovering his composure, the Tsar gathered himself up and told his wife, 'I think I'll go for a walk . . . walking always does me good.'[13] His brand of courage had a simple moral grandeur as he walked towards the Grande Allée, but to the many watching eyes, with his head bent and slow steps, he looked completely broken.

This was the beginning of five months' house arrest at Tsarskoe Selo. The royal couple had been so relieved to find each other alive that the humiliation they had now to endure was almost bearable. Many of the palace staff wept openly, but began to be more hopeful as Vladimir Voeikov, the palace commandant, assured them, 'The Sovereign and all of us are going to England.'

But the revolutionaries had no intention of allowing their prey to escape to a lair in England. When asked why the Tsar and his family should not go abroad, Nikolai Chkheidze, a Menshevik,* replied,

---

*   Member of the element of the Russian Social Democratic Labour Party, which opposed Lenin. This faction was itself split between 'liquidationalists', centrists and the followers of Leon Trotsky. In 1920, after a serious falling-out with the Bolsheviks, some Mensheviks settled in the United States. In 1922 the party in Russia was suppressed, and in 1931 there was a show trial, which foreshadowed Stalin's Great Purge.

'Never', and revealed the ominous plan that Nicholas had 'to be rendered harmless'. Inciting the comrades, he then provocatively suggested that the Tsar had 'enormous sums of money . . . 500 million roubles in gold' in European banks. This was not true, as Nicholas had removed most of his money as a personal contribution to the Russian war effort. But the revolutionaries' real fear was that, if Nicholas went abroad, he could become a rallying point for a counter-revolution.

In captivity in his own home, soldiers pushed around the former Emperor, baiting him like peasants in a Breughel painting or yokels tormenting poor 'Tom'* on a country road: 'You can't go there, Mister Colonel', or, more insultingly, 'Stand back when you are commanded.' People got used to the sight of Nicholas – now a sad, bearded woodcutter – sweeping paths.

He minded when the guards mocked him when he appeared in his treasured Lifeguards Hussars Regiment uniform. In one of the crueller strokes in the art of humiliation, he was ordered to remove from his uniform the epaulettes which carried his father Alexander III's monogram.[14, 15] This 'swinishness' Nicholas found as hard to forgive as the unnecessary confiscation of the Tsarevich's traditional toy rifle and Cossack dagger.

The arrival of Kerensky at the palace in flamboyant style, wearing an open-necked shirt and in one of the royal cars, was deliberately offensive. Marching into the sitting room, he introduced himself as the Procurator-General.[16] He later claimed that although he had nurtured a virulent hatred for the Tsar, he had to confess to being overcome by Nicholas's charm: 'this man with . . . the wistful smile and gentle manner', who 'struck him as a rather sad human being pursued by fatal misfortune'. But he was not won over by the Empress, her hauteur and bitter silence eloquently demonstrating her hostility towards the leader of the provisional government. Grudgingly, Kerensky then passed on a message from Buckingham Palace: 'The Queen of England,' he said with a smirk, 'asks for news of the ex-Empress.'

Being isolated had one advantage: Nicholas had very little news. He and Alix spoke often about England. He still took pleasure in his likeness to the King. 'Have you seen my last photograph?' asked

---

* Poor Tom, from Shakespeare's *King Lear*, Act III Scene 4: 'Poor Tom . . . who is whipped from tithing to tithing, and stock-punished, and imprisoned'.

Nicholas, picking up a photograph of George V. 'Doesn't it flatter me?'[17] he said with a shy smile.

He spent a great deal of time in his mahogany-panelled study, where he taught the Tsarevich history. He looked on house arrest at Tsarskoe Selo as a time 'to read for my own pleasure', choosing, a little late in the day, *The Tasks of the Russian Army* by Kuropatkin, a former war minister. But in one withdrawn, melancholy moment, he declared, 'I have all my life only done what I was told it was my duty to do.'[18]

In the evenings he played dominoes or bezique with the Tsarina. He even managed a wry smile when he saw sentries sprawled in gilded armchairs, with muddy boots on palace footstools, pretending to be emperors.[19] His new status sometimes sparked his dry humour. Once, trying to carve a piece of leathery meat, he remarked with a thin smile, 'This may have once been a ham but now it's only an "ex-ham".'[20] Much more painful for the couple was Kerensky's order that they now must be separated from each other, meeting only at mealtimes and to pray.

Still Nicholas refused to be despondent. With an optimism which seemed pitiful to the few courtiers still around, he expressed the hope to one of them that, as he was being freed from 'responsibilities to the nation', he hoped to 'fulfil his life's desire' to have a farm, 'somewhere in England'. 'What do you think?' he asked, but the adviser was silent.[21]

Everyone else was aware that the King would not be receiving the Tsar and his family in England. The long 'Georgie–Nicky' relationship would soon be consigned to old, crested parchment envelopes.

TWENTY-FIVE

'An Out-and-Out Backwater'

Nobody is allowed today to walk along the dank, tree-lined path, with drooping branches and climbing weeds, leading to the graceful Bow Room at the Alexander Palace, where the Tsar and his family waited to be sent to Siberia.

Kerensky, the Prime Minister, who was enjoying working at the Winter Palace with his feet up on Alexander III's desk, told Nicholas that he was sending the family to 'an out-and-out backwater'[1] called Tobolsk, claiming it was to protect them from the inevitable brutality of revolution.

Nicholas wrote in his diary on 28 July 1917 that he had 'just learned that they are going to send us not to the Crimea, but to a town in the East. But where precisely? No one can say.' Siberia was to be their destination, not Livadia, with its camellias and tender grapes, where they might have lived in elegant obscurity.

On a warm August evening, on the eve of their departure, the last of the imperial retinue at the Alexander Palace gathered in the Tsarina's green boudoir for a doleful tea party. 'It was the most mournful and depressing party I ever attended,' Charles Gibbes later recalled painfully, aware that it was the 'prelude to an inescapable tragedy'. Nicholas was devastated that they were not going to Livadia, fearing that if Moscow was the destination he would be put on trial. A far worse fate awaited them in Siberia.

The family had been told to be ready to leave the Alexander Palace at midnight. Nicholas, now looking gaunt, tried to conceal his distress as the Tsarina, their daughters and the Tsarevich endured a miserably uncomfortable night sitting on their suitcases. Occasionally they went back to their rooms to try and rest, but almost at once they were summoned back and told that the cars were on their way. They waited until six in the morning.

The Tsarina, unable to walk, was then lifted out through the French windows by servants holding her like a piece of palace porcelain.[2] Then, before the watchful guards on 1 August 1917,[3] the

Tsar 'embraced every man, the Tsarina every woman' of the remnants of their household as they left their cherished home. It was the moment when the Tsarina felt the 'the whole force of their desolation', coming face to face with the almost unbearably tragic faces of those staying behind. 'What,' she asked herself, biting back tears, 'shall the future bring to my poor children? My heart breaks thinking of them.'

At the Alexander Station, once a place of happy arrivals and departures, in an involuntary movement Nicholas automatically put his hand to his cap as he came out on to the platform, but not a single soldier returned the salute. In the menacing silence, the party, including thirty-nine courtiers, servants and retainers, made their way to the train on foot and under heavy guard.[4] The train was about fifty yards along the railway siding and, when they reached the steps, Alix stumbled and fell heavily.[5] She had to be helped on to the train, which carried the Red Cross mission emblem and flew a Japanese flag[6] to ensure they reached their destination unharmed. They reached the port of Tyumen on 18 August 1917 and then were taken on the *Rus*, a shabby, old steamer, along the Tobol river to Tobolsk.

At first sight the town appeared charmingly *en fête*, with jugglers, clowns, balalaika music, sleighs decorated with ribbons and street sellers with trays of cherry vodka, steaming blinis and gingerbread. This was not a welcoming party for the Tsar, but the final festivities on the eve of Lent. The 27,000-strong, largely Tartar population, proud of their land, was not hostile; some even waved. This confirmed the Tsarina's belief in the basic goodness of the Russian peasants; she always liked to think of them as 'big children'.

The house they were to occupy, the ironically named Freedom House, was not ready. Filthy and damp, it had been occupied by soldiers for months, the walls were streaked with grime and graffiti. The family had to stay on board their unsavoury vessel, with its almost unbearable sanitary conditions, on the swampy, storm-swollen river.

Eventually the governor's creeper-covered eighteen-roomed mansion was cleaned up, filled with aspidistras, potted palms, reading lamps and, vitally, a chaise longue for the Empress. Nicholas and the family moved in; their possessions were slight, just a few suitcases, their diaries and love letters.

Nicholas was given a food-rationing card, number 54, an excuse for more degradation. The details on the card gave his name as

Nicholas Alexandrovich Romanov, Ex-Emperor, residing on Freedom Street, with six dependants. Even his enemies were struck by the Tsar's grace under pressure. When one of the revolutionary overlords came to dictate the rules of behaviour, Nicholas asked gently, 'Why don't you let us walk in town? You can't actually be afraid that I shall run away?' Smiling at the commissar's embarrassment, he said, 'What is the matter, kind sir? I was in Tobolsk in my youth. I remember it is a very beautiful town, and I would like to see it.' Physical humiliations he handled with dignity; even when he had been knocked off his bicycle after soldiers laughingly stuck a bayonet into the spokes.

A group of local Soviets caustically described the sad occupants they encountered in the imperial suite as 'withered grandees,' and enquired with cruel, exaggerated politeness if Nicholas was satisfied with the guard and if he had any complaints.[7] And yet a visitor could sometimes have been fooled into thinking it was a happy family summer holiday as the grand duchesses spotted early blue Siberian anemones, sniffed 'the nice lilac bushes and small honeysuckle', or brought back armfuls of daisies for the Empress from the garden.[8]

Imperial valet Terenty Chemodurov was shocked by the behaviour of the 'absolutely indecent' guard making a point of jeering at the tsarinas 'as they walked to the bathroom'.[9]

But even in their spartan confinement, menus were printed for the imperial family as if they were still in the Alexander Palace. One stated simply, 'Veal, garnished with macaroni'; the previous day it had been 'Hot wild duck, salad and rice pudding'. The royal cook, Haritonov, tried his best with poor ingredients; most days, food tended to be pickles, potatoes, shredded cabbage and maybe blancmange.

Gallantly, Nicholas tried to make Tobolsk sound like a vacation. Writing to his mother on 27 October 1917, he told her, 'The food here is excellent,' complaining about a weight gain of 'eight to ten pounds'.

One of the few pleasures not denied him was manual work. He enjoyed gardening, and asked his guards, 'Can you allow me to saw firewood? I love such work.'[10] In the evenings, having decided 'to read all our best writers from beginning to end', he particularly enjoyed military histories, including Fiodor Uspensky's *History of the Byzantine Empire* and John Richard Green's *A Short History of the English People.* In his meticulous way, another trait shared with George V, he listed in his diary the number of pages and how long it had taken him to finish a book. His cultivated mind helped him endure house arrest, and he was genuinely delighted to discover some of Tolstoy's work 'I had not known before' – a quarter of *War and Peace.*

He read Turgenev's *Nest of the Gentry*[11] to Alix and the children, and, for something lighter, chose *The Haunted Armchair* and *The Perfume of the Lady in Black.* His own preference for an entertaining read was Conan Doyle's *Memoirs of Sherlock Holmes.* The children, moulded by their English tutors, enjoyed a selection of books including *The Fifth Form at St Dominic's* and Rider Haggard's *King Solomon's Mines.*

Tea was served after dinner and by eleven o'clock everyone was in bed. It was a simple routine, which for this particular family was bearable because of their closeness. The paralysing monotony of their life at Tobolsk was, in retrospect, an oasis in view of what was to come.

Now grey-bearded, with silver flecks in his hair, Nicholas, though ineffably tired, was spending his days 'like any humble serf', gardening – growing beans, turnips and lettuce. The officers assiduously ignored his courteous salutes. Once he put out his hand to one of the jailers, who replied, 'not for anything in the world', to which Nicholas said, 'But my dear fellow, why? What have you got against me?'

The King, absorbing letters 'from people in all classes of life'[12] making plain their opposition to the Tsar's settling in England, might have been dismayed had he seen his cousin in Tobolsk, this fastidious man in a shabby khaki shirt, patched trousers and worn boots, being sneered at by his guards, with cigarettes impudently hanging from their mouths.

The guards were now even more confident because they knew that on 7 November 1917 the Bolsheviks had seized real power in St Petersburg. Provisional government ministers meeting in the Malachite Hall of the Winter Palace went into a nervous huddle when the dark wintry sky dramatically lit up with red flashes from the guns of the Peter and Paul Fortress and warning shots were fired from the cruiser *Aurora.*

By 2.10 a.m., the petrified provisionals had been arrested by the Bolsehviks and frogmarched down the marble steps to the jeers and exultation of the mob. Kerensky ignominiously hid in an *isba*, a cottage; he and his provisional government were finished. Lenin was back and was quickly harnessing the new Soviet power. The Bolsheviks had increased their manpower to 52,000 and were highly organised.

Civil war now set in for the harsh winter of 1918. Filthy red rags now flew from cathedral cupolas and the Winter Palace, while Nevsky Prospekt was strangely empty. Palaces became committee rooms filled with dishevelled strikers and soldiers who spat at the portraits and took pot shots at crystal chandeliers. Carpets were used for bonfires, and rare libraries and works of art were destroyed as the often barefoot mob swarmed through the great houses and palaces. Lenin was master now, and he moved to Moscow.

A band of disorderly soldiers and workmen, 'ruffians with unshaven faces', with a 'motley collection of every kind of weapon', surrounded the British Embassy. Instead of the soft footfall of velvet-jacketed pages, all that could be heard inside the embassy now was a deafening and 'constant sound of shooting, the shouts and screams of drunken and wounded men, a medley of sobs and laughter, of maudlin voices joining in the interminable choruses of Russian folk songs'. An 'atmosphere of dread . . . seemed to brood over the town'.[13]

Lady Georgina Buchanan's sewing parties, set up during the war, went on serenely during this turbulence. Socialites in elaborate hats faced increasing danger on their way to the embassy and, in shocked voices, told each other about the horrible sights they had just witnessed: a policeman trussed up in ropes, the body of another dragged along a frozen road, an officer being shot down on a doorstep.

In typically English style, embassy secretary Evelyn Henley,[14] arriving for work in the ballroom, sniffed disapprovingly and remarked that the rebels had been most inaccurate: the Winter Palace had been hit only three times by shells from the cruiser *Aurora*, and thus she assumed that the mutinous sailors were either hopeless shots or had deliberately used blanks.

A marauding mob stormed the Winter Palace, breaking down gold-embossed doors and hauling treasured paintings off the walls. Buchanan saw the devastation for himself.[15] Lorries full of soldiers 'drove up to the Winter Palace and went away again, heavily loaded with cases of priceless wine . . . women brought packing cases, washing baskets, sacks and bags, and could be seen trying to sell bottles of champagne or valuable old liqueur to passers-by in the streets'. In Hogarthian scenes they then lay drunk in snow streaked with different shades of wine and the gold of liqueurs, and littered with broken wine bottles bearing the imperial seal, looted from the Tsar's cellars.

When Nicholas heard the news at Tobolsk he was filled with remorse about his abdication, saying, 'The Emperor abdicated because he thought it would be better for Russia. It turned out to be worse.'

In a letter to Anna Vyrubova dated 16 December 1917, Alix had nothing but admiration for Nicholas, saying, 'He is simply marvellous . . . Such meekness while all the time suffering intensely for the country'. Then she added wistfully, 'We have no news from our old home or from England.'[16] The Tsarina smuggled a letter out of Tobolsk in Gibbes's handwriting to her former governess Miss 'Madgie', Margaret Jackson, which included a clumsy floor plan of the house where they were held prisoner. But it never reached its destination.

Christmas at Tobolsk in 1917 was their last. The imperial family tried to celebrate. Alix did a drawing of a piece of holly to remind her of Christmas in England. They sat round a miniature Siberian spruce tree that was placed on the table and gave each other tiny gifts: treasured personal icons or small silver dishes, ribbons painted as home-made bookmarks and hand-knitted waistcoats; for the servants, gloves and scarves. To please the Empress there was an embroidered lilac handkerchief with a tender inscription: 'To my sweet, darling Mama dear – may God's blessings be upon you and guard you forever. Your own loving girl, Tatiana.' As entertainment, the tutors, Gilliard and Gibbes, directed the children in an English play ironically called 'Packing Up'; the biggest laugh for the sad little audience was when a gust of wind revealed that Anastasia was wearing her father's Jaeger underpants under her skirt.[17]

By spring, life had become distinctly more squalid in Tobolsk. The guards were mutinous because they had not been paid. Tension about a power struggle among the local Soviets was conveyed to Nicholas and his family via even more contemptuous treatment. Nicholas was horrified by the Treaty of Brest-Litovsk, in which Lenin agreed to part with a third of Russia's territory to placate the Germans and bring peace.

The Bolshevik commissar, Vassily Yakovlev,* told Nicholas on 12 April 1918 that he now had definite orders to move them to Moscow. A few days earlier the Tsarevich had been tobogganing down the stairs, although it was strictly forbidden, had fallen and was badly bruised, aggravating his haemophilia. Nicholas replied that he could not be separated from his son, who was now seriously ill. The commissar, impervious to the boy's pain as Alexei cried out, 'I would like to die, Mama . . . I'm so afraid of what they may do to us here' – merely said stonily that the Tsar and Tsarina must leave at once.

As a wife and mother, the Empress was now forced to make an almost biblical choice; in the end, she sacrificed her children to be with Nicholas, supporting the man she had loved unwaveringly through the best and now the worst of times. In a mood of barely disguised bitterness she said quietly to Yakovlev, 'You know what my son is to me . . . I must choose between him and my husband. But I have made up my mind. I must be firm. I must leave my child and share my husband's life or death.'

It was agony for this overprotective mother, who was also worried about her daughters at such a vulnerable stage in their young lives. She knew how the guards taunted them, shouting drunken obscenities, and making them blush when they deliberately dived naked into the ponds. They suffered and felt ashamed when faced with the degrading, crude graffiti on the walls, implying sexual adventures between Rasputin and their mother.

Grand Duchess Maria, the most resilient daughter, was chosen to accompany her parents. There was another reason for the choice: it was feared that the nubile Maria was becoming too attached to one of the guards.

In the winter months, as the river was frozen, it was impossible to leave Tobolsk by steamer. On a cruelly cold day, 26 April 1918, with icy sleet, four filthy *tarantasses* were drawn up in front of the governor's mansion.[18] These peasant carts had no seats or springs, being just huge baskets suspended between two poles; the traveller was forced to sit or lie on the floor. The imperial doctor felt sure the Tsarina would not survive this elaborately contrived, extreme discomfort over hundreds of miles of hard, bumpy, primitive tracks.

---

*   He carried out his duties ardently but later fell foul of Stalin and was executed in 1938.

Some straw from a pigsty in the backyard was brought for her.[19] The Tsarina, normally frail and enveloped in soft shawls, was now unceremoniously pushed into a cart not unlike the tumbril which took Marie Antoinette to the guillotine. All was now ready for the imperial family's last journey.

Standing in the doorway of the governor's mansion, three of the young grand duchesses, Olga, Tatiana and Anastasia, tried to wave but were overcome by tears. Then their father moved over to them and made the sign of the cross above his daughters.

The children had filled the Tsar's pockets with cheering notes; one from Olga told her father not to worry about Alexei: 'God protect you, bless you and have pity on you, my dear darling Papa'; and from his soldier-boy heir came the brave promise, 'I'm going to try to eat a lot and get well quickly. I am so glad our sharpshooters are travelling with you.'

The party endured a harrowing, 186-mile journey through snow-filled ravines, along muddy, rutted tracks and across the swollen Irtysh river; the horses waded in up to their chests, often losing their balance; twice the carts were overturned. Having given up any exercise apart from playing the piano, and hardly ever walking, the Tsarina, in a thin Persian lamb coat, at times had to be carried by her husband. In what normally would have been a touching romantic gesture, he gingerly walked across shaky wooden planks laid over the ice floes, carrying his precious cargo. The Empress wrote to a friend saying simply that all her 'soul had been shaken out'.[20] One morning the Tsarina had an unexpected glimpse of Rasputin's Siberian village when they changed horses at Pokrovskoye. In an eerie moment, the shaman's family appeared impassively at the windows of their house.[21]

The prisoners, who still thought they were bound for Moscow, found a train waiting at Tyumen which would take them to Ekaterinburg, stronghold of the Ural Soviet, where they would spend the last seventy-eight days of their lives.

TWENTY-SIX

'The Road to Calvary'

Few can avoid a cold shudder at the thought of Siberia, that desolate, barely habitable region where a tsar and later many progressive Russian writers were banished to languish and die.

The ability of the human soul to be hopeful was never more in evidence than in the Tsar and Tsarina's pleasure at the change in the weather, as they were moved from one prison to another. Like kidnap victims, they had no idea where they were going or who was going with them.

As if bound for a Siberian spring holiday, Alix recorded the day they arrived in Ekaterinburg as 'Beautiful, warm . . . glorious bright sunshine . . . and changing clouds'. This being Russia, she was reporting snow five days later. Her favourite good luck symbol was the swastika, which she engraved on the wall above what would be the Tsarevich's bed, marking the day, 30 April 1918, of their arrival.[1]

Nicholas and Alexandra tended to look at their lives in terms of 'light' or 'pitch black'.[2] Now it was becoming harder, even with their deep religious conviction, to remain optimistic. But the two intangibles which eluded the Bolsheviks were the bond between the couple and the intensity of their *charismata*, the spiritual gifts which helped them accept their wretchedness.

The Empress seemed to have been waiting all her life for this cruel test of character, declaring, 'If they do take everything from us, they cannot take our souls.' But then she was often at her best in a crisis, as witnessed during the war when she was running busy hospitals, but was not often given credit; 'she is one of those characters who rise to the sublime only in misfortune'.[3]

A power struggle in the Urals had disrupted the planned trial, so the train carrying the imperial family to Moscow was diverted instead to Ekaterinburg. This mining town in Siberia, created in 1721 by Catherine the Great 30 miles east of the border between Asia and Europe, was famous for its diamonds and subsequently infamous for the murder of the last Tsar. Visitors were seldom attracted to such an ugly town, unless they were engineers or mining technicians. Ekaterinburg had always had a reputation for violence and organised crime.

After his abdication, Nicholas declared with an intuitive despondency that he would 'go anywhere at all, only not to the Urals . . . the Urals are strongly opposed to me'.[4] Ekaterinburg was where the Russian monarchy would disappear in a round of gunfire.

A mob gathered to watch the imperial family arrive at Ekaterinburg Station on Tuesday 30 April 1918. Seeing the royal luggage being unloaded, one screamed, 'All these boxes contain the gold dresses of the wanton women.' Others took up various rallying cries: 'Death to the tyrant!'; 'Hang them'; 'Bloodsuckers'. The modest sight of six pairs of the Tsar's boots was enough to enrage them, and they began to shout raucously, 'Drown them in the lake.'

As guards rifled through their luggage, Nicholas, wearily watching this bucolic pantomime, said, 'They are taking things out of them . . . we shall never see . . . again'. He particularly hated the way the guards roughly seized the Empress and carried out an unnecessary personal body search, snatching her grey suede bag out of her hands; but all they found was a handkerchief, some smelling salts and heart drops.[5]

The family was then taken away to the Ipatiev House, a large two-storey white-brick and stone building on the side of a hill, which belonged to a local engineer. Although it had twenty-one rooms and was in fashionable Ascension Square, renamed the Square of National Vengeance, Nicholas, Alix and later with all the children were confined to four rooms.

But Nicholas even managed to even find words of praise for their new prison, saying, 'The house is good and clean.' His stoicism could hardly insulate the family from the ornate humiliation of these last few months in the 'house of special purpose', behind two huge grim fences. They could see nothing outside. Alix noted the gradual end of winter with 'snow and dirt lying'; but then to the imperial family everything looked off-white, as all their windows had been painstakingly whitewashed by an elderly man to prevent them seeing or being seen. 'Only at the top can see a bit of sky . . . it looks as if there is a fog outside the windows . . . not at all cosy', Alix wrote in her diary.[6] As the sun rises at around five in the morning in Ekaterinburg, the day started brightly enough; even the Soviets could not block out the light of dawn.

If ever there was good news or comfort for the couple, it was the arrival of the four children on 10 May 1918, bringing 'immense joy'[7] but also distressing stories about their journey. Their French tutor, Gilliard, had been forced to stifle gallant instincts: unable to help, he had to watch as the young Princesses, who had never carried anything heavier than a hoop or a skipping rope, battled with brown leather suitcases and trunks. When Tatiana, tentatively holding on to her black-and-tan Pekinese dog, slipped in the mud in driving rain, Nagorny, one of the two sailors who looked after her brother, rushed forward to help, but soldiers roughly pushed him away. The sailor then carried the crippled Tsarevich from the riverbank on to the *Rus* for the damp journey.

On this journey the tsarinas were separated from the protection of their tutors and the rest of the royal party but kept vigilantly awake; although innocent and overprotected, they were aware of the sexual attentions of some of the drunken guards and the threat of rape.[8] These sheltered girls had got used to being spied upon while dressing and undressing by some of the more prurient guards at Tobolsk. Now reunited with their parents, the children had a more contented night's sleep – even though they were lying on the floor on their cloaks – than they had known for even one night when alone at Freedom House.

Often criticised for her mournful appearance, the Tsarina now had good reason for a downturned mouth and her sad accusing eyes. She was comforted by religious books, rereading the Bible and the Life of Saint Serafim of Sarovsk. Though needlework could aggravate her migraines, dutifully, like a serf's wife, she patched the Tsar's trousers and her daughters' nightdresses, and knitted socks for 'Little One'. Sometimes she mustered enough strength to cut her husband's hair; he seemed not to complain, revealing in his diary how 'Alix cut my hair quite well'.

On 19 May 1918, Nicholas's fiftieth birthday was marked with a small parcel of chocolate and coffee which arrived from Grand Duchess Elizabeth 'Ella' Feodorovna, his sister-in-law in Moscow. Ella was dear to him; she had been the go-between, the romantic alchemist in his pursuit of Alix. Now all that they had to remember her by were the albums of enchanting drawings of children, flowers, cherubs, clowns, bumblebees and butterflies she had once drawn for her little sister, sending them to Darmstadt, addressed to Prinzessin Alix von Hessen.

The unkempt, slovenly guards, who had been drawn from the local factories, joined the imperial family at poor meals of mainly dry black bread, ageing greasy cabbage soup and mildewed potatoes, reaching insolently across them with filthy hands into the one dish, nudging the Tsar and Tsarina as they grabbed at any elusive piece of meat being saved for the Tsarevich.[9]

Sometimes the less brutish guards stopped in their tracks when they heard the high voices of the grand duchesses singing wistful Russian psalms, briefly charmed by their innocent grace; occasionally, they asked the girls to play the piano for their amusement.

Olga, aged twenty-three, was blonde, artistic, close to her father and protective of the Tsarevich. An attractive twenty-year-old, Tatiana had her mother's reserve, while Maria, then aged eighteen, was extrovert, slightly overweight and the most popular with the soldiers, always asking them about their families. Anastasia had not been blessed with the willowy beauty of her older sisters, but she had a strong sense of mocking humour. Her mother would refer to her as 'my legs!', as the girl – she was seventeen and the most outgoing of them all – willingly ran endless errands for the ailing Empress.

A new jailer, beetle-browed Yankel Yurovsky, was now appointed grand commander of the Ipatiev House. Nicholas called him 'the dark gentleman' – 'this specimen we like least of all' – he recorded in his diary.[10] Black-bearded and always in a black leather jacket, the former jeweller and photographer's assistant was chillingly efficient, obsessional about discipline; he put a stop to the crude taunting of the tsarinas.

The sailor Derevenko, once so solicitous of the Tsarevich, now instinctively sensing the captors' even uglier mood towards the prisoners, took advantage. Swaggeringly, legs outstretched to trip up the Tsarevich, he bullied him, ordering him to fetch and carry, and taught him crude swear words. The child, bewildered, kept running from one object to another, doing whatever the sailor told him.[11] It was Nagorny who protected the frail boy, and he was also murdered.

Nuns from a nearby convent had been allowed to send eggs and pastries to the prisoners, particularly for the Tsarevich. The day before the assassination, the guards ordered fifty eggs, which were hard-boiled by the chef, Haritonov. But these were not for the royal captives; instead they were eaten at a ghoulish picnic by their bloodstained murderers, who watched grimly as the corpses took their time to burn, even with liberal amounts of paraffin.

There were continuing rumours about rescue attempts; more than once the imperial family was told to listen out for a whistle in the dead of night. Believing intrepid agents might be hiding in the nearby fir forests, the Tsar and family lay on their beds by the windows 'fully dressed', hugging their most precious possessions, icons and jewellery, waiting for the elusive sound of rescue. Alix and her daughters had stitched 'the medicines'[12] – code for 'jewels' – into their bodices, fur hats, the hems of their skirts, even behind the buttons on their jackets.

There was one cackhanded attempt at rescue by two young imperial officers who brought a car to Ekaterinburg. They found Nicholas sitting on a bench with Alexei in the garden, and hissed, 'Jump in, we're going to save you.' But Nicholas refused, saying with dignity, 'It does not behove a Russian Tsar to flee from his own country. The Russian people will not harm me, for I have never wished them ill.'[13] In spite of everything, he still loved Russia and believed his people loved him.

Any pretence of putting the Tsar on trial was abandoned. The Ural Regional Soviets were acting independently and sent Lenin a starkly worded telegram, informing him that 'the agreed trial' could not be delayed. 'Trial' was code for murder. One telegram to Moscow announced that 'the Ekaterinburg detachment' had only one goal, which was to 'annihilate the luggage', code for the imperial family. 'Chimney-sweep' was the word devised for the execution. The extermination of the Romanov family was seen as a clean sweep of filthy chimneys.

When Father Storozhev, a Russian Orthodox priest, was called to the 'house of special purpose' to say Mass for the Tsar and his family at 10.00 a.m. on 14 July 1918, he sensed a change in the atmosphere thinking that they were all different, particularly sad, as if 'something has happened to them'. They were no longer happily talkative among themselves.

The Tsar's beard was unkempt, the grand duchesses' hair had grown back again after being shaved off when they had had measles, giving them the haunted look of starving prisoners. When the Song of Cherubim, 'Who resteth with the Saints', was sung, the imperial family knelt and bowed their heads.

The telegram Yurovsky had keenly awaited from Moscow arrived on 16 July 1918, bearing the long-awaited instructions to 'exterminate the R—vs'. In his version of events years later, he pointed out the difficulties he faced: 'Shooting people,' he suggested, 'isn't the easy matter it might seem to some.' To make things swift and more efficient, he employed 'the same number of gunmen as victims'.

'We must shoot *them all* tonight,' he told Paul Medvedev, commander of the guard at the Ipatiev House, but had some difficulty finding volunteers prepared to kill the tsarinas; even the guards who had tormented them were reluctant. Handing out a dozen Nagants,* Yurovsky instructed the assassins that they were to pepper the eleven victims with bullets but that they must leave the choice target for their master.

On their last day, the family got up at nine, looking forward to the simple pleasure of eggs for breakfast. But the Tsarina, always intuitive, was uneasy when guards came to take away Leonid Sednev, the kitchen boy, giving as a fatuous reason for his removal that he had to visit his uncle. Later he was seen sitting on the window sill of the house across the lane, weeping bitterly.

Nicholas's last diary entry inevitably has a mention of the weather, which he recorded as being 'warm and pleasant'. One of the guards said afterwards that, in spite of their hatred for the 'German whore', they had always been struck by the Tsar's humble bearing and his 'kind eyes'. Suffering lent him more majesty than he had ever mustered during his ill-starred reign. He too had a premonition; his valet Chemodurov was shocked when he found the Emperor lying on a little bed fully clothed, something which was completely out of character. The manservant offered to prepare the bed, but Nicholas replied gently, 'Don't trouble, old man, I feel in my heart I shall live only a short time.'[14]

That night the imperial family went to bed at the usual time, around 10.30 p.m. Just after midnight, Yurovsky allowed himself the pleasure of waking them himself for their appointment with death. He told them that, as the White Army was approaching and

---

*   A 7-shot revolver designed in Belgium by Émile and Léon Nagant of Liège but made by Russia's Tula Arsenal from 1898, and was still being issued to Soviet police in the 1950s. Paradoxically, in view of its use here, it was almost unique among contemporary designs in being capable of being fitted with a silencer.

there was unrest in the town, they would be better off moving down to the cellar. It would not do for them to be exposed to any danger.

The Empress and her daughters took forty minutes to dress, carefully putting on their jewel-laden corsets. Struggling in night-clothes, the Tsarevich, nodding sleepily, was carried in his father's arms. Although fourteen, he had been so ill he could no longer walk; he insisted that Joy, his spaniel, should accompany them.

The party, including Anna Demidova, the Empress's chamber-maid, carrying a cushion stuffed with jewels, valet Alexis Trupp, the chef Haritonov and burly old Dr Botkin, all biddably followed Yurovsky down the stairs. But the tsarinas, dressed in blue wool cloaks and also carrying small cushions, were frightened, sobbing and 'clutching each other'.[15]

They trailed across the courtyard to a lower room with incongruously flowery wallpaper. 'What, there isn't a chair?' the Empress asked. 'One isn't even allowed to sit down?' As a chair was brought in, the maid put down the cushion she was carrying for the Empress. Yurovsky then asked the imperial family to pose for a photograph. With grim satisfaction he spoke the immortal lines, 'Your relatives have tried to save you, they have failed, and we are now obliged to shoot you all.' Leaping to his feet, the Tsar incredulously asked, 'What?'[16] 'What does this mean?' At this Yurovsky raised a Browning pistol and, pointing it at the Tsar, responded viciously, 'This! Your race must cease to live.'

The Emperor was first to get a bullet through his head; through all the crying and butchery, the Empress began to recite the 'Our Father' and tried to cross herself, but was blown from her chair, killed instantly. In the light of a cold Siberian summer dawn, as the shooting began, the blood of the imperial family splattered the walls of the cellar, which was so small that 'murderers and victims almost stood on each other's toes'.

The shooting of all eleven people began around one o'clock in the morning. Four of the Tsar's dogs started howling outside and there was a brief lull while they were hanged. The shooting was hap-hazard, taking twenty minutes altogether because the children were slow to die. 'Aim straight for the heart,' Yurovsky irritably instructed the gunmen, who found their bullets were ricocheting off the princesses' jewelled bodices. Anastasia and Maria cowered,[17] trying to shield their heads. Anastasia also 'rolled about and screamed . . . and when one of the murderers approached [she] desperately tried to fight him off until he killed her'.[18] Another, whimpering faintly as the bodies were being loaded like sacks of waste on to a lorry, was also battered into infinity.

The air was now filled with the acrid stench of cordite. Ironically, of all the family, the frail Tsarevich was the last to survive, writhing on the floor, trying to reach for the lapel of his father's coat. Yurovsky indulged himself by kicking him in the head with his boot, and then fired point-blank twice into the boy's ear.[19] 'I finished him off,' he reported triumphantly, but still found that Alexei had a 'strange vitality' and took longer to die than was altogether 'convenient'.

The loyal Anna Demidova, with extraordinary strength, grabbed at her assassin's gun barrel with both hands, but he simply plunged his bayonet through her chest.[20]

Orders were given to 'wash up' the bloody walls and floor of the death chamber, but for years afterwards these shameful marks on the walls could not be erased. When they threw the bodies on to primitive stretchers, someone reported the sound of 'rustling', and it is claimed that one of the grand duchesses sat bolt upright, only to be clubbed on the head.

Undressing the bodies, they found that the Tsarina was wearing an elaborate pearl-studded belt, and that her daughters Olga, Tatiana and Maria had solid rubies, sapphires, emeralds, huge pearls and eighteen pounds of diamonds in their bodices. Later, when the bones and skulls were found, there was also a manicured woman's finger, believed to be the Tsarina's.

The disfigured 'bloody bundles'* were then loaded on to a lorry and driven 12 miles towards Four Brothers' Wood, a forest near the village of Koptyaki. On the way, the murderers came across a village woman setting out early with her fish to put up her stall in the town, but she was ordered home, escorted by a guard who forbade her to look back.

The assassins prepared a pit around 6 feet deep and 8 feet square. They then splashed sulphuric acid and 150 gallons of petrol on to the faces and naked bodies of the imperial family and their servants. A few branches and brushwood were thrown into the pit before the pyre was set alight. Yurovsky, the chief assassin, fled on the last train out of Ekaterinburg, taking with him the Tsar's diaries, bound

---

* Yurovsky's assistant, Rudolf Lacher, never forgot the sight.

in black morocco leather, which he had begun at the age of fourteen.[21]

The White Army marched on Ekaterinburg on 25 July 1918, and immediately seized the 'house of special purpose'. The Tsar and his family had missed being rescued by a week. One eyewitness described the 'chilling disorder' of the cellar, its walls riddled with bullets and smeared with congealed blood. Scrawled caricatures on the lavatory walls of Rasputin and Alexandra were like something from the Kama Sutra.

The children's tutors, Gibbes and Gilliard, were now allowed to go through the house, where they found the Tsarevich's pet spaniel, Joy,* half-starved,[22] shivering and blinded, standing near the door of the cellar, waiting to be let in by his young master.

They recognised so many personal things: the wooden board which was used as a tray for the boy's meals in bed when he was too ill to join the family; the small basket for his hairbrushes; the Empress's lilac silk jewel case; her wheelchair; a copy of *Tales from Shakespeare*; a child's belt; a decorative paste shoe buckle; and a Maltese cross with emeralds. Scrupulously catalogued by the Bolsheviks, they put these items on show later along with other poignant exhibits in the nearby Museum of the People's Vengeance, and included the Tsarevich's wooden toy soldier and books with the initials A.F.†

A small book was found hidden in a ventilator in the Ipatiev House, bearing the inscription, 'For my own beloved Nicky, dear, to use when he is absent from his *Spitzbube* Fr. His, lovingly, Alice', a sentimental treasure belonging to Nicholas conveying ineffably happy memories of the early days of his engagement. A ruby stone, which had been part of a ring given to her by Nicholas when she was fifteen, was found round the Tsarina's neck.[23]

The first the world knew about the murder of the Tsar and his family was from a revolutionary radio station today operating from Tsarskoe Selo. Trotsky was told by Sverdlov, Chairman of the All-Russian Central Executive Committee of Soviets, that the Tsar had been shot because 'Ilyich (Lenin) decided we shouldn't leave the Whites a live banner to rally round.'[24]

The King and Queen heard the news about the murder of 'poor Nicky of Russia' a week after it happened. 'Shot', Queen Mary

---

*   Joy was later brought to England and given a good home near Windsor Castle.

†   Alexandra Feodorovna, the Tsarina.

recorded in her diary, 'by those brutes of Bolsheviks'. It was all, she declared 'too horrible and heartless'. It was too late for any mementos – virtually everything had been destroyed by the Bolsheviks – but the King had precious photographs: family shots of 'Nicky' and 'Georgie' together sailing, picnicking, splendid in uniform – two cousins enjoying warm, affectionate confidences.

Gibbes returned to England with his keepsake of the Tsarevich; he had chosen his bloodstained bandages. He became a priest in Oxford, a sad and contemplative figure who died in 1963 at St Pancras Hospital in London. His indelible memory of the Romanovs was of a family 'so sweet, so sad . . . leading lives of utter simplicity on the road to Calvary'.

TWENTY-SEVEN

Small Humiliations

'I was devoted to Nicky, who was the kindest of men and a thorough gentleman.' This was the King's sad entry in his diary on 25 July 1918, when told about the murder of the Tsar.

He had assumed that only Nicholas had been killed at Ekaterinburg and was outraged when he heard that the Tsarina and those 'poor innocent children' had also been murdered. 'It's too horrible,' he said. 'It shows what fiends those Bolshevists are.' In a letter to the Tsarina's sister, Princess Victoria, Marchioness of Milford Haven, he suggested by way of comfort that it was probably best, as, 'after dear Nicky's death, Alix could not have wished to live. And the beautiful girls' had surely been 'saved from worse at the hands of those horrible fiends'.[1]

It was painful, too, hearing about the ignominious end of the Tsarina's sister Ella, Grand Duchess Elizabeth, murdered at Alapaevsk in Siberia on 8 January 1919 with four grand dukes, one of them found cradling his Persian cat. Wearing her nun's habit, Ella had kept up a chant of 'Lord, forgive them, for they know not what they do.' Later, Princess Victoria arranged for Ella's burial in the peace of the Orthodox convent on the Mount of Olives in Jerusalem.

News of the Tsar's gruesome end sent shock waves through European royal houses. There were dismaying accounts of Bolshevik atrocities as remaining Romanovs were murdered in the 'Red Terror' campaign. The Tsar's able younger brother, Grand Duke Michael, was shot in the temple by revolutionaries on 13 June 1918. An earlier message from the British Ambassador to Lord Stamfordham, protesting against the humiliating treatment Michael had endured, was, in retrospect, a classic piece of understatement: 'The poor Grand Duke,' Buchanan had declared, 'has, I am afraid, had rather a bad time of it lately.'[2]

As Bolshevik domination increased, British diplomats in Russia were viewed with hostility as imperialist lackeys, and their lives were in danger. 'Too long have we calmly endured the mockery of the representatives of Allied imperialism' the Russian newspaper *Izvestiya* protested. Capturing the mood of the country, it continued, 'We allow people who once licked the boots of tsarism to remain in Russia although they do not recognise the workers' government.'[3] The King believed that, at the cost of cancelling the offer of safe haven to the Tsar, he had prevented the spread of Bolshevism to Britain.

He was now carrying out a carefully orchestrated plan aimed at nurturing the monarchy. Events in Ekaterinburg, combined with postwar unrest had accelerated the need for a more democratic royal approach. Lord Stamfordham made the radical suggestion that 'There would seem to be no reason . . . why the King should not both visit hospitals and . . . meet shop stewards and trade union secretaries and form personal and first-hand opinions of their grievances, aims and aspirations.'

This innovative campaign to make the monarchy more popular, resulted in a cross section of society now being invited to lunch or tea at the palace; part of an offensive against the socialist promise of true equality and the destruction of the class system in Britain.

By January 1924, the King was ready to cope with his first Labour government, if at first he was a little puzzled. Writing to his mother, as if explaining a new species of human being, he told her he was surprised how they 'all seem to be very intelligent'. They referred to him as the 'little quiet man'.[4] But he was loud enough in his fierce disapproval of their wish to recognise the new Soviet regime in Russia. He told Prime Minister Ramsay MacDonald that he would find it 'abhorrent' to have to accept the presence on British soil of any representative of Russia 'who, directly or indirectly', had been connected with the 'abominable murder of the Emperor, Empress and their family.'[5] Nevertheless, he later told MacDonald, 'You have been the Prime Minister I liked best.'[6]

The King's defensive anger was sometimes an expression of his pent-up anguish about the Tsar's death. He resisted the appointment of any ambassadorial British presence in Russia's new regime. Later, indignantly he asked Sokolaikov, the first Soviet Ambassador to London, who was presenting his credentials at Windsor Castle in 1930,[7] 'What do you think it means to me to be forced to shake hands with a man of the party that murdered my cousin?'

All around Europe, monarchies were collapsing, or, as Herbert Asquith succinctly observed,* there now appeared to be a distinct 'slump in emperors'. The King expressed little regret when Wilhelm II was forced to give up his throne. 'I look upon him,' he said of the Kaiser, 'as the greatest criminal known for having plunged the world into this ghastly war.'† The defeat of the German Army had resulted in the signing of the Armistice on 11 November 1918. Fleeing into exile in Holland on 11 November 1918, one of the first things the deposed Kaiser did was to request 'a nice cup of English tea'. He now had time to reflect on his theory that 'Monarchy is like virginity: once you've lost it, you can't get it back.'

Not lacking in compassion, George was stirred by the plight of the Tsar's mother Dagmar, his beloved 'Aunt Minnie', who was marooned in the Crimea with her daughter Xenia, held by a gang calling themselves 'The Soviet of Workers and Soldiers' Deputies'. But even under these degrading conditions, one of the family had the foresight to bury some of the imperial jewels in cocoa tins behind a rock on the seashore, marking the spot with the bleached skull of a dog.

The Dowager Empress, then seventy-three years old, had been sustained by the wildly improbable but optimistic belief that Nicholas was still alive somewhere in the far north of Russia, a place that could only be reached in summer and was being protected by a group of 'Old Believers', a breakaway branch of the Orthodox Church.

It was with the greatest reluctance that she left Russia on 25 March 1919, Good Friday, a suitably sombre day. Nineteen Romanovs with retainers had boarded a British warship, HMS *Marlborough*. As they set sail, Xenia enquired, 'What are those little black things all along the shore?'[8] The captain, who had lent her his binoculars, replied, 'Madam, that is your silver.' The servants, scrambling aboard with understandably indecent haste, had abandoned any attempt at loading all 200 tons of royal baggage.

---

* Asquith had been Home Secretary, Chancellor of the Exchequer and, in 1909, Prime Minister.

† Despite this, 'the English royal family had a soft spot for William II', according to James Lees-Milne in his biography of Harold Nicholson, who had been asked by Queen Mary to excise an unkind reference to the Kaiser in his own biography of George V. She had always enjoyed the ex-Kaiser's 'very affectionate letters' from his exile in Doorn.

Dagmar stood motionless on deck as the band played 'God Save the Tsar', leaving the country which she had loved as home for more than half a century. The voyage to safety was like a sad, floating house party. The women exchanged gifts appropriate for a restrained Easter on board – not Fabergé any more, but simple painted boiled eggs. Children, each carrying a white flower, 'bowed and kissed the Empress's hand', offering the traditional Russian Easter greeting '*Khristos voskrese*' [Christ is risen], and receiving the answer '*Voistinu voskrese*' [In truth he is risen].

When the ship berthed in Malta, Dagmar sent a message to the King suggesting she might settle there, as she thought the Mediterranean port charming. But George, who had mixed memories of the little island, insisted they must come to England. This rebuff was a painful reminder of her newly vulnerable position as a stateless person without much say in her own destiny. They sailed from Malta on board HMS *Lord Nelson*.

When the ship docked in Portsmouth on 9 May 1919, Queen Alexandra, now seventy-four years old, was waiting at the quayside. Tenderly she embraced her 'little sister', who was wearing a sequinned hat and showing a touch of her old style. Together they left by train for London, where the King and Queen were waiting at Victoria Station.

Grand Duchess Marie Pavlovna, a granddaughter of Alexander II, sourly described the 'welcome' as 'somehow lacking . . . the station was virtually deserted'. Whether it was to save his aunt's feelings or his own, the King had insisted on a 'members of the royal family only' reception. He had been warned by advisers to be cautious about any royal public endorsement of the deposed Russian imperial family.*

Once used to the deference of the imperial court, Dagmar, now without her exotic Circassian guards with their flashing swords, was escorted by a top-hatted stationmaster. A few of her retainers had prostrated themselves on the platform: they had been so struck by the King's likeness to the Tsar that they crossed themselves, believing it was a miracle.

Dagmar found her new circumstances almost intolerable. Sharing Marlborough House in London with her sister was a strain on both

---

* Besides, just over a week after Nicholas had given up the throne, the British government had speedily recognised the provisional government in Russia.

women, although they loved each other dearly. But they had become crotchety, one buffeted by deafness and memories of Edward VII's chronic philandering ('my naughty little man', she once called him),[9] the other by the death of her husband and three sons.

Soon Dagmar returned to Copenhagen, where she settled in her last home, Hvidøre, a Victorian villa with a rose garden and orchard. The British royal family had not been entirely sorry to see her go. Sensitive to atmosphere, with a hint of sarcasm Dagmar expressed in a letter the hope 'that my absence will help to calm everyone'.[10] Assuaging his feelings of guilt, the King, with help from his mother and his sister, Princess Victoria, now made her an allowance of £10,000 a year. Laconically, Dagmar observed that it was 'better to be number one at Hvidøre, than number two at Sandringham', and pinned a homely motto, 'East or West, Home is Best', above the mantelpiece.[11]

But when Queen Alexandra died Dagmar was inconsolable, remembering their golden days as admired Empresses. Failing to find much happiness in her native Denmark, where she was under sufferance again, this time plagued by economies imposed by her parsimonious nephew King Christian X, she felt elderly, poor and unwanted. Her daughters were at her bedside in Denmark when she died, aged eighty, in November 1927. The Duke of York, the future King George VI, attended her funeral there in Roskilde Cathedral.

Soon after her death, alarm bells rang insistently at Buckingham Palace about the contents of those cocoa tins, which had been smuggled out of Russia and stashed away under the Dowager Empress's bed in Denmark.* Swiftly, they were brought to England and opened at Windsor Castle on 22 May 1929.

In a reverent silence they watched as 'ropes of the most wonderful pearls, all graduated, the largest being the size of a big cherry',[12] were laid out on a mahogany table, a reassuring sight for the King, Queen Mary, Grand Duchess Xenia and a few hand-picked courtiers. The little party stood transfixed as jungle-green emeralds, ruby-and-diamond tiaras, four-row pearl chokers, twenty pink diamond stars and huge cabochon sapphires twinkled, brightening the castle drawing room on a grey, early summer's day.

It was Queen Mary's good fortune that she found herself in the happy position of being able to acquire diamond necklaces, tiaras

---

* The Tsar's own estate in England had been valued at a pitiful £500.

and stomachers 'at knock-down prices'[13] because of the plight of the surviving Romanovs.

Apart from the few trinkets they personally retained, the sale of the jewellery was never enough to prevent the Tsar's two sisters from being poverty-stricken in England. 'Sometimes Xenia had almost to beg for help.'[14] Sonia Goodman, whose husband Phillip is a grandson of Lady Ottoline Morrell, recalls how even as a child she was aware of their hardship, so stoically endured.

Her parents, Count and Countess Kleinmichael, had been favourites at the Russian court. After the Revolution, they came to England, where the Count joined Baring Brothers. Soon he was swept up as Xenia's confidant and executor, and as such he tried to make her life more tolerable: 'My father looked after her although Buckingham Palace handled her money.' Asked how the Tsar's sisters were treated in exile in England, Mrs Goodman shakes her head.

A fetching photograph is produced of an elderly Count Vladimir Kleinmichael doing tapestry for cushions, which his daughter proudly points out are still decorative in the Goodman drawing room in London's Notting Hill. Another photograph is of a party on the lawn at Marlborough House, where an unsmiling Queen Mary is looking glum in a long white dress, while Alexandra and Dagmar are laughing like schoolgirls behind a tree. The Queen always felt uneasy about her mother-in-law's sister, who, although widowed, as Dowager Empress still expected a certain precedence.

Xenia never lost her feeling of dependence and was forced to live at a succession of addresses in England. First she was given shelter at Buckingham Palace, where wisely she did not outstay her welcome, but moved on with her six sons to the Savoy Hotel, and from there to a couple of addresses in Kensington. The King felt impelled to offer her £2,400 a year and white-painted Frogmore Cottage, about half a mile from the castle near the Long Walk at Windsor, although it was in a 'deplorable condition'.[14] He agreed to pay for renovations, but insisted that Xenia be careful about the use of gas fires. The message conveyed from Sir Frederick 'Fritz' Ponsonby, the King's Private Secretary, was not one of ecological sensitivity, more of economy: 'HM hopes you will put up a notice in each room asking that fires might not be lit until the heating is actually required.'[15] But they did find her an old gas cooker that was no longer needed at Windsor Castle.

Lord Wigram, a kindly royal adviser and the last Private Secretary to George V, thought Xenia 'very badly off' by royal standards. But she managed to create a homely Russian atmosphere with a pleasantly cluttered sitting room with embroidered shawls and photographs of the Tsar – looking hesitant, smiling or serious in full uniform. However, visitors given tea from a samovar, with lemon, cherries and spicy raisin cake, knew that he was a forbidden topic.

Friends and family saw for themselves how Xenia struggled to look after her virtually unemployable sons. Lean-hipped, with smooth black hair and in well-cut suits, draping their elegant shapes like Noel Coward characters over small damask sofas, they toyed languidly with cigarette holders.

The Tsarina had always been patronising about 'poor little Xenia, with such boys and her daughter married into that wicked family and with such a false husband'. The marriage had not been strong enough to survive the strain of impecunious exile.

During the Second World War, Xenia faced yet another move; already she had been forced to give up Frogmore and had been living in a grace-and-favour house at Hampton Court. Now she was being sent to Craig Gowan in Scotland, with the excuse that it was a peaceful, safe hideaway where the royal family 'could keep an eye' on her. But dispatching her to this gaunt nineteenth-century shooting lodge, which they used twice a year at most, was to condemn her to even more loneliness. 'She was booted out,' Sonia Goodman mockingly intones in a suitably sonorous voice. 'His Majesty offers Craig Gowan,'[16] impersonating a royal emissary.

A great-niece of the Tsarina, Countess Mountbatten of Burma, was also acutely aware of Xenia's poverty in Scotland. 'They were sweet, as poor as church mice. I always remember, at Craig Gowan. Xenia would bravely tell us the remote countryside reminded her of Russia and take us off looking for mushrooms.'[17] The Queen Mother remembered Xenia in Scotland as a 'dear, small and kind' figure, 'dressed in black, who never complained and taught the Queen and Princess Margaret to sing the song of the Volga Boatmen'.[18] Xenia died in April 1960.

This uneasy existence gives some idea of how the Tsar might have fared in England, except that as a fellow emperor, and for security reasons, he might have been given a more sizeable house, one in which he could be protected from all manner of intrusions, though not perhaps from the small humiliations. After some years in

Denmark, his other sister, Olga, at the age of sixty-six gamely went
to Canada as an agricultural immigrant, where a sad picture
emerged of her life in a small bungalow in Toronto. When Sonia
Goodman visited her she thought the grand duchess seemed
preoccupied by gnats. 'She was always fascinated by flies and
catching them, and, like Australians, kept inspecting the jar put out
to catch wasps.' Even boredom under a cherry tree in a Russian
orchard had a weary glamour compared to fly-swatting in Ontario.
'Carrots featured rather a lot,' Sonia Goodman dryly recalls,
remembering Olga's struggle to be a farmer.

When the Queen and Prince Philip visited Canada in 1959, Olga
was invited to join them aboard the royal yacht *Britannia*. Her
excited neighbours urged her to abandon her usual old beret, grey
smock and brown brogues, and to buy something new. Olga
resisted. 'All this fuss, just to go and see Lizzie and Philip,' she
grumbled, setting off in a plain blue and white cotton frock. She
died of cancer, aged seventy-eight, in a small flat over a Toronto
barber's shop in November 1960; Olga had stayed close to the
Orthodox Church and was occasionally sent honey by monks at a
Russian monastery in America.

The Duke of Windsor always claimed that his father had wanted
to rescue the Tsar, long before he was seized by the Bolsheviks, but
that his plan had been thwarted.[19] Romantics also liked to believe
that at least one or two of the young duchesses were saved, literally
thrown into a tiny plane* at Ekaterinburg and whisked across the
Siberian steppe to Vladivostock,[20] a journey of 3,000 miles. The
loudest voice claiming to be the Tsar's youngest daughter,
Anastasia, was that of an eccentric and slightly frumpy woman,
who for years hoodwinked the susceptible with tales of her life in
St Petersburg.

Married to a local businessman, Anna Manahan fantasised about
life as a Romanov princess in Charlottesville, Virginia, a town
celebrated for its Thomas Jefferson University with its Georgian
colonnades and elegant lawns. 'When the so-called "Anastasia" was
given little tests asking if she remembered how the Tsarevich hated
having his hair cut or about a tablecloth which the Empress loved,
she never knew the answer; for sixty-four years she tried to cheat
us.' She was a fraud or, at best, a fantasist, and her claims have

---

*   The DH 4, made of struts and string and looking rather like a box kite.

always been dismissed with ill-concealed contempt by Romanov experts. 'The wretched Anastasia was just an illiterate Polish girl.'[21]

The general view, according to a former White House aide who lives in Charlottesville, was that 'she was crazy. One hot summer's day she was seen sitting in her husband's pick-up truck naked, with nothing more on than a fur scarf, insisting that the doctor should come out and examine her in the street.'[22]

Prince Nicholas Romanov can hardly bring himself to speak about the 'poor lady' who 'looked so vulgar. She could never be mistaken for one of the Tsar's daughters who could not look vulgar if they tried.' When she died in Charlottesville in 1984, DNA tests established conclusively that she had deceived the world for years and had not a drop of Romanov blood in her veins.

Rumours about the plight of surviving Romanovs continued to buzz uncomfortably in the King's ears. He complained that he personally had to deal with more difficulties during his reign than ever Queen Victoria experienced in her sixty-three years on the throne. 'Will there never be an end of them?' he asked the Archbishop of Canterbury, Dr Cosmo Lang, as they walked together in Scotland.

Having rescued his aunt and her daughters, now another first cousin, Prince Andrew of Greece, was in trouble. While the memory of the Tsar's murderous end rankled, it was not enough to make the King feel obliged to rescue this cousin either. Prince Andrew, who was Prince Philip's father and a grandson of King Christian IX of Denmark, was being held by revolutionaries in Greece in 1922, and was facing death. Queen Olga of Greece* in desperation appealed to the King – 'I implore you to save him' – but he was deaf to her pleas. A telegram sent in December 1922 by Sir Eyre Crowe to Lord Hardinge at the Foreign Office emphasised the King's view that it was 'most undesirable that Prince Andrew should come to England at [the] present time'.

Eventually, as a result of Foreign Office intervention, the Prince was taken to safety on board the cruiser HMS *Calypso*, though he was never particularly grateful and resentfully led a nomadic life travelling around the sunnier parts of Europe. His wife, Princess Alice, a niece of the Tsarina and considered one of the most

---

* Grand Duke Constantine's daughter; he was the second son of Nicholas I, and she married George of Greece, 'Greek Georgie'.

attractive princesses in Europe, had been rescued a year earlier from Corfu with her son, Prince Philip, and four daughters.

Earl Mountbatten of Burma, a nephew of the Tsarina,* had always been inordinately proud of his relationship with the British royal family. For years he boasted about the King's role in rescuing Prince Andrew because he was, Mountbatten later explained, 'deeply concerned at having failed to take active steps to save his other first cousin Nicholas II', and had no wish 'to repeat the unfortunate state of affairs'. But this has proved to be nothing more than a personally comforting version of events.

The truth is less palatable. The King had not intervened as Mountbatten longed to believe. Instead he made it abundantly plain that Prince Andrew was not welcome in England. 'Don't want him here,' he declared. It was no secret that he considered his playboy Greek cousin an 'awful fellow' who enjoyed 'nightclubs and smoking'.

A proud man, Mountbatten was eventually forced to accept the factual account held in the Public Record Office, now the National Archives. In a private letter, he blamed his romantic view of the King's intervention† on 'his rather defective memory'.[23] This blow to Mountbatten's harmless familial vanity came towards the end of his life, just before he was killed at the age of seventy-nine by an IRA bomb. He had been on board his boat in the west of Ireland in August 1979 when the terrorists struck, also killing his fourteen-year-old grandson, Nicholas Knatchbull, the boy's paternal grandmother, Dowager Lady Brabourne, and Paul Maxwell, a fifteen-year-old local boy. His daughter, Countess Mountbatten of Burma, was seriously injured. For most people such dismaying memories might provoke hatred, but, dark-haired and calm, the Countess remains contained, kind and gently attentive.

Her great-aunt Alice, Prince Philip's mother, who lived in exile at Buckingham Palace, she remembers as suffering from 'awful depression and nervous breakdowns'. The Countess wonders out loud if there was something in the Hesse genes which made their

---

*   His mother was her sister, Princess Victoria of Hesse.
†   Mountbatten was indulged in this pleasant fantasy by members of the royal family; except the Queen Mother, who thought him a social climber who had engineered the marriage between his impecunious nephew, Prince Philip, and her daughter, the Queen.

women mentally fragile. The Tsarina was often prone to bouts of melancholy introspection, which were damaging to her image at the Russian court.

Princess Alice set up her own religious order and because of her nun's robes was known as 'The Grey Lady'. Countess Mountbatten's grandmother, Princess Victoria, was not that impressed by her niece's new-found spirituality, remarking acerbically, 'Who ever heard of an abbess who smokes and plays canasta?'

The Countess particularly admired her other great-aunt, Ella, who made a point of visiting Ivan Kaliaev, the revolutionary who had murdered her husband, Grand Duke Sergei. With a slight smile, her great-niece observes, 'But he wasn't a bit pleased to see her and not at all repentant.' This 'turning of the other cheek' is not an example the Countess, who still feels anguished over the actions of the IRA, is tempted to follow.

Her grandmother, the great survivor of the Hesse sisters, was a 'cheerful, spirited character who liked to wear a long black skirt with a black-and-white-checked skirt underneath and a pocket where she kept her cigarettes hidden'. When she was told in her eighties that she must cut down on smoking, with Alice in Wonderland logic the Marchioness* interpreted the doctors' advice literally. 'She would cut her cigarettes in half, so when she said, "Dear child run and get my cigarettes", we had to run twice instead of once.'

Queen Victoria was not meant to know about her grand-daughter's love of tobacco, but had an uncanny way of knowing the very things being kept secret from her. 'Once in Scotland, Queen Victoria said to my grandmother, "I hear you smoke"; a frightened silence followed but then the Queen said, "Well you may have one now because of the midges."'

The King felt helpless when he heard about the hardship endured by many of his homeless, impoverished but often gallant relatives. Queen Alexandra died from a heart attack at Sandringham in 1925, and George felt remorseful because he knew how she had worried and wept over her sister Dagmar and the murder of her nephew the Tsar and his family. He loved his mother, no matter how forgetful she became – even her unpunctuality was always forgiven – and

---

* Of Milford Haven, having married Prince Louis of Battenberg, who changed his name in 1917.

cherished her letters, so full of warmth, laughter and concern. He adored her gaiety, her child-like spontaneity, qualities he himself lacked, and her wry humour. At his parents' silver wedding celebrations in 1888, Alexandra was wreathed in orange blossom, but she also had an orange on her head. Asked about this unusual accessory, the Princess of Wales airily explained it was because she was no longer a bud but a ripened fruit.

Her death and the General Strike in 1926, prompted by a crisis in the coal industry when foreign competition threatened the livelihood of the nation's miners, wore him down physically and emotionally. When it was called off after nine days, aware of how badly the Tsar had handled strikes in Russia, George spoke with feeling: 'Our old country can well be proud of itself as during the last nine days there has been a strike in which four million men have been affected; not a single shot has been fired and no one killed; it shows what a wonderful people we are.'[24]

By 1928 he was feeling low, and needed emergency surgery to drain an abscess which had developed on his right lung. The Prince of Wales, hearing that George was close to death, returned swiftly from Africa on 11 December 1928, and was shocked to find the King had become 'a little shrunken old man with a white beard' who appeared unconscious. But suddenly his father stirred and, opening 'half an eye', seeing his son and heir by his bed, reacted smartly. 'Damn you, what the devil are you doing here?'[25] he asked in a remarkably strong voice and, recovered, he was sent to recuperate in Bognor, a stay not engraved on his heart as one of unadulterated happiness.* He continued to worry about his blond, self-absorbed heir, fearing he would squander the hard-earned legacy of a stable monarchy.

---

* His recovery was helped by the concern shown by the British people, who now wrote him encouraging letters and subscribed a gratifyingly generous £689,597 to a thanksgiving fund.

TWENTY-EIGHT

A Chorus of Disapproval

The King had to live with constant, painful reminders of
Nicholas's death which, in a strangely detached comment, he
once described as 'an alien stunt'.[1]

When a service of remembrance for the murdered Tsar was held at
the Russian Church in Welbeck Street in London, he was advised
not to attend, both to spare the feelings of the Romanovs and for his
own protection. But, accompanied by Queen Mary, George went to
the service, where the deep, mournful chant of the Russian
Orthodox choir rising to a crescendo sounded to him like a rebuke.

He also had to bear with Romanov recriminations. Some talked
intemperately about a cold-blooded King who had abandoned the
Tsar, his wife and children.

In a stinging criticism, Prince George of Greece, writing to Grand
Duchess Xenia from St Cloud on 2 November 1920, declared,[2]
'There is *one*, who might have stuck to principle and to nobel [*sic*]
acts, only one, and this is English Georgie.' And angrily he went on,
implying that in his opinion George was 'hiding behind the words
"constitutional King"' and so allowing 'the evil to conquer over
everything that is good and right, so as to stick to his damned
throne, which nowadays is no better than a WC.'[3] 'It's hard to
realise that people can have so little heart . . . May God help us all.'[4]

Joining this chorus of disapproval, 'Ducky', Grand Duke Kyril's
wife,* took an equally jaundiced view. 'Georgie' had been instrumental in inviting the Bolsheviks, 'the scum of the earth', to the 1919
Versailles Peace Treaty talks.[5] Frostily he told her that everyone in
England was aware of the ruthless behaviour of the Bolsheviks, and
had been 'appalled at and outraged by their revolting crimes'.
Instead of his usual loving signature, there was a strictly formal 'Rex
Imperator', just in case 'Ducky' had forgotten his position as King
and Emperor. She would have been even more furious if she had

---

* She was the daughter of Queen Victoria's son Alfred, Duke of Edinburgh.

known that he thought she had 'lost much of her beauty' and now looked 'aged and battered'.[6]

Princess Paley was never liked by either family, and was described as 'a fornicator'[7] when she eloped with Nicholas's uncle, Grand Duke Paul.* She blamed Buchanan, the British Ambassador, who had, she believed, deliberately disobeyed a 'Royal command' by not 'safely conveying the King's invitation to the Emperor'.[8]

Some thought Buchanan a far too gullible ambassador who had been hoodwinked by the revolutionary leaders. Humiliated, and seen as a poor player in the tragedy, he returned in 1918 to England, where he was warned that any reference by him to the failure of attempts to get the Tsar out of Russia would result in his being charged with an infringement of the Official Secrets Act, and, even worse, his pension would be stopped. He never received the peerage he expected, and his last years were full of bitterness and disappointment.

The Tsar's sister, Grand Duchess Olga, believed that 'had a braver and more imaginative man than Buchanan been at the British Embassy in St Petersburg in 1917', there was no doubt that 'Nicky's life would have been saved'.

However critical some of the Romanovs were of the King's attitude to the Tsar, they may not have known how desperately he wanted to see the Bolsheviks 'smashed'. On the eve of the Genoa Conference in 1922 he asked his liberal-socialist Prime Minister, Lloyd George, if he intended to meet Lenin and Trotsky.[9] 'Sir, I am not able to choose between the people I am forced to meet in your service,' the Prime Minister replied, his Welsh tongue firmly in his cheek. They may not have always seen eye to eye, and they certainly had an abrasive relationship, but the King's response now was 'to roar with laughter'.[10]

However, Buchanan's daughter was always convinced that it was Lloyd George and not the King who had put her father in an impossible situation with the Russians by the sudden withdrawal of the safe haven invitation. She blamed the Prime Minister's 'lack of decision and apprehension', which, in her opinion, had led to the refusal 'to lend a helping hand to the cousin of his King'.[11] But the

---

*   A divorcee, formerly Mme Olga Pistolker, her greatest crimes were being a commoner and wearing diamonds which had belonged to her mother-in-law Empress Maria, wife of Alexander II.

opposite was true. In Lloyd George's papers an impeccable source is quoted: 'Most people think the invitation was initiated by the King. In fact, it was initiated by the government. From the first, the King was aware of the difficulties.' The author was Lord Stamfordham, the King's most trusted adviser, who was determined that his master should not carry any blame.[12] But this document actually presents the King as callous and indifferent, as if he had never wanted the invitation to be extended to the Tsar in the first place.

When Lloyd George was working on his memoirs, he was surprised to find that some 332 telegrams were missing from the file on the Tsar. Stung by the accusation that he had been partly responsible for Nicholas's death, he confirmed that an invitation to take refuge in England had been extended 'by the British Crown and Government . . . an offer', he firmly declared, 'which remained open and was never withdrawn'.[13]

For many years, official biographers of George V were advised by Buckingham Palace to 'omit things and incidents which were discreditable'[14] to the King. Most obeyed, dutifully accepting the courtiers' view that it had been the Prime Minister who was partly responsible for the Russian tragedy.

But in 1983, a new life of George V dramatically altered these perceptions.[15] Respected writer Kenneth Rose put a microscope to 'the persistent myth that it was the King who strove to rescue his cousin from the perils of the Russian Revolution only to be thwarted by a heartless and opportunist [Prime Minister]'.[16] During his research, he was aware 'certain efforts' being made by the palace to get him to 'tone down sensitive material on the Tsar'.[17] He refused, but was not censured, despite establishing conclusively that the British government would have offered asylum to the Tsar 'but for the fears expressed by Buckingham Palace'. The painful reality was that, 'at the most critical moment in their fortunes', Nicholas, his wife and children were 'deserted not by a Prime Minister appeasing his supporters by saying no to asylum, but by their ever-affectionate Cousin Georgie'.[18]

There was no denial by the palace; the evidence was incontrovertible. Familial ties had not been strong enough to warrant any risk to the monarchy. Nicholas and Alix would not have been welcome in England, where the Tsar was seen as a tyrant by the British people and his forbidding wife was not trusted because of her German background. George had no dewy memories of Alix or of shared childhood days at Osborne and Windsor, at one time confiding in General Wallscourt Waters,* 'I've known her all my life ... but I hate her'.

The Tsarina's great-niece, Countess Mountbatten of Burma, views some of the catastrophic events in her family history with an inspiring lack of bitterness. Partly deaf as the result of an IRA bomb, she admits, 'Yes, it was true that King George V was always concerned about revolutionary possibilities in Britain,' and sadly adds, 'My grandmother [Princess Victoria of Hesse, Alix's sister] never got over the Tsarina's murder.'[19]

Prince Nicholas Romanov, a patrician 83-year-old, and a distant cousin of Nicholas II who has the same vulnerable eyes as the last Tsar, remains utterly rational about events in 1917. Speaking in his home in the Gruyères Mountains in Switzerland, where the windows are wide open to a bright blue sky, and the sun glints on the medal he has just been awarded by President Putin, he chuckles, 'One minute they want to shoot you, next they give you a medal.'

His view of Nicholas is one of compassion, but he also understands the King's reasons for refusing safe haven. 'The essential difference between the two cousins was,' he says, 'that in a crisis the King behaved without sentimentality. He did not hesitate to make a decision as a head of state. He acted not as "Cousin Georgie" but as King George V.' Drawing on a favourite analogy, he sees the King 'acting like the commander of a ship', which he was – at heart, anyway.

'His duty was to his country and to his people; just like the captain of a destroyer when a huge wave approaches, he acts. It is not that the King was leaving his cousin to drown, more that he was thinking of his crew.'

However, he also acknowledges that the King need not have panicked, as revolution was unlikely. He does not think that the phlegmatic British people would have risen up and revolted because a small, bedraggled imperial family had come to stay as the guests of their Windsor cousins, quietly picking lilac or mushrooms. No Russian can ever pass a mushroom; it reminds them of their homeland.

When asked what would have happened if the position had been reversed, if it had been the King needing safe haven, Prince Nicholas

---

* Former British Military Attaché in Moscow.

does not hesitate, replying with a mournful shake of the head, 'Unfortunately I fear that Nicholas would have followed his impulse as a relative; he would have welcomed the British royal family to Russia. Unlike the King, he never made the distinction between private, cousinly intimacy and being ruler of one of the greatest empires. He always acted with his heart. Perhaps he was too human.' His voice trails off.

Political historian Dominic Lieven, who does not share his fellow aristocrat's view, is uncompromisingly critical of both Emperors. The cousins, he disparagingly suggests, 'were alike, each with limited intellect'. In his opinion, there is no doubt, 'George V was ratlike and self-serving'.[20] He speaks not only on the grounds of being an historian but also as one of the Latvian Lievens, an important family at the court of the last Tsar.

Not mincing his words, Lieven believes that 'The British royal family was most anxious not to be associated with an autocratic regime which had collapsed'. But he, too, admits that, if the King's life had been in danger, 'There is absolutely no doubt that Nicholas, with that warm, generous, Russian spirit, would unhesitatingly have made room for George and his family'.

Count Nicolai Tolstoy, a Russian historian born in London in 1935, talks about the Tsar's abdication as if it happened yesterday. It all seems as freshly painful as the unsatisfactory campaign he led in 1991 for the return of the imperial jewels from Windsor Castle.

Speaking as the great-grandson of Tsar Nicholas I's Chamberlain, he admires Nicholas's courage, which, he says, is not often praised in accounts of the harrowing months before his assassination. 'He lived in terrible times and was aware of the danger, particularly the hatred towards the Tsarina, but showed such dignity.'

He believes the King was ludicrously oversensitive in 1917 about anti-German feeling in England. 'He listened to all those rumours about people throwing stones at dachshunds. With ill-disguised cynicism, Tolstoy believes the King's overreaction was close to panic. 'As for his ridiculous change of name in 1917 to Windsor, it was all so unnecessary.'

If Nicholas had been given sanctuary in England, Tolstoy believes he would have lived the life of a country gentleman. 'The children would have made dynastic marriages. They were very beautiful.' The suggestion of any mingling of imperial blood with that of the Hanoverian House of Windsor prompts a mirthless 'ha-ha'.[21]

Kyril Zinoviev, a scholarly 94-year-old aristocrat who lives in London, is not so sure. Tall and spare in dark cords and a sports jacket with superior leather trim, he grew up in St Petersburg and saw the damage done to the Winter Palace by the revolutionaries in 1917. 'I have also,' he says, 'the dubious distinction of being one of the last people to see Rasputin alive.' His family lost everything and came to England, where he wrote under the pseudonym Fitzlyon, as there was some danger of his being assassinated.*

He believes that, had the Tsar settled in England, he would not have minded a simple life, but suggests that 'The Tsarina would have been a very difficult customer.' Now almost blind, he shrugs in a gesture of despair, and with upturned palm says, 'But the Tsarina would always have imagined she was being slighted, overlooked, or that her due was not being given. The trouble was Alix was a stupid woman, mulish, not well educated at all, but thought she knew better.' Zinoviev's mother was one of her ladies-in-waiting.

He is not the sort of person who stirs up controversy but was always troubled by the lack of any accurate account of events in 1917. 'I wanted to investigate the King's reasons for reneging on his invitation to the Tsar.' A trusted ambassadorial figure, moving comfortably in Russian and British royal circles, he approached the Tsarina's nephew, Lord Mountbatten, whom he knew socially, to ask him for help or access to relevant 1917–18 royal papers. Mountbatten's immediate reaction was, 'Yes, certainly', without any hesitation.

Zinoviev's old-fashioned, clipped BBC English accent lends a seasoned authority to the account of his subsequent astonishment when Mountbatten's attitude suddenly changed, almost to the point of rudeness. 'Someone had obviously got hold of him. "All the records have been destroyed." A door was firmly closed,' he told me bluntly.

A yawning gap remains in the Royal Archives, and also at the National Archives, covering the vital period from April 1917 until the assassinations at Ekaterinburg. Zinoviev is uncompromising in his belief that it was 'the King's ruthless instinct for self-preservation in putting personal and family affection to one side' which forced him to make 'such a harsh decision'.

---

*   He is the co-author of the recent *Companion Guide to St Petersburg*, with Jenny Hughes, published in 2003.

He re-enacts a scene where he visualises Lloyd George's startled expression when told by the King that he was withdrawing the invitation of safe haven. Lloyd George 'pointed out that the letter of invitation had already been sent and he thought that the King would understand what that meant'.

Warming to his theme, Zinoviev describes how the King angrily replied that he understood perfectly well, but his answer was still 'No'. 'He looked Lloyd George in the eye and told him, "From now on, it is understood that I wanted to save my cousin's life more than anything, but you absolutely refused to save him. Is that clear?"'

Zinoviev adds diplomatically, 'Of course, in all fairness the King had foreseen the growing influence of Labour in 1917 even though at the time the government was still a Liberal Party under Lloyd George. He was also coping with a backlash of discontent stirred up by the trade unions.'*

There was of course another reason for the refusal of safe haven. With a smile he says, 'A much simpler one. The Emperor was not wanted here because he would cost too much.'

Resentment of the old imperial regime still hovers in Russia, but there has also been a dawning recognition of some of the Tsar's gentler qualities. Lenin's 'radiant way' did not fulfil its promise, and only the powerful few prospered after the murder of the Tsar, who, unlike Stalin, never gave orders for the disposal of some 15 million Russian civilians.

In 1991 the Soviet Union began to disintegrate. Mikhail Gorbachev had introduced the ideas of personal freedom, *glasnost* and *perestroika*.† This was followed by an attempt at reconciliation in 1992, when Boris Yeltsin as President of the Russian Federation welcomed back one of the principal claimants to the tsarist throne, Grand Duke Vladimir's son Kyril, the sad-faced head of the imperial house. He apologised for the rough treatment meted out to Russia's 'moral and intellectual elite', forced out by the Bolsheviks in 1917.[22]

---

* The miners' strike of 1912 had lasted for five weeks.

† *Glasnost*: Commonly held to be Gorbachev's idea, the whole notion of openness and free discussion was tentatively introduced into Russia in the nineteenth century. *Perestroika*: A reform programme introduced by Gorbachev, geared to the economy and an improvement in the political climate.

This fitted in nicely with the newly fashionable trend for historical atonement. Labour Prime Minister Tony Blair was quick to apologise to the Irish for the famine of 1865. As yet, there has been no expression of regret from the British royal family about the wretched fate of their cousin Nicholas. Neither is there any desire in Russia for the restoration of a Tsar.

The Romanovs and the Vladimirs are still the two leading royal families in Russia. Each has a legitimate claim to the Tsar's throne; so too does the Duke of Kent through his late mother Princess Marina. She was the granddaughter of the compellingly attractive Marie Pavlovna, who was married to the powerful Grand Duke Vladimir, one of Nicholas II's uncles.* It is Prince Michael of Kent, his younger brother, who relishes most this strain of the blood imperial dating back to 1797. He enjoys the startled looks his cultivated resemblance to the last Tsar creates; his beard helps.

In St Petersburg, he is proprietorial about the old Vladimir palace, his great-grandmother's ancestral home, opposite the Peter and Paul Fortress. On a bitterly cold day, a group of musicians in shabby grey astrakhan hats, with red sashes over their greatcoats, stand outside, stamping their feet as they play a reedy version of 'God Save the Queen'. As a weak sun melts the black ice, they visibly cheer up with 'Roll out the Barrel'.

Prince Michael strides purposefully into the hall of the palace, past two stuffed brown bears and a marble nude which, at a touch, whirls on her plinth showing all her curves. The palace is still a handsome town house, with its art deco mirrors decorated with painted pink roses and without the melancholy air of so many of the palaces in St Petersburg today. Most of the original furniture is still in place, including the sauna with tiled stove which the comrades considered decadent.

The Vladimirs, patrons of the arts, were sought-after stars in St Petersburg, and Marie Pavlovna's brilliantly exotic parties attracted a glamorous, celebrated coterie. After the Tsarina and the

---

*   Grand Duke Vladimir Alexandrovich was one of the Tsar's most influential uncles. Rich and successful, he ruled St Petersburg socially until the Revolution. The Vladimirs' youngest child Helena married Prince Nicholas of Greece; their daughter Princess Marina was also a first cousin of Prince Philip. Their fathers were brothers; although considered Greek the bloodline was Danish through their paternal grandparent Christian IX of Denmark.

Dowager Empress, she was the 'third most important lady in the land', a responsibility she embraced enthusiastically. Before the season, Cossack convoys on winter sleighs delivered barrels of beluga caviar and the best sturgeon to the palace, along with vineyards of wine. In winter, in rich damasks, jewels and furs, guests made their willing way up the golden staircase, past a cartouche of two putti holding the entwined gold initials of the Vladimirs, to the glowing, berry-red Raspberry Parlour, where they looked out across the sparkling, white Neva, in warm and delicious anticipation of incomparable hospitality.

But in 1917 this conviviality was shattered as dramatically as a cartoonist's idea of drunken Russian cavalry officers with waxed whiskers smashing crystal glasses against marble fireplaces. The Bolsheviks seized the palace, relishing its opulence, but found their talent as meticulous list-makers was sorely stretched. It took them weeks to catalogue the contents of the cellars alone. They refrained from resentfully burning the Vladimir Library. Instead, the priceless volumes inherited from Alexander II, on three floors, were sold by weight to American universities and the Library of Congress.

As President of the Romanov Family Association, Prince Nicholas has been instrumental in gently reintroducing the family of the last Tsar to the Russian people, 'if only', he wryly suggests, 'as honoured guests'. With weary relief, he says, 'No longer are they showing the Tsar as a slobbering idiot and his wife as a whore on television and in films in Russia.'

He himself would be as acceptable a claimant* to the Russian throne as any of the contenders, but this elderly ambassador for the Romanovs laughs at the very idea: 'Haven't you heard?' he says. 'I am a republican.'

---

* There are two factions within the Romanov family. One supports George, Grand Duke Kyril Vladimirovich's grandson, the other, Prince Nicholas Romanov, a great-great-grandson of Tsar Nicholas I, who looks the part of an urbane emperor. In 1944, while in exile, the Grand Duke pronounced himself Tsar, Emperor Kyril I, and head of the dynasty, much to the chagrin of the Romanovs. His son Vladimir was born in Finland in 1917 and moved to France. He had no heir, so that when he died his daughter Marie Vladimirovna, who in 1976 married Prince Franz Wilhelm of Prussia, took up the cudgels on behalf of her son Grand Duke George. The boy, who struggles with his weight, was unable to get into Oxford and lives with his mother in Madrid.

TWENTY-NINE

Imperial Requiem

'All this fuss and expense . . . What will people think about it in these hard and anxious times?' The King fretted about the cost of his Silver Jubilee, which fell on 6 May 1935. Surprised by the determination of the British people to mark the occasion, he engagingly suggested, 'I am sure I cannot understand it . . . for after all I am only a very ordinary fellow', unconsciously revealing the secret of his success.

In an exemplary long reign, it was not just his humanity and steadfastness, but his insularity and distrust of anything 'unEnglish', which made George popular. His strength was also a single-minded devotion to duty, to the monarchy and to the men and women who had fought for their country during the First World War. Ex-servicemen, those 30,000 wounded soldiers and sailors who, as he liked to say, 'paid the price for us', were close to his heart. Obstinately, he insisted on hiring a one-legged war veteran as a lodgekeeper at Windsor Castle in spite of protests by the police. After three years he reluctantly gave in, agreeing that a fit, two-legged guard was needed for such a high-security job.[1]

George inspired a reassuring feeling of continuity. When 4,406 people gathered in St Paul's Cathedral on 6 May 1935 for a thanksgiving service for the life of this modest man, he was genuinely overwhelmed. A boisterously warm reception in the East End astonished him: 'I had no idea they felt like that about me,' he murmured disbelievingly. 'I am beginning to think they must like me for myself.'[2]

This show of appreciation, the nearest the British people got to adulation, bolstered the King towards the end of his life, when he was burdened by illness and worry. He had reluctantly come to terms with the notion of home rule for Ireland. He had always been interested in the Irish problem, but his concern was more to do with an acquisitive, proprietorial attitude than any real wish to seek an acceptable, democratic solution. He saw himself as father of the empire and was not prepared to yield a jot of territory in Ireland or India.

Against all his instincts, in 1931 he was obliged to receive Mahatma Gandhi, who was leading a successful campaign of civil disobedience in India. He could hardly take his eyes off the 'rebel fakir' who he later described as a 'little man with no proper clothes on and bare knees'. He also warned the polished, adroit lawyer, 'Remember, Mr Gandhi, I won't have any attacks on my empire.'

But he was weary, worn down by too many crises, including the Great Depression and the financial backlash after the Wall Street Crash of 1929. The general election of that year had ushered in a short-lived 'National Government'; now the Conservatives in 1931 were faced with dole queues and nearly three million unemployed.[3]

He worried about the Prince of Wales, with his 'dentist's smile', his obvious lack of enthusiasm for the sacrament of marriage and his generally cavalier attitude to the monarchy. There had been a succession of mistresses; the latest, Mrs Wallis Simpson, a loud American divorcee, was not even kept discreetly in the wings but was all too evident on yachts in the south of France dressed in shorts and drinking cocktails.

George began to retreat into his shell, withdrawing from social life, which he had never liked much anyway. Now, ambitious hostesses lamented that he 'could only be persuaded to dine out four or five times in the London season'.[4] The world as he knew it was finished. He was not comfortable with the 1930s, and hated the way modern women looked. 'Good God,' he called out once to the Queen, 'look at those short skirts, look at that bobbed hair!' as a group of young women walked up the hill at Windsor, unaware that the King had his eye on them.[5] The sight was enough to bring on a bout of irascibility.

In his marriage, the King, like many of his subjects, found that he and his wife had less to say to each other and shared fewer interests as the pace of their life together gently wound down. On the other hand, they were not particularly desolate when their children left and married. Yet George showed a surprising tenderness when, on 28 February 1922, Princess Mary married Henry Viscount Lascelles, who was fifteen years older than his bride. The King liked his son-in-law; both men enjoyed field sports and disapproved of 'modern girls'. After the wedding, George went to Mary's room in the palace to say goodbye to this unbending 24-year-old daughter, and 'quite broke down'.[6] In recent years she had provided him with companionship and, a year later, she gave him a first grandson.* He thought the baby 'a beauty', but complained, 'It makes me feel very old to be a grandfather.'[7]

'There you go again, Mary: furniture, furniture, furniture,' the King grumbled when the Queen tried to tell him what an enjoyable afternoon she had spent looking at antiques.[8] Once, after a rewarding visit to the Schönbrunn Palace in Vienna, she remarked in a tone of barely concealed exasperation, 'Alas, for my poor George all these things are a sealed book, such a pity and so deplorable in his position! And he misses so much that is interesting in one's life.'[9]

While the King may not have shared Queen Mary's obsession with *objets d'art*, his regard for her remained unaltered and was always tinged with gratitude. Towards the end of his life, when making a speech that was also being recorded,† he asked that the reference he was making to his wife should come at the end, in case he broke down: 'I can't trust myself to speak of the Queen,' he said, 'when I think of all I owe her.'[10] He was more vulnerable than ever he wanted anyone to know.

Another blow that increased his feeling of isolation was the death on 3 December 1935 of Princess Victoria, his favourite sister. She had given him his beloved parrot Charlotte.[11] Brother and sister spoke on the telephone every day. Connecting them for one of their regular 9.30 a.m. telephone calls, the royal telephonist heard the Princess say, 'Hello, you old fool!' and he had to break in discreetly saying, 'Beg pardon, Your Royal Highness, His Majesty is not yet on the line.' His sons never enjoyed this sort of joshing camaraderie with their father.

It was Christmas 1935 when George made his last broadcast from Sandringham. These were always seen as innovative events and were appreciated by the British public. But he had suffered another attack of bronchitis, his breathing was erratic and his voice

---

*   Viscount Lascelles, later 6th Earl of Harewood, born 7 February 1923.

†   At Westminster Hall, in response to the homage being paid by the Commons and the Lords as part of the Jubilee celebrations.

lacked its usual vigour. Sitting at a favourite small table, he delivered his short message, written for him by Rudyard Kipling: 'My words,' he said, 'will be very simple, but spoken from the heart on this family festival of Christmas.'

'I feel rotten' was the last entry in his diary, dated 17 December 1935.* Later he seemed to recover slightly and went out on Jock, his white pony, through the woods at Sandringham. But this was a false dawn. He had a relapse, and needed to muster all his reserves of will-power to attend a meeting of the Privy Council, where he wore his favourite yellow, blue and green Tibetan dressing gown. Had he been his usual vigorous self, he would have been outraged by this sartorial laxity. Now he struggled to sign an order, apologising for the delay, saying, 'Gentlemen, you see I cannot concentrate.'[12]

He told Sir Frederick Willans, who like all his medical advisers wore full court dress with gold buttons and velvet knee-breeches, 'I'm not taking any more of your blasted muck.'[13] Courtiers were encouraged by this hint of the King's old hectoring style. A favourite chef from Buckingham Palace was asked to make some broth and gruel with, the patient suggested, a few drops of warm brandy 'as a treat'.[14]

Hardly able to speak, still there was one last deathbed enquiry about the health of the empire. He had been worrying about, and disapproved of, India's call for independence.[15] Now hearing his private secretary, Lord Wigram, say, 'All is well, sir', he felt reassured and drifted off into the sleep of death. His physician, Lord Dawson of Penn, scribbled a note: 'The King's life is moving peacefully to a close.' Then, at five minutes before midnight on 20 January 1936, he died behind a double circle of high screens after a massive injection of cocaine and morphine, enabling *The Times* to carry the story of his death the following morning.

The grand procession for his funeral on Tuesday 28 January 1936 included representatives of the Union of Soviet Socialist Republics,[16] five kings and several royal princes, all walking in step to the measured sound of the 'Funeral March'. Jock, the pony, led by his groom, and Charlotte, the parrot, perched in a carriage, brought up the end of the procession.

---

*   He had kept a diary since childhood, written in large uncomplicated hand-writing and bound in cloth.

George was buried at Windsor, where official mourning dictated that there would 'be no music or dancing at hotels until further notice'.[17] A black band of crêpe was worn around the left arm during the services.* The Australian Prime Minister, Sir Robert Menzies, declared that King George V was 'the first great constitutional monarch', a view appreciated by the British people.

In his poem 'Death of King George V', Sir John Betjeman captured some of the essence of the private man, forced to become King, who at heart was a sailor, and on dry land was happiest being a country squire:

> Spirits of well-shot woodcock, partridge, snipe
> Flutter and bear him up the Norfolk sky:
> In that red house in a red mahogany bookcase
> The stamp collection waits with mounts long dry.
>
> The big blue eyes are shut which saw wrong clothing
> And favourite fields and coverts from a horse . . .[18]

The King had few regrets, but until the end of his life he grieved about the death of the Tsar, his remorse compounded by the appealing beauty of the young tsarinas. Nicholas himself would probably have understood the reasons why he had to be refused safe haven in England. He was in awe of the British monarchy and so respected the bonds which had been formed four centuries earlier between Tudor England and Ivan the Terrible's Russia.

The exceptional harmony and affectionate mutual regard of the Emperors was re-emphasised towards the end of 1915 when the King, 'as a mark of his affection', appointed Nicholas to the rank of Field Marshal. 'If you accept,' he said, as if Nicholas might have turned down such a token of the King's esteem, 'it will be a great pleasure to me and an honour to the British Army and especially at a time when our two armies are fighting against a common enemy.'[19]

---

*   Gloves for national mourning were advertised by the London Glove Company. Ladies' 4 Button BLACK FRENCH KID, 2s 6d per pair. For men 1 Button strong Black Cape Driving Gloves, British made, 3s per pair. *Morning Post*, 9 May 1910.

The Tsar was already Colonel-in-Chief of the Royal Scots Greys,* a connection which Scotland's premier cavalry regiment treasures to this day.[20] A portrait of Nicholas by the distinguished Russian artist Serov hangs in the officers' mess and is given a place of honour wherever the regiment is serving. The Russian imperial anthem is included in music played at regimental dinners.

During the Revolution in 1917, when Nicholas was stripped of all honours, his association with this Scottish regiment appeared lost as a ragged army in coarse shirts and tattered greatcoats surged through the the tsarist palaces, tearing down all the links with an imperial past created by Peter the Great.

But in a strangely apt and graceful footnote to Nicholas's life, many decades later four Royal Scots Dragoon Guards officers† escorted his body to its last resting place in the St Peter and Paul Fortress in St Petersburg. The regiment had never forgotten the Tsar, who had been their Colonel for twenty-two years, and stood over his coffin at the reburial ceremony in 1998.

For over sixty years, the bodies of Nicholas, his family and their retainers lay undetected in a dense birch forest near Ekaterinburg. Then in 1979, in an almost miraculous breakthrough, they were discovered. Two men, Alexander Avdonin, a Russian geologist, and crime writer Geli Ryabov, had been given vital clues by Alexander Yurovsky, son of one of the Tsar's chief executioners. The white-haired, bearded, retired Vice-Admiral confessed that he could no longer live with the detailed account of the murders in 1918 left by his father,[21] regarding it as 'this most horrible page' in his father's life.[22]

The two men went first to Koptyaki Forest, where gingerly they followed a track until they reached the Four Brothers' Mine; as they had been told to expect, this was where they found the bodies of the Tsar, his wife, three of the children, the doctor and three servants underneath a makeshift platform of pine planks.

Today the forest is a place of pilgrimage. The spring there is considered the holiest place in Russia, attracting newly-weds,

---

*   The Royal Scots Greys were merged with the 3rd Dragoon Guards (The Carabiniers) under 'Options for Change' in 1997 to create the Royal Scots Dragoon Guards.

†   Lt-Col Phillips, Maj Mark Ravnkilde, RSM Cochlan and Pipe Major Brotherton.

middle-aged couples, children and students, who stoop to fill containers with water from the well. It is not an easy or cheap journey for many of them.

The two men had to swear each other to secrecy about their discovery. Their fear was that, if Leonid Brezhnev learned of their discovery, they would have been sent to the Gulag for their association, even in death, with the imperial family. It was not until 1989 that they were able to tell the world that they had found the Tsar's bullet-riddled skull, though they had to admit that there had been no trace of the two youngest children. The bleak view taken was that Alexei and Anastasia's fragile bones had been taken by wolves.

A feeling of revulsion across Russia followed these revelations. Even as early as 1977, there had already been some embarrassment about the Ipatiev House, then called the Museum of the People's Vengeance. It was a macabre tourist haunt during the repressive years. Schoolchildren and important government visitors were photographed in the cellar beside the bullet holes, and lectured about the 'heroes' who had murdered the Tsar. They were also told how some had met unexplained, violent deaths,[23] shuddering at the thought of the 'Tsar's curse'.[24]

The Ipatiev House was demolished in 1999 on orders from President Boris Yeltsin, who had been born in the Urals. A pink-and-grey-marble church, the Cathedral of the Spilt Blood, with five gold onion domes with crosses,* and costing £7.5 million,[25] was built on the unhappy site. The cellar now attracts pilgrims who, as a priest spoons out more incense, kiss the icons of the new Russian martyrs Nicholas and Alexandra, whose abused bodies were exhumed from a mass grave in 1991.

The Russian authorities had been reluctant to allow DNA evidence to be tested at Aldermaston in England, but eventually agreed. A nephew of the Tsar's, Tikhon Kulikovsky, should have provided the ideal link, but he refused to cooperate. He gave two reasons.[26] One was his inability to forgive the King for refusing his uncle safe haven in 1917. He also was firmly convinced that 'the British royal family had personally swindled his mother, Grand

---

* Crosses on tiny onion-domed churches symbolising the victory of Christendom over the Golden Horde denote that Ivan IV, the Terrible, inflicted a final defeat in 1552 on the Golden Horde at the Battle of Kazan.

Duchess Olga, 'out of hundreds of thousands of dollars following the sale of certain jewellery to Queen Mary'. It was Prince Philip who provided the incontrovertible imperial DNA proof, as his mother had been a niece of the Tsarina.*

Nicholas and his family were reburied with honour, but this took seven years of arguing, cajoling and smooth-talking. There was a simmering uneasiness about the new wave of sentimental regret about the Tsar's murder; a reburial ceremony was seen as a provocative swing back towards Russia's imperial past.†

The Queen would have liked to go to the ceremony, seeing it as a 'dignified closing of a great cycle of dynastic history'.[27] But somehow she never received a formal invitation. Prince Michael, sombrely dressed, looking more than ever like Nicholas II's double, was the only senior member of a European royal family to attend.

The last big gathering of the imperial family had been in 1913, ironically to celebrate the dynasty's 300 years of absolute power. Now coveys of Romanovs flew in from all over the world, and, as pilots announced the descent into St Petersburg, some stared stonily at the bleak landscape, while others prayed. The atmosphere was taut. Prince Nicholas Romanov, who did so much to make the reburial not only possible but also a gracious and moving occasion, remarked philosophically, 'We Romanovs are part of Russian history. You turn a page.'[28]

Friday 17 July 1998 was oppressively hot for the four Royal Scots Dragoon Guards officers lined up at Pulkova Airport waiting for the flight from Siberia carrying the Tsar's remains. Standing to attention on the red-carpeted tarmac for nearly an hour, they hoped to catch a glimpse of the aeroplane emerging with its sad cargo from the cloudy heat haze. They were not to know that the local bureaucrats in Ekaterinburg were refusing to let the bodies go. They had cherished dreams of building a tourist

---

* Princess Alice of Greece was the daughter of the Tsarina's sister Victoria, who married the Marquis of Milford Haven.

† In 1992, one of the first Romanovs to return to Russia was Grand Duke Vladimir, then aged seventy. He was welcomed back by big, blustering Boris Yeltsin, President of the Russian Federation. A restrained, dignified man, the Grand Duke listened to Yeltsin's apology and said simply that he had never expected to visit Russia.

complex around the imperial remains. Eventually, after much argument, they were persuaded to release the nine cheap plywood coffins.

When the plane landed, an hour late, the British escort party lowered their swords in salute when the Tsar's coffin, with its Romanov coat of arms, was carried down the steps, and the military band switched to the hymn 'How Glorious'. The coffins, still with their tacky customs seals, were then placed in limousines with Mafia-style blacked-out windows for the journey to 'Peter', the affectionate name for the old tsarist city.

The Dragoons gratefully marched off before racing into the city to form up in an honour guard. One or two found their legs had seized up, but, in spite of this and the humidity, they felt their performance 'had been rather better than the Russians'. In classic understatement, they agreed that the Russian goose-step was 'different to say the least', but that it was easier 'to slow march in British fashion than goose-step in Russian style'.[29]

The procession into St Petersburg moved at 30mph along the desolate 20-mile highway, past brutalist blocks of flats and sad allotments. When the cortège reached the city, where flags flew at half mast, it slowed down outside the Winter Palace, in keeping with an old Russian custom in which remains are traditionally taken past their last home. An impressive 2,000-strong army, navy and air force honour guard had formed up outside the palace to pay homage to the Tsar on his final journey.

It was not the 35,000 soldiers and police, or the gathering of Romanovs waiting outside the Peter and Paul Fortress, but the sight of the 'pale, grief-stricken' Russians which was so unexpected. 'Every tiny street and sidewalk was crammed with people waving imperial flags and holding up icons; some genuflected, others crossed themselves. One shook his fist.'[30]

As bells tolled over St Petersburg, the gates of the fortress opened slowly and the regimental piper struck up. The four British military ambassadors now took their places behind the grand Russian honour guard, but were directly in front of the small coffins covered with the yellow and black Romanov flag.

They slow-marched to the cathedral, the cobbled streets echoing with a haunting selection of slow laments, later to be heard on news programmes worldwide. The Russian soldiers now had to march to the Dragoon Guards' regimental piper: 'They were a bit sniffy, but

"Pipey" was an impressive figure in kilt and with skiandu;* he did awfully well and played a slow march so they could goose-step away. There was hardly a dry eye when he finally played "Going Home".'[31]

In St Catherine's Chapel, where Nicholas and the family liked to worship, a reverent invited crowd holding melting candles waited for the Tsar. Even for those not invited, like one or two politicians who had simply vaulted over the railings, oblivious to the impressively awesome atmosphere, it was an occasion not to be missed. Others bullied their way in to hear Boris Yeltsin's speech of repentance. 'The greatest sin', he intoned, looking suitably mournful, 'that any nation could commit was regicide.' The very word 'regicide' sent a shiver of horror through the Romanovs present.[32] Some crossed themselves, murmuring '*Gospodi pomiliu*', Lord have mercy.

This imperial requiem epitomised all the lusciously emotional extravagance of the Russian Orthodox Church; the music had never sounded more poignant, as the bearded priests in gold and cream-embossed silk robes recited the canticles in deep, resonant voices.

As Nicholas II's coffin was lowered into the earth to the sound of muffled drums, the entire Romanov family sank to their knees. His simple coffin was placed in a vault in the whitewashed crypt, the traditional resting place of the Romanov ancestors, and a nineteen-gun salute was fired across the Neva.

As the Romanovs left after the ceremony, a press of people crowded round them, saying, 'Forgive us, forgive us . . .'.[33] This recurring lament was almost too much to bear for some of the Tsar's more elderly relatives.

'The scenes were extraordinary, like something straight out of Dostoevsky',[34] the Russian writer so preoccupied with psychology and the forces of good and evil. Even the British officers were a little overcome as people rushed up to them in a show of emotion, saying, 'Thank you, thank you for being here.'

A reception was held for the Tsar's family at the recently restored Marble Palace, which had been built as a token of Catherine II's love for Grigory Orlov, who had captured the throne for her; it took seventeen years to complete, by which time he was no longer her lover. Distinguished still by some thirty-three different shades of

---

* Skean-dhu: a dirk worn with Scottish formal dress, usually tucked into the top of a sock.

marble, including pale pistachio and apricot, in 1917 the Bolsheviks turned it into a museum dedicated to the worship of Lenin.

Over a glass of champagne in the *piano nobile*, the Romanovs were asked if they realised what had been said to them by the tearful crowd outside the fortress. 'Of course we understood,' they said, 'but we thought it wiser to pretend not, and just gave a blessing and a low, traditional Russian bow.'[35] Prince Michael thought the ceremony had been a milestone in Russian history.

That evening the Scottish officers chartered a launch which they later moored alongside the Adamant restaurant, where Prince Michael was having dinner. He came out and stood by the railings to listen as the pipe major played from the boat. Their last task was to present the head of the Romanov family with a history of the regiment. Prince Nicholas was touched and wrote to the Queen, the regiment's Colonel-in-Chief, to thank her for honouring her cousin, the last Tsar.

After the reburial, the Romanovs scattered again into exile, Prince Nicholas to a Swiss village and others to Florida, Paris, Copenhagen and London. They smile at the clichéd myths about Russians in exile listening dolefully to the music of Shostakovich, drinking too much, smelling of expensive cologne, soulfully yearning for a return of old imperialist Russia. But one did admit, 'We all, whatever age, want to cry about Russia.'[36] But they are too sophisticated, too battered by life, to harbour any unrealistic fantasies about the restoration of the Tsar, and most agree with Grand Duchess Marie Pavlovna that the past is 'like a dusty diamond'.

There is little bitterness about events in Ekaterinburg. They are generous about the King and acknowledge that he was as immovable about what he believed was right as the oldest stone in Westminster Abbey. Even if that meant turning away the Tsar.

In his lifetime, George V saw the end of five emperors, eight kings and eighteen small dynasties,[37] and is credited with safeguarding the history and traditions of the British monarchy.

The Tsar, on the other hand, lost everything, but to his people he has become a saint.*

---

*   In August 2000 Nicholas II was canonised by the Synod of Bishops of the Russian Orthodox Church.

APPENDIX ONE

Genealogical table showing links between the royal family of Great Britain and the imperial family of Russia

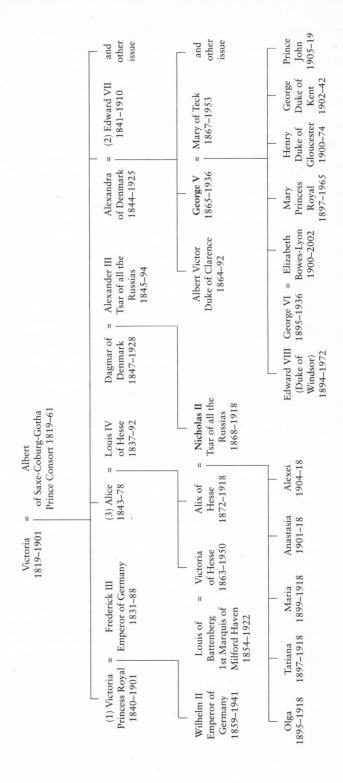

Victoria 1819–1901 = Albert of Saxe-Coburg-Gotha Prince Consort 1819–61

(1) Victoria Princess Royal 1840–1901 = Frederick III Emperor of Germany 1831–88

(3) Alice 1843–78 = Louis IV of Hesse 1837–92

Alexander III Tsar of all the Russias 1845–94 = Dagmar of Denmark 1847–1928

Alexandra of Denmark 1844–1925 = (2) Edward VII 1841–1910   and other issue

Wilhelm II Emperor of Germany 1859–1941

Louis of Battenberg 1st Marquis of Milford Haven 1854–1922 = Victoria of Hesse 1863–1950

Nicholas II Tsar of all the Russias 1868–1918 = Alix of Hesse 1872–1918

Albert Victor Duke of Clarence 1864–92

George V 1865–1936 = Mary of Teck 1867–1953   and other issue

Olga 1895–1918   Tatiana 1897–1918   Maria 1899–1918   Anastasia 1901–18   Alexei 1904–18

Edward VIII (Duke of Windsor) 1894–1972   George VI 1895–1936 = Elizabeth Bowes-Lyon 1900–2002   Mary Princess Royal 1897–1965   Henry Duke of Gloucester 1900–74   George Duke of Kent 1902–42   Prince John 1905–19

APPENDIX TWO

The British Royal Family

Queen Victoria (1819–1901)	Daughter of Duke of Kent, fourth son of George III. Succeeded to the throne 1837. Married (1840) Albert Duke of Saxony, Prince of Saxe-Coburg-Gotha.
Victoria, Princess Royal (1840–1901)	Eldest child of Queen Victoria and Prince Albert, and sister of Edward VII. Married (1858) Frederick, Crown Prince of Germany and German Emperor.
Edward VII (Albert Edward) (1841–1910)	Eldest son of Queen Victoria. Married (1844) Princess Alexandra of Denmark.
Princess Alice (1843–78)	Sister of Edward VII. Married (1862) Prince Louis, Grand Duke of Hesse. Mother of Alix of Hesse, last Tsarina of Russia
Albert Victor (Duke of Clarence) (1864–92)	Elder son of Edward VII. Engaged to Princess Mary (May) of Teck. Died of a fever aged twenty-eight.
George V* (George Frederick Albert Edward of Saxe-Coburg) (1865–1936)	Second son of Edward VII. Succeeded to the throne 1910. Married (1893) Princess Victoria Mary of Teck.

* George V's three sisters were:

Louise, Princess Royal (1867–1931)	Eldest daughter of Edward VII. Married (1899) Duke of Fife.
Princess Victoria (1868–1935)	Second daughter of Edward VII. Unmarried.
Princess Maud (1869–1938)	Third daughter of Edward VII. Married (1896) Haakon VII, King of Norway.

Edward VIII
(Edward Albert Christian
George Andrew Patrick
David) Prince of Wales
and Duke of Windsor
(1894–1972)

Eldest son of George V. Briefly reigned in 1936 before abdicating to marry Mrs Wallis Simpson.

George VI
(Albert Frederick
Arthur George, Duke
of York) (1895–1952)

Second son of George V; came to the throne in 1936. Married (1923) Lady Elizabeth Bowes-Lyon, Queen, later Queen Elizabeth the Queen Mother.

Mary, Princess Royal
(1897–1965)

Only daughter of George V. Married (1922) the 6th Earl of Harewood.

Prince Henry
(Duke of Gloucester)
(1900–74)

Son of George V. Married (1935) Lady Alice Montagu-Douglas-Scott, daughter of 7th Duke of Buccleuch (Princess Alice, Duchess of Gloucester).

Prince George
(Duke of Kent)
(1902–42)

Fourth son of George V. Married (1934) Princess Marina of Greece and Denmark. Killed in an aircraft crash while on active service in the RAF during Second World War.

Prince John
(1905–19)

Youngest son of Edward VII. Suffered from epilepsy; during his brief life was kept from public view and had little contact with his own family.

APPENDIX THREE

The Russian Imperial Family

Tsar Nicholas II (1868–1918)	Succeeded his father in 1895. Married (1895) Alix of Hesse.
Alicky (1872–1918)	Tsarina Alexandra Feodorovna. Born Princess Alix of Hesse; granddaughter of Queen Victoria.
Olga (1895–1918) Tatiana (1897–1918) Maria (1899–1918) Anastasia (1901–18)	Tsarinas and daughters of Tsar Nicholas II.
Alexis (1904–18)	Tsarevich Alexei Nikolaievich. Heir to Nicholas II.
Alexander III (1845–95)	Tsar from 1855 and father of Nicholas II.
Dagmar (1847–1928)	Princess Maria Feodorovna, Dowager Empress and mother of Nicholas II; sister of Queen Alexandra of Great Britain.
Misha (1878–1918)	Grand Duke Michael Alexandrovich; brother of Nicholas II.
Xenia (1875–1960)	Grand Duchess Xenia Alexandrovna, sister of Nicholas II and wife of Sandro.
Olga (1882–1960)	Grand Duchess Olga Feodorovna; younger sister of Nicholas II.
Sandro (1866–1933)	Grand Duke Alexander Mikhailovich; cousin of Nicholas II.
Sergei (1857–1905)	Grand Duke Sergei Alexandrovich; uncle of Nicholas II and brother-in-law to Alix through marriage to her sister Ella.

APPENDIX FOUR

A Comparative Chronology

	Russia		Britain
	Russia		*Britain*
862	Rurik the Viking settles on River Neva	865	Great Viking invasion of Eastern England
1485/95	Moscow Kremlin built by Italian architects	1485	Henry Tudor crowned Henry VII at Battle of Bosworth Field
1553	First trade routes set up between Russia and England	1553	Mary Tudor becomes Queen of England
1584	Boris Godunov becomes tsar	1587	Execution of Mary Queen of Scots
1591/ 1613	Time of troubles; feeble rulers produce lawlessness and widespread devastation	1588	Defeat of Spanish Armada
1613	First Romanov chosen as tsar by Land Assembly	1611	Authorised (King James) Version of the Bible
1682	Accession of Peter the Great	1685	Judge Jeffreys transports 800 supporters of the Monmouth Rebellion to Barbados and executes 200
1697	Great Embassy to Europe	1697	Peter the Great stays in Deptford; studies shipbuilding

1703	Foundation of St Petersburg	1703	Marlborough destroys French army at Blenheim
1712	Capital moved to St Petersburg from Moscow	1714	Treaty of Utrecht cedes Newfoundland and Nova Scotia to Britain
1762–96	Reign of Catherine the Great	1760–1820	Reign of George III
1775	Old Hermitage built to house Catherine's jewels and *objets d'art*	1773	Boston Tea Party
1784	Conquest of the Crimea and naval dominance of Black Sea	1788	George III manifests first visible signs of madness
1787	Grigory Potemkin creates fake villages to convince Catherine II the countryside is populated	1789	French Revolution and MCC celebrates second birthday
1797	Law of Succession establishesmale primogeniture	1797	Horatio Nelson loses his right arm at the Battle of Santa Cruz
1812	Moscow destroyed by fire to thwart Napoleon's occupation	1815	Final defeat of Napoleon ar Battle of Waterloo
1853/6	France and Britain support Turkey against Russia in the Crimean War which ends inconclusively	1855	Florence Nightingale revolutionises nursing
1867	Alaska sold to USA for $7 million	1863	Bertie, Prince of Wales marries the Sea King's daughter, Princess Alexandra of Denmark
1881	Tsar Alexander II assassinated by Nihilists outside the Winter Palace	1881	First Boer War

1893	Lenin organises Socialist Workers' Party in St Petersburg	1893	Second Home Rule (for Ireland) Bill
1894	Nicholas II becomes Tsar of All the Russias, Emperor and Autocrat, Supreme Commander, Little Father, Lord and Judge	1898	Winston Churchill in the Battle of Omdurman against the Dervish Army in Sudan
1901	Political killing gathers pace with the assassination of Education Minister Nicholas Bogolepov	1901	Queen Victoria dies
1903	Trans-Siberian Railway opens	1903	Edward VII visits Paris: better relations between Britain and France
1904/5	Military and naval defeats in the Russo-Japanese War	1905	George, Prince of Wales, tours India
1905	Abortive revolution sparked by mass shooting of peaceful protestors	1905	L'Entente Cordiale
1911	Prime Minister Peter Stolypin assassinated at gala performance in the Kiev Opera House	1910	George V crowned King of the United Kingdom of Great Britain and Ireland, and of the British Dominions beyond the Seas, Defender of the Faith, Emperor of India
1914	Russia supports the Allies in the First World War and suffers severe defeat at Tannenberg	1914	War with Germany and retreat from Mons
1916	Murder of Rasputin	1916	Abortive Easter Rising to overthrow British rule in Ireland

| 1917 | October Revolution and abdication of Nicholas II | 1917 | US declares war on Germany |
| 1918 | Citizen Romanov and his family murdered by his former subjects | 1918 | Armistice and King George V drives 9 miles through deliriously cheering crowds |

Notes

Some of the following abbreviations may be found in the text:

GARF   Gosudarstvenny Arkhiv Rossiiskoi Federatsii, State Archives of the Russian Federation, Moscow
LRA   Leeds Russian Archive, Brotherton Library, University of Leeds
NA   National Archives
RA   Royal Archives

Introduction

1. Maurice Baring, *The Collected Poems of Maurice Baring*. John Lane, Bodley Head, 1911.
2. Miriam Kochan, *The Last Days of Imperial Russia*, p. 10.
3. Dimitri Obolensky, *Bread of Exile*.
4. Meriel Buchanan, *Recollections of Imperial Russia*, p. 258.
5. Buchanan, *Recollections of Imperial Russia*, p. 470.
6. Bowman manuscript.
7. Eugenie Fraser, *The House by the Dvina*.
8. Geoffrey Hosking, *Russia: People and Empire 1552–1917*.
9. Victor Alexandrov, *The End of the Romanovs*, p. 157.

1: Grandmother of Europe

1. Diana Souhami, *Mrs Keppel and Her Daughter*.
2. Kenneth Rose, *George V*, p. 5.
3. John Gore, *King George V*, p. 9.
4. Georgina Battiscombe, *Queen Alexandra*, pp. 5 and 86.
5. Battiscombe, *Queen Alexandra*, p. 87.
6. Denis Judd, *The Life and Times of George V*, p. 64.
7. *New Penny* magazine, 1901, pp. 224–5.
8. Arthur Bryant, *George V*, p. 16.
9. Kenneth Rose, *George V*, p. 4.
10. James Lees-Milne, *Harold Nicolson: A Biography*, p. 224.
11. Lees-Milne, *Harold Nicolson*, p. 232. Harold Nicolson in conversation with Queen Mary at Marlborough House on 21 March 1949.
12. Michaela Reid, *Ask Sir James*, p. 122.

13. Ian Vorres, *The Last Grand Duchess*.

14. *Ibid*.

15. *The Times*, 17.2.94.

2: *Motherless Alicky*

1. David Duff, *Hessian Tapestry*, p. 101.

2. Greg King, *The Last Empress*, p. 4.

3. King, *The Last Empress*, p. 14.

4. Richard Hough, *Advice to a Granddaughter: Letters from Queen Victoria to Princess Victoria of Hesse*, p. 9.

5. King, *The Last Empress*, p. 18, n. 25.

6. Duff, *Queen Mary*, p. 118.

7. Sophie Buxhoeveden, *The Life and Tragedy of Alexandra Feodorovna, Empress of Russia*, p. 15.

8. King, *The Last Empress*, p. 22.

9. Lily Dehn, *The Real Tsaritsa*, p. 185.

3: *'We Bathe Every Day'*

1. John Gore, *King George V: A Personal Memoir*, p. 26.

2. Carolly Erickson, *Alexandra: The Last Tsarina*, p. 8.

3. David Duff, *Queen Mary*, p. 38.

4. Stephen Poliakov, *The Lost Prince*.

5. HRH the Duke of Windsor, *A King's Story*.

6. *Girl's Realm*.

4: *Their Mothers' Darling Boys*

1. Greg King and Coryne Hall, *Once a Grand Duchess*.

2. Historian Dominic Lieven in conversation with the author.

3. Catherine Radziwill, *Nicholas II: The Last of the Tsars*, pp. 25–6.

4. Radziwill, *Nicholas II: The Last of the Tsars*, p. 25.

5. In conversation with a future Archbishop of Canterbury, Randall Davidson.

6. Georgina Battiscombe, *Queen Alexandra*, p. 60.

7. Battiscombe, *Queen Alexandra*.

8. Greg King and Penny Wilson, *The Ruin of an Empire*, p. 31, n. 5.

9. Denis Judd, *The Life and Times of George V*, p. 24.

10. Sir Arthur Bryant, *George V*, 1936, p. 19.

11. Bryant *George V*, p. 78.

12. Judd, *George V*, p. 7.

13. Kenneth Rose, *George V*, p. 8.

14. Judd, *George V*, p. 15.

15. King and Wilson, *The Fate of the Romanovs*, p. 32.

16. *New Penny* magazine, 1899.

5: 'Little Darling'

1. Mark D. Steinberg and Vladimir M. Khrustalëv, *The Fall of the Romanovs*, p. 7, n. 13, *Nicholas to Alexandra*, 3 September 1902 GARF, f. 640, op. 1 d. 102, l. 600 b.
2. John Perry, *The Flight of the Romanovs*, p. 57.
3. James Lees-Milne, *Harold Nicolson*, p. 230.
4. John Gore, *King George V*, p. 276.
5. *Ibid.*, p. 109.
6. *Ibid.*, p. 72.
7. Gore, *King George V: A Personal Memoir*. A diary entry, 1887, by Prince George, referring to the novel by Vin Vincent, published by Farren Oakden & Walsh in 1885.
8. Donald and Rosemary Crawford, *Michael and Natasha*, p. 11.

6: 'Dearest Pussy'

1. Arthur Bryant, *George V*, p. 28.
2. David Duff, *Queen Mary*, p. 69.
3. Christopher Hibbert, *Queen Victoria in Her Letters and Journals*, p. 315.
4. Duff, *Queen Mary*, p. 39.
5. *Ibid.*, p. 27.
6. Kathleen Woodward, *Queen Mary*, p. 52.
7. Duff, *Queen Mary*, p. 41.
8. Giles St Aubyn, *The Royal George*, p. 320.
9. Duff, *Queen Mary*, p. 40.
10. *Ibid.*, p. 77.
11. James Pope-Hennessy, *Queen Mary*, p. 222.
12. Duff, *Queen Mary*, p. 79.
13. James Pope-Hennessy, *Queen Mary*, p. 242.
14. Duff, *Queen Mary*, p. 820.
15. James Lees-Milne, *Harold Nicolson*, p. 232, Queen Mary in conversation with HN.
16. Pope-Hennessey, *Queen Mary*, p. 259.
17. Herbert Bury, *Russian Life Today*, A.R. Mowbray, 1915, in conversation with the Tsar.
18. John Curtis Perry, *The Flight of the Romanovs*, p. 163.
19. Harold Nicolson, *King George V*, p. 50.
20. Edward O'Connor MP, *Impression of Nicholas in the House of Commons*.

7: Carefree in Coburg

1. E.M. Almegedin, *An Unbroken Unity: A Memoir of Grand Duchess Serge of Russia*, p. 35.
2. Charlotte Zeepvat, *Romanov Autumn*, p. 102.

3. Andrei Maylunas and Sergei Mironenko, *A Lifelong Passion*, p. 20.
4. *Ibid.*, p. 45.
5. Greg King, *Last Empress*, p. 23.
6. Carolly Erickson, *Alexandra: The Last Tsarina*, p. 49.
7. *The Letters of the Tsaritsa to the Tsar.*
8. Maylunas and Mironenko, *A Lifelong Passion*, p. 48.
9. Vladimir Poliakov, *The Tragic Bride*, p. 47.
10. Maylunas and Mironenko, *A Lifelong Passion*, p. 58.
11. Catherine Radziwill, *Nicholas II: The Last of the Tsars*, p. 59.
12. Lili Dehn, *The Real Tsaritsa*, p. 59.

8: *Sweet Kisses*

1. Andrei Maylunas and Sergei Mironenko, *A Lifelong Passion*, p. 70.
2. Maylunas and Mironenko, *A Lifelong Passion*, p. 67.
3. Michael Allen in conversation with the author.
4. *Ibid.*
5. *Ibid.*
6. Maylunas and Mironenko, *A Lifelong Passion*, p. 70.
7. *Ibid.*, p. 71.
8. Letter dated 18 June 1894 in possession of Michael Allen.
9. Carolly Erickson, *Alexandra: The Last Tsarina*, p. 55.
10. Maylunas and Mironenko, *A Lifelong Passion*, p. 74.
11. Erickson, *Alexandra: The Last Tsarina*, p. 56.
12. Nicholas's diary, 21 July 1894.
13. Catherine Radziwill, *Nicholas II: The Last of the Tsars*, p. 66.

9: *A Sharp Intake of Breath*

1. John Gore, *King George V: A Personal Memoir*, p. 120, citing George's diary entry for 1 November 1894.
2. Andrei Maylunas and Sergei Mironenko, *A Lifelong Passion*, p. 99.
3. Marc Ferro, *Nicholas II*, p. 1.
4. Ian Vorres, *The Last Grand Duchess*.
5. Carolly Erickson, *Alexandra: The Last Tsarina*, p. 64.
6. Vorres, *The Last Grand Duchess*, p. 68.
7. Georgina Battiscombe, p. 159.
8. Peter Kurth, *The Lost World of Nicholas and Alexandra*, p. 49.
9. Graham and Heather Fisher, *Bertie & Alix*, p. 149.
10. Coryne Hall, *Little Mother of Russia*, p. 67.
11. Michael Ignatieff, *The Russian Album*.
12. General Yepanchin.
13. Maylunas and Mironenko, *A Lifelong Passion*, p. 109, citing diary of Konstantin Romanov.
14. *Ibid.*, p. 61.

15. Catherine Radziwill, *Nicholas II: The Last of the Tsars*, p. 87.
16. Maylunas and Mironenko, *A Lifelong Passion*, p. 112, citing letter dated 16 November from Anichov Palace.
17. *Ibid.*, p. 111, diary entry dated 15 November 1894.
18. Radziwill, *Nicholas II: The Last of the Tsars*, p. 89.
19. Denis Judd, *The Life and Times of George V*, p. 89.
20. GEO VAA 43129.
21. Maylunas and Mironenko, *A Lifelong Passion*, p. 332.
22. Rosemary and Donald Crawford, *Michael and Natasha*, p. 98, Michael's diary, 27 April 1910, GARF 601/1301.
23. Kenneth Rose, *King George V*, p. 81 citing conversation between the King and Lord Esher.
24. Harold Nicolson, *King George V: His Life and Reign*, p. 123.
25. Maylunas and Mironenko, *A Lifelong Passion*, p. 333.
26. Rose, *King George V*, p. 85.
27. *Ibid.*, p. 84.
28. Gore, *King George V: A Personal Memoir*, p. 415.
29. *Ibid.*, p. 258.
30. *Ibid.*, p. 259, citing diary entry 'Thursday 22 June. Our Coronation Day Buckingham Palace.'
31. Denis Judd, *The Life and Times of George V*, p. 92.
32. Rose, *King George V*, p. 103, citing a letter from The Master of Elibank to his wife.
33. Nicolson, *King George V*, p. 147, citing diary entry 22 June 1911.
34. Gore, *King George V: A Personal Memoir*, p. 147, citing diary entry for 23 June 1911.
35. *The Times*, 27 May 1896.
36. Sophie Buxhoeveden, *The Life and Tragedy of Alexandra Feodorovna, Empress of Russia*, p. 65.
37. George Buchanan, *My Mission to Russia*.

10: Cup of Sorrows

1. Greg King, *The Last Empress*, p. 109, n. 24, citing Sidney Harcave, *Years of the Golden Cockerel*, New York, Macmillan, 1964.
2. Catherine Radziwill, *Nicholas II: The Last of the Tsars*, p. 117.

11: 'I Like My Wife'

1. Harold Nicolson, *King George V*, p. 51.
2. James Lees-Milne, *Harold Nicolson*, Diary entry 4.10.1949.
3. John Gore, *King George V: A Personal Memoir*.
4. Letter to Sir Francis de Winton from the Duke of York, 23 January 1893.
5. *New Penny* magazine, 1899, vol. 4 no. 40.
6. David Duff, *Queen Mary*, p. 139.
7. Giles St Aubyn, *The Royal George*, p. 300.

8. Lord Burnham, *Royalty Digest*.

9. A.J.P. Taylor, *British Prime Ministers and Other Essays*, p. 318.

10. Lees-Milne, *Harold Nicolson*, p. 229 n. 81 (H.N. in conversation with Sir Kenneth Clark).

11. Frankland Noble, *Prince Henry, Duke of Gloucester*, p. 4.

12. Gore, *King George V*, p. 114.

13. Aubrey Buxton, *The King and His Country*, p. 6.

14. Denis Judd, *The Life and Times of George V*, p. 87.

15. Harold Nicolson, *King George V*, p. 51.

16. Tranby Croft was a house in Yorkshire where the Prince of Wales was a house guest and where on 8 September 1890 Colonel Sir William Gordon-Cumming was accused of cheating at baccarat which was illegal at the time. The Colonel was outraged by the suggestion and the result was a court case when he claimed damages for slander. The Prince of Wales was cited as a witness. The Colonel lost the case, but it had been hugely damaging to the reputation of the Prince of Wales, and his mother Queen Victoria was mortified.

17. Ian Shapiro archives.

18. Letter from George V. Argyll Etkin Collection.

19. Lees-Milne, *Harold Nicolson*, p. 233.

20. Judd, *The Life and Times of George V*, p. 208.

21. Nina Epton, *Victoria and her Daughters*, New York, Norton, 1971 (cited in C. Erickson, *Alexandra: The Last Tsarina*, p. 109).

22. Andrei Maylunas and Sergei Mironenko, *A Lifelong Passion*, p. 131.

23. Osbert Sitwell, *Queen Mary and Others*, p. 27.

24. Lees-Milne, *Harold Nicolson*, p. 72.

25. *Ibid.*, p. 268 n. 24, H.N. diary 4.1.1953.

26. Duff, *Queen Mary*, p. 110.

27. Nicholas II, The Imperial Family State Archive of the Russian Federation fund 642, 1.1 no. 2324 ff. 56–56v.

28. *Ibid.*, fund 601, 1.1 no. 1194, ff. 95v–96.

12: 'A Charming, Dear, Precious Place'

1. Greg King, *The Last Empress*, p. 116.

2. Sophie Buxhoeveden, *The Life and Tragedy of Alexandra Feodorovna, Empress of Russia*.

3. Lili Dehn, *The Real Tsaritsa*, p. 57.

4. Marfa Mouchanow, *My Empress*, p. 40.

5. Major-General Andrei Elchaninov, *Tsar Nicholas II*, p. 30.

6. M. Eager, *Six Years at the Russian Court*, p. 21.

7. Dehn, *The Real Tsaritsa*, p. 60.

8. Marc Ferro, *Nicholas II: The Last of the Tsars*, p. 50.

9. Anna Vyrubova, *Memories of the Russian Court*.

10. Meriel Buchanan, *Petrograd: The City of Trouble*, p. 74.

11. Wilfred Blunt, *Lady Muriel*.

12. Dehn, *The Real Tsaritsa*, p. 51.

13. Curator Alexandra Valentina Vaileva, in conversation with the author.

13: Learning to Rule

1. Nicholas and Maria Feodorovna, *Letters of Tsar Nicholas and Empress Marie*, p. 35.

2. Nicholas to his mother, 27 September 1906, GARF, f. 642, op. I, d. 2329 l.

3. Denis Judd, *The Life and Times of George V*.

4. Simon Courtauld, re: King Carlos of Portugal, *Spectator* magazine p. 58, May 2005.

5. John van der Kiste, *Crowns in a Changing World*.

6. Kenneth Rose, *King George V*, p. 71.

7. Arthur Bryant, *George V*, p. 146.

8. George V to de Winton, Argyll Etkin Archive.

9. Lady Longford, *The Royal House of Windsor*.

10. Judd, *The Life and Times of George V*, p. 72.

11. David Duff, *Queen Mary*, p. 119.

12. John Gore, *King George V: A Personal Memoir*, p. 162.

13. *Ibid.*, p. 377.

14. Duff, *Queen Mary*, pp. 174–5; Lady Cynthia Colville, *A Crowded Life*, p. 120.

15. Gore, *King George V: A Personal Memoir*, p. 202.

16. *Ibid.*, p. 220.

17. *Ibid.*, p. 368, n. 1.

18. *Ibid.*, p. 360, n. 1.

19. James Lees-Milne, *Harold Nicolson: A Biography*, p. 224; H.N. diary (unpubl.) 7 September 1948.

20. Bryant, *George V*, p. 120.

21. Duke of Windsor, *A King's Story*.

22. The nickname was coined by American writer Henry James.

23. Gore, *King George V: A Personal Memoir*, p. 328.

24. Rose, *George V*, p. 294.

25. Hugo Vickers, *Alice, Princess Andrew of Greece*, p. 11.

26. James Pope-Hennessy, *Queen Mary*, p. 448.

27. Gore, *King George V*, p. 264.

28. *The Times*, 21 April 1917.

29. Harold Nicolson, *King George V*, p. 308; David Duff, *Queen Mary*, p. 110.

30. Rose, *George V*, p. 345.

31. Andrei Elchaninov, *Tsar Nicholas II*, p. 112.

32. A description of Nicholas by Grand Duke Alexander.

33. V.N. Kokovtsov, *Out of My Past: The Memoirs of Count Kokovtsov*, p. 519.

34. Andrei Elchaninov, *Tsar Nicholas II*.

35. Anna Vyrubova, *Memories of the Russian Court*, p. 93.

36. *Ibid.*, p. 74.

37. Sir Bernard Pares, *My Russian Memoirs*.
38. *Ibid*.
39. Count Alexander Grabbe, *The Private World of the Last Tsar*, p. 30.
40. *Ibid*., p. 236.
41. Letter from York Cottage dated 17 January 1917.
42. Rose, *King George V*, p. 217.

14: Their Wives and Mothers Did Not Compare

1. Marc Ferro, *Nicholas II: The Last of the Tsars*, p. 52 from Vyrubova, Anna, *A Journal Secret, 1909–17*, Paris, 1928.
2. David Duff, *Queen Mary*, p. 96.
3. Ian Vorres, *The Last Grand Duchess*.
4. Alexander Mossolov, *At the Court of the Last Tsar*.
5. Duff, *Queen Mary*, p. 63.
6. *Ibid*., p. 36.
7. Osbert Sitwell, *Queen Mary and Others*, p. 28.
8. *Ibid*., p. 37.
9. *Ibid*., p. 27.
10. Kenneth Rose, *George V*, p. 72.
11. Denis Judd, *The Life and Times of George V*, p. 109.
12. Sitwell, *Queen Mary and Others*, p. 26.
13. *Ibid*., p. 32.
14. Sophie Buxhoeveden, *The Life and Tragedy of Alexandra Feodorovna, Empress of Russia*, p. 128.
15. Marfa Mouchanow, *My Empress: Twenty-Three Years of Intimate Life with the Empress of All the Russias, from Her Marriage to the Days of Her Exile*, p. 50.

15: A Special Gaiety of Spirit

1. Peter Kurth, *Tsar: The Lost World of Nicholas and Alexandra*, p. 68.
2. Lili Dehn, *The Real Tsaritsa*, p. 81.
3. Marfa Mouchanow, *My Empress*, p. 161.
4. Charlotte Zeepvat, *Romanov Autumn*, p. 254.
5. Rosemary and Donald Crawford, *Michael and Natasha*, p. 10.
6. Rt Revd Herbert Bury, *Russian Life Today*.
7. Charles Gibbes, *Tutor to the Tsarevich*, p. 33.
8. Alexander Mossolov, *At the Court of the Last Tsar*, p. 53.
9. Opinion expressed to the author by Elliot Philipp, an eminent gynaecologist.
10. Opinion of Russian psychiatrist Bechterev.

16: 'Get That Damned Child Away from Me'

1. Frances Welch, *The Romanovs and Mr Gibbes*.
2. Marc Ferro, *Nicholas II*, p. 133.

3. Alexander Mossolov, *At the Court of the Last Tsar*.
4. James Lees-Milne, *Harold Nicolson*, diary entry for 21.7.48, conversation with Earl of Cromer, formerly Lord Chamberlain of the Household.
5. Arthur Bryant, *George V*, p. 30.
6. Lord Harewood in an interview with *Tatler* magazine, February 2004, p. 109.
7. David Duff, *Queen Mary*, p. 106.
8. Lees-Milne, *Harold Nicolson*, p. 230, Morshead in conversation with H.N. 1949.
9. Stephen Poliakov, *The Lost Prince*.
10. The Duke of Windsor, *Letters from a Prince*, p. 128, letter dated 20 January 1919.
11. *Ibid.*, p. 128.

17: *Seeds of Unrest*

1. Astolphe de Custine, *Letters from Russia*, p. 273.
2. Norman Davies, *Europe*, p. 836.
3. Coryne Hall, *Imperial Dancer*, p. 99.
4. Mark Ferro, *Nicholas II: The Last of the Tsars*, p. 159.
5. Recalled by Osip Mandelstam.
6. John Curtis Perry, *The Flight of the Romanovs*, p. 96.
7. Ian Vorres, *The Last Grand Duchess*, p. 114.
8. William Gerhardi, *The Romanovs*, p. 502.
9. Michael Hughes, *Inside the Enigma*, p. 41.
10. V.N. Kokovtsov, *Out of My Past*.
11. Alexander Mossolov, *At the Court of the Last Tsar*, p. 139.
12. *Ibid.*, p. 130.
13. Denis Judd, *The Life and Times of George V*, p. 78.
14. Kenneth Rose, *King George V*, p. 66.
15. Meriel Buchanan, *The Dissolution of an Empire*, p. 55.
16. *Ibid.*, p. 55.
17. Letter from Nicholas II, RA geo AA 43 146 Nov. 15/28 1910.

18: *Hollowness and Vodka*

1. Meriel Buchanan, *The Dissolution of an Empire*, p. 41.
2. *The Times*, 3 August 1914.
3. Greg King, *The Last Empress*, p. 221, citing N.N. Golovine, *The Russian Army in World War I*, p. 53.
4. Diary 29 July.
5. Diary 31 July.
6. *Ibid.*
7. George Buchanan, *My Mission to Russia*, vol. I, p. 204.
8. Anna Vyrubova, *Memories of the Russian Court*, p. 104.

9. John Gore, *King George V*, p. 305, n. 1.
10. *Ibid.*, p. 305.
11. Denis Judd, *The Life and Times of George V*, p. 131.
12. Gore, *King George V*, p. 348.
13. *Pearson Weekly*, 'The King and War News', 27 March 1915.
14. Marc Ferro, *Nicholas II*, p. 23.
15. Catherine Radziwill, *Nicholas II: The Last of the Tsars*, quoting Petrograd correspondent of English newspaper, p. 223.
16. V.N. Kokovtsov, *Out of My Past*, p. 28.
17. Norman Davies, *Europe*, p. 836.
18. AF to Nicholas, p. 453.
19. Davies, *Europe*, p. 915.
20. Donald and Rosemary Crawford, *Michael and Natasha*, p. 197.
21. Lili Dehn, *The Real Tsaritsa*, p. 197.
22. From the Bowman manuscript – impressions from her mother.
23. King, *The Last Empress*, p. 257.
24. Sir Robert Bruce-Lockhart, *Memoirs of a British Agent*, p. 102.
25. Davies, *Europe*, p. 914.
26. Kenneth Rose, *King George V*, p. 223.

19: *Sparkling Cyanide*

1. V.N. Kokovtsov, *Out of My Past*, p. 297.
2. Nicholas Romanov in conversation with the author.
3. Alfred Knox, *With the Russian Army*, p. 334.
4. Kokovtsov, *Out of My Past*, p. 296.
5. Norman Davies, *Europe*, p. 915.
6. Donald and Rosemary Crawford, *Michael and Natasha*, p. 90.
7. Miriam Kochan, *The Last Days of Imperial Russia*, p. 35.
8. Edvard Radzinsky, *Rasputin: The Last Word*.
9. George Buchanan, *My Mission to Russia*, vol. 2, p. 37.
10. Greg King, *The Last Empress*, p. 275.

20: *Jaded Eau-de-Nil*

1. Sir Robert Bruce-Lockhart, *Memoirs of a British Agent*, p. 115.
2. Meriel Buchanan, *Recollections of Imperial Russia*, p. 26.
3. W. Somerset Maugham, 'His Excellency' from *Collected Short Stories*, vol. 3.
4. Bernard Pares, *My Russian Memoirs*, p. 275.
5. Michael Hughes, *Inside the Enigma*, p. 90 n. 28, citing Samuel Hoare, *The Fourth Seal*, p. 242.
6. Buchanan, *Recollections of Imperial Russia*, p. 410.
7. Hughes, *Inside the Enigma*, p. 25.
8. Buchanan, *Recollections of Imperial Russia*.
9. *Ibid.*, p. 11.

10. Bruce-Lockhart, *Memoirs of a British Agent*, p. 116.

11. Buchanan, *Recollections of Imperial Russia*, p. 13.

12. Buchanan, *An Ambassador's Daughter*, p. 105.

13. Buchanan, *Recollections of Imperial Russia*, p. 85.

14. Buchanan, *The Dissolution of an Empire*, p. 15.

15. Lili Dehn, *The Real Tsaritsa*, p. 45.

16. George Buchanan, *My Mission to Russia*, vol. 2, p. 141.

17. Meriel Buchanan, *Recollections of Imperial Russia*, p. 47.

18. *Ibid.*, p. 41.

19. FO800/205.

20. Michael Hughes, *Inside the Enigma*, p. 288,.

21. Robert Bruce-Lockhart, *Memoirs of a British Agent*, p. 119.

22. George Buchanan, *My Mission to Russia*, vol. 2, p. 43.

23. *Ibid.*, vol. 2, p. 46.

24. *Ibid.*, vol. 2, p. 49.

25. Meriel Buchanan, *Recollections of Imperial Russia*, p. 1.

26. Pierre Gilliard, *Thirteen Years at the Russian Court*, p. 99.

27. George Buchanan, *My Mission to Russia*, vol. 2, p. 50.

28. Princess Catherine Radziwill, *The Last of the Tsars*, p. 268.

29. Buchanan, *My Mission to Russia*, vol. 2, p. 238.

30. *Ibid.*, vol. 2, p. 31.

31. Meriel Buchanan, *Recollections of Imperial Russia*.

32. George Buchanan, *My Mission to Russia*, vol. 2.

21: *The Crow's Nest*

1. Count Grabbe, *The Private World of the Last Tsar*.

2. Zoia Belyakova, *The Romanovs, The Way it Was*, p. 143.

3. Lili Dehn, *The Last Tsaritsa*, p. 237.

4. Meriel Buchanan, *The Dissolution of an Empire*, p. 135.

5. Sophie Buxhoeveden, *The Life and Tragedy of Alexandra Feodorovna, Empress of Russia*, p. 179.

6. Major-General Andrei Elchaninov, *Tsar Nicholas II*, p. 36.

7. Charlotte Zeepvat, *Romanov Autumn*, p. 153.

8. Buxhoeveden, *The Life and Tragedy of Alexandra Feodorovna, Empress of Russia*, p. 178.

9. Carolly Erickson, *Alexandra: The Last Tsarina*, p. 201.

22: *In a Snowbound Siding*

1. Bernard Pares, *My Russian Memoirs*, p. 396.

2. Meriel Buchanan, *The Dissolution of an Empire*, p. 156.

3. Marc Ferro, *The Last Tsar*, p. 144.

4. Pierre Gilliard, *Thirteen Years at the Russian Court*, p. 181.

5. George Buchanan, *My Mission to Russia*, p. 77.

6. Donald and Rosemary Crawford, *Michael and Natasha*, p. 255.

7. Miriam Kochan, *The Last Days of Imperial Russia*, p. 208.

8. Robert Bruce-Lockhart, *Memoirs of a British Agent*, p. 101.

9. John Curtis Perry, *The Flight of the Romanovs*, p. 67.

10. Lili Dehn, *The Real Tsaritsa*, pp. 140–1.

11. Donald and Rosemary Crawford, *Michael and Natasha*.

12. Diary, 2 February 1917 (Russian calendar).

13. Dehn, *The Real Tsaritsa*, p. 139.

14. William Gerhardi, *The Romanovs*, p. 34 – Nicholas diary entry.

15. Charles Sydney Gibbes, *Tutor to the Tsarevich*

16. Meriel Buchanan, *The Dissolution of an Empire*, p. 163.

17. George Buchanan, *My Mission to Russia*, vol. 1, p. 79.

18. *Ibid.*, p. 61.

19. Mark D. Steinberg and Vladimir M. Khrustalëv, *The Fall of the Romanovs*; Document 5, Letter from Alexandra to Nicholas, 25 February 1917, GARF f. 601, op. 1, d. 1151, l. 490–493 ob. Manuscript, Steinberg and Khrustalëv.

20. Dehn, *The Real Tsaritsa*, p. 137.

21. Steinberg and Khrustalëv, *The Fall of the Romanovs*, p. 50.

22. *Ibid.*, p. 50 n. 22, testimony of Count Frederik.

23. Catherine Radziwill, *Nicholas II: The Last of the Tsars*, p. 283.

24. Diary of Nicholas II, 27 February–3 March 1917 (Russian calendar).

25. *Ibid.*, 1 March 1917 (Russian calendar).

26. Dehn, *The Real Tsaritsa*, p. 193.

27. Steinberg and Khrustalëv, *The Fall of the Romanovs*, pp. 57–8.

28. Meriel Buchanan, *The Dissolution of an Empire*, p. 175.

29. Dehn, *The Real Tsaritsa*, pp. 194–5.

30. Buchanan, *The Dissolution of an Empire*, p. 176.

31. George Buchanan, *My Mission to Russia*, p. 69.

32. Steinberg and Khrustalëv, *The Fall of the Romanovs*, p. 97.

33. Nicholas's diary, March 1917.

34. Andrei Maylunas and Sergei Mironenko, *A Lifelong Passion*, p. 550.

35. From a photo of a telegram which appeared in *Illyustrirovannaya Rossiya*, Donald and Rosemary Crawford, *Michael and Natasha*.

36. Meriel Buchanan, *The Dissolution of an Empire*, p. 202.

37. Steinberg and Khrustalëv, *The Fall of the Romanovs*, p. 114.

38. Buchanan, *The Dissolution of an Empire*, p. 189, Petrograd.

39. Protocol of Talks, GARF 601/2099 State Archive of the Russian Federation.

40. Bernard Pares, *My Russian Memoirs*, p. 469 citing Diary of Nicholas II, 2 March 1917 (Russian calendar).

41. Diary of Nicholas II, 3 March 1917 (Russian calendar).

42. *Ibid.*, 8 March 1917 (Russian calendar).

43. George Buchanan, *My Mission to Russia*, vol. 2, p. 88.

44. V.N. Kokovtsov, *Out of My Past*, p. 470.

45. Michael Hughes, *Inside the Enigma*, p. 54, quoting Professor Norman Stone *The Eastern Front, 1914–17* (London: Macmillan, 1976), p. 151.
46. Meriel Buchanan, *The Dissolution of an Empire*, p. 181, from *Nicholas II as I Knew Him* by Sir John Hanbury-Williams.
47. Victor Alexandrov, *The End of the Romanovs*, p. 136.
48. Victor, *The End of the Romanovs*, p. 137.
49. Kenneth Rose, *George V*, p. 209. King's diary, RA.
50. Harold Nicolson, *King George V*, p. 299.

23: 'The End Is Inevitable'

1. Meriel Buchanan, *The Dissolution of an Empire*, p. 195.
2. Michael Davies, *Inside the Enigma*, p. 890 (Lord Bertie to Lord Hardinge).
3. Buchanan, *The Dissolution of an Empire*, p. 193.
4. *Ibid.*, p. 194.
5. Peter Kurth, *Tsar: The Lost World of Nicholas and Alexandra*, p. 154.
6. Buchanan, *The Dissolution of an Empire*, p. 190.
7. Kurth, *Tsar: The Lost World of Nicholas and Alexandra*, p. 154.
8. *Ibid.*, p. 197.
9. FO/800/205, Stamfordham to Balfour 30 March 1917.
10. Buchanan, *The Dissolution of an Empire*, pp. 196–7.
11. Stamfordham letters, Royal Archives.
12. House of Lords Records Office – Royal Family.
13. The *Sunday Times* on previously unpublished extracts from George V's diaries, 2004.
14. Kenneth Rose, *King George V*, p. 211.
15. *Ibid.*, p. 316.
16. Meriel Buchanan, *An Ambassador's Daughter*, p. 156.
17. William Clarke, *The Lost Fortune of the Tsars*, p. 357.
18. *Ibid.*, p. 38.
19. Rose, *King George V*, p. 215.
20. Robert Wilton, *The Last Days of the Romanovs*, from 15 March 1917, Robert Wilton, special correspondent of *The Times*, author of *Russia's Agony*.
21. Meriel Buchanan, *Petrograd: The City of Trouble*, pp. 1140–1.
22. Buchanan, *The Dissolution of an Empire*, p. 202.
23. *Ibid.*, pp. 201–2.

24: A Sad, Bearded Woodcutter

1. Lili Dehn, *The Real Tsaritsa*, p. 153.
2. Donald and Rosemary Crawford, *Michael and Natasha*, p. 271, n. 15.
3. Dehn, *The Real Tsaritsa*, p. 178.
4. *Ibid.*, p. 162.
5. *Ibid.*, p. 165.
6. Meriel Buchanan, *Petrograd: The City of Trouble*, p. 108.

7. Carolly Erickson, *Alexandra: The Last Tsarina*, p. 289.

8. Mark D. Steinberg and Vladimir M. Khrustalëv, *The Fall of the Romanovs*, p. 146 (Afanasy Beliaev, Archpriest at Tsarskoe Selo).

9. Pierre Gilliard, *Thirteen Years at the Russian Court*, pp. 214–15.

10. William Gerhardi, *The Romanovs*, p. 31.

11. Steinberg and Khrustalëv, *The Fall of the Romanovs*, p. 156 (note, Diary of Nicholas II, 9 March–31 July 1917, GARF).

12. Anna Vyrubova, *Memories of the Russian Court*, p. 212.

13. Dehn, *The Real Tsaritsa*, p. 89.

14. Steinberg and Khrustalëv, *The Fall of the Romanovs*, p. 178.

15. Robert Wilton, *The Last Days of the Romanovs*, p. 612.

16. Vladimir Poliakov, *The Tragic Bride*, p. 262.

17. Dehn, *The Real Tsaritsa*, p. 199.

18. Gerhardi, *The Romanovs*, p. 32.

19. Steinberg and Khrustalëv, *The Fall of the Romanovs*, p. 124 (note 17, Diary of Nicholas II, 13 March and 18 April 1917).

20. Dehn, *The Real Tsaritsa*, p. 199.

21. Count Alexander Grabbe, *The Private World of the Last Tsar*.

25: 'An Out-and-Out Backwater'

1. Robert Wilton, *The Last Days of the Romanovs*.

2. Peter Kurth, *Tsar: The Lost World of Nicholas and Alexandra*, p. 165.

3. Sophie Buxhoeveden, *The Life and Tragedy of Alexandra Feodorovna, Empress of Russia*, p. 307.

4. Mark D. Steinberg and Vladimir M. Khrustalëv, *The Fall of the Romanovs*, p. 169.

5. Paul Benckendorff, *Last Days at Tsarskoe Selo*, p. 112.

6. Steinberg and Khrustalëv, *The Fall of the Romanovs*, p. 169.

7. *Ibid.*, p. 238, n. 107 GARF.

8. Alexandra Feodorovna's diary, June 1918.

9. Steinberg and Khristalëv, *The Fall of the Romanovs*, p. 280.

10. Steinberg and Khristalëv, *The Fall of the Romanovs*, p. 260.

11. Carolly Erickson, *Alexandra: The Last Tsarina*, p. 316.

12. Kenneth Rose, *King George V*, p. 212 (Lord Stamfordham to A.J. Balfour, 24 March 1917, from Windsor Castle).

13. Meriel Buchanan, *Petrograd: The City of Trouble 1914–18*.

14. *Ibid.*, p. 183.

15. George Buchanan, *My Mission to Russia*, vol. 2, p. 208.

16. Steinberg and Khristalëv, *The Fall of the Romanovs*, p. 213 (GARF).

17. Charles Sydney Gibbes, *Tutor to the Tsarevich*.

18. Pierre Gilliard, *Thirteen Years at the Russian Court*, p. 262.

19. Carolly Erickson, *Alexandra; The Last Tsarina*, p. 325.

20. Lili Dehn, *The Real Tsaritsa*, p. 331.

21. Andrei Maylunas and Sergei Mironenko, *A Lifelong Passion*, p. 616 (Nicholas's diary).

26: 'The Road to Calvary'

1. Pierre Gilliard, *Thirteen Years at the Russian Court*, p. 274.
2. Vladimir Oustimenko and Lyubov Tyutyunnik, *The Family Life of Nikolai and Alexandra*, p. 106.
3. Peter Kurth, *Tsar: The Lost World of Nicholas and Alexandra*, p. 161.
4. Mark D. Steinberg and Vladimir M. Khrustalëv, *The Fall of the Romanovs*, p. 277.
5. Carolly Erickson, *Alexandra: The Last Tsarina*, p. 329.
6. Andrei Maylunas and Sergei Mironenko, *A Lifelong Passion*, p. 622.
7. *Ibid.*, p. 624.
8. Kurth, *Tsar: The Lost World of Nicholas and Alexandra*, p. 190.
9. Robert Wilton, *The Last Days of the Romanovs*, p. 79.
10. Kurth, *Tsar: The Lost World of Nicholas and Alexandra*, p. 193.
11. Victor Alexandrov, *The End of the Romanovs*, p. 164.
12. Kurth, *Tsar: The Lost World of Nicholas and Alexandra*, p. 187.
13. William Gerhardi, *The Romanovs*, p. 515.
14. Testimony of Terenti Chemodurov.
15. Kurth, *Tsar: The Lost World of Nicholas and Alexandra*, p. 193, evidence of Austrian prisoner of war who was an orderly to Yurovsky.
16. Robert K. Massie, *The Romanovs*, p. 5.
17. *Ibid.*, p. 6.
18. Wilton, *The Last Days of the Romanovs*, p. 90.
19. Massie, *The Romanovs*, p. 6.
20. Kurth, *Tsar: The Lost World of Nicholas and Alexandra*, p. 197.
21. Edward Radzinsky, *The Last Tsar*.
22. Massie, *The Romanovs*, p. 747.
23. Wilton, *The Last Days of the Romanovs*, p. 157.
24. Leon Trotsky, *Diary in Exile – 1935*.

27: Small Humiliations

1. Robert K. Massie, *The Romanovs*, p. 17.
2. Sir George Buchanan to Lord Stamfordham, 7 September 1917, RAGV, p. 284, A/26.
3. Appeal from the Council of People's Commissars to the Toiling Masses of England, America, France, Italy and Japan on Allied Interventions in Russia, 1 August 1918, in degrees, Soviet Documents on Foreign Policy, vol. 1, pp. 88–92, Michael Hughes in *Inside the Enigma*, p. 137.
4. Harold Nicolson, *King George V*, p. 386, citing J.R. Clynes, *Memoirs*.
5. Denis Judd, *The Life and Times of George V*, p. 178.
6. A.J.P. Taylor, *British Prime Ministers and Other Essays*, pp. 106–7.
7. Mabell Airlie, *Thatched with Gold*, p. 231.

8. Coryne Hall and John Van der Kiste, *Once a Grand Duchess*, chapter 'It All Seems Like a Terrible Nightmare'.

9. Coryne Hall, *Little Mother of Russia*.

10. *Ibid.*, p. 329.

11. Sir Frederick Ponsonby, *Recollections of Three Reigns*.

12. Suzy Menkes, *The Royal Jewels*.

13. Sonia Goodman in conversation with the author.

14. Ian Vorres, *The Last Grand Duchess*, p. 189, ministry of works report.

15. *Ibid.*, p. 202; Arthur Ponsonby, *His Life from His Letters*.

16. Hall and Van der Kiste, *Once a Grand Duchess*, p. 216.

17. Lady Brabourne in conversation with the author.

18. Coryne Hall in personal conversation. Researching her book *Little Mother of Russia*, she visited Clarence House. Frightened of dogs, she asked if the Queen Mother's corgis could be shut away during her visit; they were and not a bark or snuffle was heard.

19. HRH the Duke of Windsor, *A King's Story*, p. 131.

20. Richard Meinertzhagen, a soldier and adventurer, made such a claim, and his colourful diaries are tantalising, although many entries are sparse. '1 July 1918: . . . Success was not complete and I find it dangerous to give details. One child was . . . much bruised and brought to Britain where she still is.'

21. Professor Zoia Belyakova in conversation with the author.

22. Mrs Philippa Bowers in conversation with the author.

23. Kenneth Rose, *King George V*, p. 348.

24. Judd, *The Life and Times of George V*, p. 183.

25. Rose, *King George V*, p. 357.

28: A Chorus of Disapproval

1. Denis Judd, *The Life and Times of George V* (King in conversation with Lady Asquith), p. 148.

2. Ian Shapiro Archives.

3. Coryne Hall and John van der Kiste, *Once a Grand Duchess*, p. 159, n. 37.

4. Hall and Van der Kiste, *Once a Grand Duchess*, p. 158.

5. John Curtis Perry, *The Flight of the Romanovs*, pp. 226–7.

6. *Ibid.*, p. 228, citing a letter from Lord Acton, the British minister in Helsinki.

7. Perry, *The Flight of the Romanovs*, p. 71.

8. Meriel Buchanan, *The Dissolution of an Empire*, p. 189.

9. Frances Stevenson, *Lloyd George: A Diary*, entry February 1922.

10. *Ibid.*, 3 February 1922.

11. Buchanan, *The Dissolution of an Empire*, p. 199.

12. Kenneth Rose, *King George V*, p. 215.

13. David Lloyd George, *War Memoirs*.

14. Robert K. Massie, *The Romanovs – The Final Chapter*, p. 86.

15. Rose, *King George V*.

16. *Ibid.*, p. 210.
17. Kenneth Rose in conversation with the author.
18. Rose, *King George V*, p. 210.
19. Kenneth Rose in conversation with the author.
20. Dominic Lieven in conversation with author.
21. Nicolai Tolstoy in conversation with the author.
22. *The Times*, 8 February 1992.

29: Imperial Requiem

1. *Independent on Sunday*, 20 February 2000, from documents released at the National Archives (Public Record Office).
2. James Pope-Hennessy, *Queen Mary*, p. 555.
3. Denis Judd, *The Life and Times of George V*, p. 192.
4. David Duff, *Queen Mary*, p. 174.
5. Christopher Hibbert, *The Court at Windsor*, p. 264.
6. John Gore, *King George V*, p. 335.
7. Ian Shapiro Archives, George V to Evelyn Forbes from Buckingham Palace, 13 February 1923.
8. Duff, *Queen Mary*, p. 175.
9. *Ibid.*, p. 122.
10. *Ibid.*, p. 199.
11. Cynthia Colville, *A Crowded Life*, p. 120.
12. Kenneth Rose, *King George V*, p. 402.
13. *Ibid.*, p. 361.
14. *Time*, 27 January 1936.
15. Mark D. Steinberg and Vladimir M. Khrustalëv, *The Fall of the Romanovs*, p. 156 (note Diary of Nicholas II, 9 March–31 July 1917, GARF).
16. Sir Arthur Bryant, *George V*, p. 177.
17. *Daily Mail*, 22 November 1936.
18. *The New Oxford Book of English Verse 1250–1950*, published by Clarendon Press, Oxford, chosen and edited by Helen Gardner. 'Death of King George V', no. 848, p. 911. Reprinted by permission of John Murray publishers.
19. George V to Emperor of Russia, 27 December 1916.
20. Colonel Roger Binks, the regimental secretary.
21. Report dated 6 July 1918 to the Ekaterinburg Soviet of Deputies.
22. Robert K. Massie, *The Romanovs: The Final Chapter*, p. 30.
23. Voikov, who had been ambassador to Poland, was recalled to Moscow, where a young man came up to him and shot him dead on arrival at the railway station. Another commissar, Yakovlev, was blown up by a car bomb in 1938; the secret police claimed 'it was an explosion of the motor'. Veteran revolutionary Yakov Sverdlov, who gave the original order for the murder of the Tsar, simply disappeared in 1919. The case was filed away under 'Crimes unsolved'. Yakov Yurovsky, the prime mover and murderer, died of cancer in 1938.

24. *London Evening Standard*, 1937.

25. Clem Cecil, *The Times*, 17 July 2003 p. 3.

26. Greg King and Penny Wilson, *The Fate of the Romanovs*, p. 446, n. 37 in conversation with one of the authors.

27. *Ibid.*, p. 484, Buckingham Palace source.

28. Prince Michael Romanov in conversation with the author.

29. *Eagle and Carbine* (regimental magazine), p. 103, vol. 28, 1999 (Major Ravnkilde).

30. Major Ravnkilde, Royal Scots Dragoon Guards, in conversation with the author.

31. *Ibid.*

32. Kyril Zinoviev in conversation with the author.

33. *Ibid.*

34. *Ibid.*

35. Zinoviev.

36. Nicolai Guedroitz, a London art dealer.

37. Harold Nicolson, *King George V*, p. 106.

Bibliography

Airlie, Mabell, Countess of, *Thatched with Gold*, Hutchinson, 1962

Almedegin, E.M., *An Unbroken Unity: A Memoir of Grand Duchess Serge of Russia*, Bodley Head, London, 1964

Alexandrov, Victor, *The End of the Romanovs*, trans. William Sutcliffe, Hutchinson, 1966

Baring, Maurice, *Russian Essays and Stories*, Nelson & Co., 1908

——, *What I Saw in Russia*, Thomas Nelson & Sons, 1913

Battiscombe, Georgina, *Queen Alexandra*, Constable, 1969

Belyakova, Zoia, *The Romanovs, The Way it Was*, Ego Publishers, St Petersburg, 2000

——, *The Romanov Legacy: The Palaces of St Petersburg*, Hazar Publishing, 1996

Benckendorff, Count Constantine, *Half a Life*, Richards Press, 1954

Benckendorff, Count Paul, *Last Days at Tsarskoe Selo*, William Heinemann, 1927

Blunt, William, *Lady Muriel*, Methuen, London 1962

Bokhanaov, *The Romanovs*, trans. Lyudmila Zenofontova, Leppi, 1993

Bruce-Lockhart, Sir Robert, *Memoirs of a British Agent*, Putnam, 1932

Bryant, Sir Arthur, *George V*, Peter Davies, 1936

Buchanan, Sir George, *My Mission to Russia* Vols 1 and 2, Cassell, 1923

Buchanan, Meriel, *Petrograd: The City of Trouble 1914–1918*, Collins, 1918

——, *Recollections of Imperial Russia*, Hutchinson, 1923

——, *The Dissolution of an Empire*, London, Murray, 1932

——, *An Ambassador's Daughter*, London, 1958

Bury, Right Revd Herbert, *Russian Life Today*, A.R. Mowbray, 1915

Buxhoeveden, Sophie, *The Life and Tragedy of Alexandra Feodorovna, Empress of Russia*, Longmans, Green, 1928

Buxton, Aubrey, *The King and His Country*, Longmans, Green, 1955

Clarke, William, *The Lost Fortune of the Tsars*, Orion, 1996

Cocker, Mark, *Richard Meinertzhagen: Soldier, Scientist and Spy*, Mandarin Paperback, 1989

Colville, Cynthia, *A Crowded Life*, London, Evans Brothers, 1963

Cooper, Duff, *Old Men Forget*, Rupert Hart-Davis, 1953

Cowles, Virginia, *The Last Tsar and Tsarina*, Weidenfeld & Nicolson, 1977

Crawford, Rosemary and Crawford, Donald, *Michael and Natasha, The Life and Loves of the Last Tsar of Russia*, Weidenfeld & Nicolson, 1997

Custine, Astolphe de, *Letters from Russia*, trans. and ed. Anka Muhlstein, New York Review Books, 2002

Davies, Norman, *Europe: A History*, Oxford University Press, 1996

Dehn, Lili, *The Real Tsaritsa*, Thornton Butterworth, 1922

Duff, David, *Hessian Tapestry*

——, *Queen Mary*, Collins, 1985

Eager, M., *Six Years at the Russian Court*, Hurst & Blackett, 1906

Edwards, Anne, *Matriarch Queen: Mary and the House of Windsor*, Hodder & Stoughton, 1984

Elchaninov, Major-General Andrei, *Tsar Nicholas II*, London, Hugh Rees, 1913

Epton, Nina, *Victoria and Her Daughters*, New York, Norton, 1971

Erickson, Carolly, *Alexandra: The Last Tsarina*, Constable, 2002

Ferro, Marc, *Nicholas II: The Last of the Tsars*, trans. Brian Pearce, Viking, 1991

Figes, Orlando, *Natasha's Dance: A Cultural History of Russia*, Allen Lane, 1996

Fisher, Graham and Heather, *Bertie and Alix, Anatomy of a Royal Marriage*, Robert Hale, London, 1974

Frankland, Noble, *Prince Henry, Duke of Gloucester*, Weidenfeld & Nicolson, 1980

Fraser, Eugenie, *The House by the Dvina*, Corgi, 1986

Fuhrmann, Joseph, *Rasputin: A Life*, New York, Praeger, 1990

Gerhardi, William, *The Romanovs*, London, Rich & Cowan, 1940

Gibbes, Charles Sidney, *Tutor to the Tsarevich*, ed. J.C. Trewin, Macmillan, 1976

Gilliard, Pierre, *Thirteen Years at the Russian Court*, trans. F. Appleby Holt, Pavlosk Press and Hutchinson, 1921

Glenny, Michael and Stone, Norman, *The Other Russia*, Faber & Faber, 1990

Golovine, N., *The Russian Army in World War I*, Oxford University Press, 1932

Gore, John, *King George V: A Personal Memoir*, John Murray, 1941

Grabbe, Count Alexander, *The Private World of the Last Tsar*, ed. Paul and Beatrice Grabbe, London, Collins, 1985

Greig, Geordie, *Louis and the Prince*, Coronet, 1995

Guitaut, Caroline de, *Fabergé in the Royal Collection*, Royal Collection Enterprises, 2003

Hall, Coryne, *Little Mother of Russia*, Shepheard Walwyn, 1999

——, *Imperial Dancer: Mathilde Kschessinska and the Romanovs*, Sutton, 2005

Hanbury-Williams, Major-General Sir John, *The Emperor Nicholas II as I Knew Him*, Arthur L. Humphreys, 1922

Hibbert, Christopher, *The Court at Windsor*, Longman, 1964

——, *Queen Victoria in Her Letters and Journals*, New York, 1985

Hingley, Ronald, *Russia: A Concise History*, Thames & Hudson, 1991

Hoover War Library Publications, No. 6, Stanford University Press, 1935

Hosking, Geoffrey, *Russia and the Russians*, Penguin, 2001

Hough, Richard, *Advice to a Granddaughter*, Letters from Queen Victoria to Princess Victoria of Hesse, London, Heinemann, 1975

Hughes, Michael, *Inside the Enigma: British Officials in Russia, 1900–39*, Hambledon Press, 2000

Ignatieff, Michael, *The Russian Album*, Penguin, 1988

Jones, Thomas, *Lloyd George*, Harvard University Press, 1961

Judd, Denis, *The Life and Times of George V*, Weidenfeld & Nicolson, 1973

Kelly, Laurence, *A Traveller's Companion to St Petersburg*, Robinson, 2003

King, Greg, *The Last Empress*, Aurum Press, 1995

—— with Wilson, Penny, *The Fate of the Romanovs*, John Wiley, 2003

King, Stella, *Princess Marina, Her Life and Times*, Cassell, 1969

Knight, E.F., *With the Royal Tour*, Longman, Green, 1902

Knox, Alfred, *With the Russian Army*, New York, Dutton, 1921

Kochan, Miriam, *The Last Days of Imperial Russia*, Weidenfeld & Nicolson, 1976

Kokovtsov, V. N., *Out of My Past: The Memoirs of Count Kokovtsov*, Stanford University Press, 1935

Kschessinska, Mathilde, *Dancing in St Petersburg*, trans. A. Haskell, Victor Gollancz, 1960

Kurth, Peter, *Tsar: The Lost World of Nicholas and Alexandra*, Madison Press, 1995

Lacey, Robert, *Elizabeth II and the House of Windsor*, Hutchinson, 1977

Lees-Milne, James, *The Bachelor Duke*, John Murray, 1991

——, *Harold Nicolson: A Biography*, Chatto & Windus, 1981

Letters of the Tsar to the Tsaritsa 1914–17, London, John Lane, 1929

Letters of the Tsaritsa to the Tsar 1914–16, Hoover Institute Press, 1973

Lieven, Dominic, *Emperor of All the Russias*, John Murray, 1993

Lincoln, W. Bruce, *The Romanovs, Autocrats of all the Russias*, Anchor Books, Doubleday, 1981

Lloyd George, David, *War Memoirs*, Nicholson & Watson, 1933–6

Longford, Elizabeth, *Victoria R.I.*, Weidenfeld & Nicolson, 1964

Maclean, Fitzroy, *Holy Russia*, Century, 1978

Malcolm, Janet, *Reading Chekhov – A Critical Journey*, Random House, 2001

Massie, Robert K., *The Romanovs – The Final Chapter*, Jonathan Cape, 1995

Maylunas, Andrei and Mironenko, Sergei, *A Lifelong Passion: Nicholas and Alexandra, Their Own Story*, Weidenfeld & Nicolson, 1996

McNeal, Shay, *The Plots to Rescue the Tsar*, London, Century, 2001

Menkes, Suzy, *The Royal Jewels*, Grafton, 1985

Meshcherskaya, Ekaterina, *Comrade Princess: Memoirs of an Aristocrat in Modern Russia*, Doubleday, 1990

Mossolov, Alexander, *At the Court of the Last Tsar*, Methuen, 1935

Mouchanow, Marfa, *My Empress*, New York, John Lane, 1918

Nicholas II, *Letters of the Tsar to the Tsarina 1914–17*, London, Bodley Head, 1929

Nicholas II and Maria Feodorovna, *Letters of Tsar Nicholas and Empress Marie*, ed. Edward J. Bing, London, 1937

Nicolson, Harold, *King George V, His Life and Reign*, Constable, 1952

Obolensky, Dimitri, *Bread of Exile: A Russian Family*, trans. Harry Willetts, Harvill Press, 1999

Occleshaw, Michael, *The Romanov Conspiracies*, London, Chapmans, 1993

Oustimenko, Vladimir and Tyutyunnik, Lyubov, *The Family Life of Nikolai and Alexandra*, p. 106

Packard, Jerold M., *Victoria's Daughters*, Sutton, 1999

Paléologue, Maurice, *An Ambassador's Memoir*, Hutchinson, 1973

Pares, Bernard, *My Russian Memoirs*, Jonathan Cape, 1931

Pavlovna, Grand Duchess Marie, *Things I Remember*, London, 1931

Paxton, John, *Companion to Russian History*, B.T. Batsford, 1984

Perry, John Curtis, *The Flight of the Romanovs*, New York, Basic Books, 1999

Poliakoff, Stephen, *The Lost Prince*, Methuen, 2003

Poliakov, Vladimir, *The Tragic Bride: The Story of the Empress Alexandra*, New York, Appleton, 1927

Ponsonby, Sir Frederick, *Recollections of Three Reigns*, New York, Dutton, 1952

Pope-Hennessy, James, *Queen Mary*, George Allen & Unwin, 1959

Radzinsky, Edvard, *The Last Tsar: The Life and Death of Nicholas II*, New York, Doubleday, 1992

——, *Rasputin: The Last Word*, trans. Judson Rosengrant, Phoenix Paperback, 2000

Radziwill, Princess Catherine, *Nicholas II: The Last of the Tsars*, Cassell, 1931

Reid, Michaela, *Ask Sir James*, Hodder & Stoughton, 1987

Rodzyanko, M.V., *The Reign of Rasputin*, Philpot, 1927

Rose, Kenneth, *King George V*, Weidenfeld & Nicolson, 1983

St Aubyn, Giles, *The Royal George*, Constable, 1963

Shelayev, Yuri, Shelayeva, Elizabeth and Semenov, Nicholas, *Nicholas Romanov, Life and Death*, Liki Rossii, St Petersburg, 1998

Sitwell, Osbert, *Queen Mary and Others*, Michael Joseph, 1974

Somerset Maugham, W., 'His Excellency', from *Collected Short Stories*, vol. 3, London, 1976

Souhami, Diana, *Mrs Keppel and her Daughter*, HarperCollins, 1996

Steinberg, Mark D. and Khrustalëv, Vladimir M., *The Fall of the Romanovs*, Yale University Press, 1995

Stevenson, Frances, *Lloyd George: A Diary*, ed. A.J.P. Taylor, London, Hutchinson, 1971

Summers, Anthony and Mangold, Tom, *The File on the Last Tsar*, Fontana/Collins, 1981

Taylor, A.J.P., *British Prime Ministers and Other Essays*, ed. Chris Wrigley, Allen Lane, Penguin, 1999

Van der Kiste, John, *Crowns in a Changing World*, Alan Sutton, 1993

——, *The Romanovs 1818–1959*, Sutton, 1998

—— with Hall, Coryne, *Once a Grand Duchess*, Sutton, 2002

Vickers, Hugo, *Alice, Princess Andrew of Greece*, Hamish Hamilton, 2003

Vitale, Serena, *Pushkin's Button*, Fourth Estate, 1995

Vorres, Ian, *The Last Grand Duchess*, London, Hutchinson, 1964

Vyrubova, Anna, *Memories of the Russian Court*, New York, Macmillan, 1923

Watson, Sophia, *Marina, The Story of a Princess*, Weidenfeld & Nicolson, 1994

Welch, Frances, *The Romanovs and Mr Gibbes*, London, Short Books, 1993

Wilton, Robert, *The Last Days of the Romanovs*, Thornton Butterworth, 1920

Windsor, HRH the Duke of, *A King's Story*, Cassell, 1951

——, *Letters from a Prince (to Mrs Freda Dudley Ward) March 1918–Jan 1921*, ed. Rupert Godfrey, Little Brown, 1998

Woodward, Kathleen, *Queen Mary*, Hutchinson, 1927

Zamoyski, Adam, *Napoleon's Fatal March on Moscow*, HarperCollins, 2004

Zeepvat, Charlotte, *Romanov Autumn*, Sutton, 2000

Ziegler, Philip, *King Edward VII: The Official Biography*, London, Collins, 1990

Zinoviev, Kyril and Hughes, Jenny, *The Companion Guide to St Petersburg*, Companion Guides, 2003

Index

Note: Major entries are in chronological order, where appropriate.

Darmstadt 16, 18, 44, 51, 54
David, Duke of Windsor 24, 68–9, 119
Davidson, Emily 108
de Custine, Marquis 124
de Winton, Sir Francis 75, 94
Demidova, Anna 201, 202
Denmark 10–11, 12, 209
Derevenko, Andrei 113, 198
Diaghilev, Sergei 2, 40
diphtheria 17–18
DNA testing 233
Dostoyevsky, Fyodor 144–5
'Ducky' 217–18
Dudley Ward, Freda 121
Duma 127–8, 129, 163, 165

Eddy, Prince, Duke of Clarence 12, 24–5, 30
  and Alix 24–5, 43–4
  appearance 43
  character 33, 43
  and May of Teck 45–6
  death 46
Edward VII 6–7, 19, 32, 59, 61, 116, 126
  extravagance of 11, 26, 33
  as father 11–12, 35, 36, 47, 95, 118
  as grandfather 96
  marriage to Alexandra 9–10
  mistresses 9–10, 35, 98, 209
  death 65–6, 152–3
Edward VIII 109, 121, 216, 227
  born 59, 77
Effrossina, Sestra 179
Ekaterinburg 194–203, 212, 233–4, 236
Eliot, Sir Charles 153
Elizabeth II 118, 212, 233
Ella Feodorovna, Princess of Hesse 50, 54,
    126, 163–4, 197
  murdered 205
Epps, John 116
Ernst, Grand Duke 51, 164
Esher, Lord 11, 128–9, 177
Europe, royal families of 9, 12, 29, 205, 207

Fabergé 103–4
Fabrice, Baroness 56

Feodorov, Sergei 169
Fetherstonhaugh, Fred 78–9
First World War 57, 68, 109, 132, 133–43,
    163, 192, 230
Fisher, Admiral 108
Four Brothers' Wood 202
France 99, 133, 179
Francis, Duke of Teck 44, 45, 46
Franklin, Elizabeth 29
Franz Ferdinand, Archduke 134
Fredericks, Count Vladimir 100
Freedom House 188–93
French culture 2, 5
Frogmore Cottage 210–11
Futurists 2–3

Galicia 138
Gandhi, Mahatma 227
Gapon, Father George 125
Gatchina Palace 59
Gautier, Théophile 1
General Strike 216
George, Duke of Kent 78, 84
George I of Greece 29, 38, 217
George V 5–6, 60, 66–7, 82–3, 94–9
  appearance 5, 48, 95, 119
  character 77, 94–5, 136
    domineering/opinionated 97
    insular 77, 98, 99
    sober 7, 24–5, 33, 83, 95
    straightforward 94–5, 96–7
    volatile 82
  childhood 10, 11–12
  in Navy 30–1, 35, 43, 46, 93, 119
  coronation 68–9
  as father 95–6, 118–20, 121
  fosters popular feeling 177–8, 206, 216
  and George Buchanan 152
  as grandfather 118, 119
  health/illness 43, 47, 136, 216
  hobbies 78–9, 82–3, 98
  and Kaiser Wilhelm 68, 131–2, 139, 207
  marriage *see under* Mary, Princess of Teck
  and Nicholas *see under* Nicholas II
  refuses to help Andrew of Greece 213–14